The Music of

WOLFGANG AMADEUS MOZART

The Symphonies

In the same series

The Music of Joseph Haydn: The Symphonies
The Music of Johannes Brahms
The Music of Johann Sebastian Bach: The Choral Works
The Music of Dmitri Shostakovich: The Symphonies

Forthcoming
The Music of Jean Sibelius
The Music of Pyotr Tchaikovsky
The Music of Richard Wagner: The Ring and Parsifal

THE MUSIC OF WOLFGANG AMADEUS MOZART
MOZART
THE SYMPHONIES
ROBERT DEARLING

22035

Fairleigh Dickinson University Press
Rutherford • Madison • Teaneck
Associated University Presses
London

Mannes College of Music
The Harry Scherman Library
157 East 74th Street, New York 21, N. Y.

© 1982 by Associated University Presses, Inc.

Associated University Presses, Inc.
4 Cornwall Drive
East Brunswick, NJ 08816

Associated University Presses Ltd
27 Chancery Lane
London WC2A 1NS, England

Associated University Presses
Toronto M5E 1A7, Canada

Library of Congress Cataloging in Publication Data

Dearling, Robert, 1933–
  The music of Wolfgang Amadeus Mozart, the symphonies.

  Bibliography: p.
  Discography: p.
  Includes index.
  1. Mozart, Wolfgang Amadeus, 1756–1791. Symphonies.
I. Title.
MT130.M8D33   785.1'1'0924   78-68625
ISBN 0-8386-2335-2   AACR2

Printed in the United States of America

To
GEORGES de SAINT-FOIX (1874–1954)
a pioneer of Eighteenth-century musical research

Contents

Acknowledgements	9
Editorial Preface	11
Introduction	13
Mozart the Man	26
1: Youthful Works: Symphonies Nos. 1–14 (1764–71)	57
First Movements	57
Slow Movements	78
Minuets and Trios	83
Finales	87
2: Consolidation: Symphonies Nos. 15–34 (1772–80)	92
Overture Symphonies	93
Three-Movement Non-Overture Symphonies	104
Four-Movement Symphonies	112
Sturm und Drang	129
Horn Symphonies	132
Serenade Symphonies	135
3: High Maturity: Symphonies Nos. 35–38 (1782–86)	139
4: The Last Symphonies: Nos. 39–41 (1788)	150
5: Conclusion	162
Appendix	167
Selected Writings	169
The Music in Print	170
Musical Instruments of Mozart's Time	172
Recommended Recordings	173
Reconstructed Timpani Parts	195
Köchel Numbers	204
Table of Mozart's Symphonies	208
Indexes	220
Index of Mozart's Works	220
General Index	221

Acknowledgements

In the important and complicated task of securing illustrations for this book my gratitude is due to the staffs of the Austrian National Tourist Office and the Austrian Institute Library, London; to Miss Frances Cooper of the Horniman Museum, London, to Andrew Dalton of the Decca Record Co., Ltd., and to Antony Hodgson for much practical help and many suggestions. Also to timpanist János Keszei, whose patience and knowledge were put unstintingly at my disposal over matters both photographic and percussive.

Thanks go also to Michael Downey for providing valuable details about modern publications of the symphonies of Mozart.

Derek Elley worked with me to prepare the typescript for publication and showed great tact and consideration; similarly, Sarah Halpern of the Associated University Presses, gave invaluable assistance in the final stages of production. To them I express my deep gratitude.

Editorial Preface

This series is specifically designed to explore the sound of each composer as his most distinctive feature, and, to this end, recognises the equally important role that recordings now play in musical life. Footnotes throughout the main text contain critical references to such recordings when it is felt that they clarify or highlight the composer's intentions. In the Appendix, these and other recommended recordings are re-grouped in a purely factual listing of catalogue numbers, performance details and any divergencies from the composer's expressed wishes.

Since the aim of the series is to clarify each composer's sound, particularly for the non-specialist, this approach should prove doubly rewarding: treating concert music as a living rather than an academic entity and showing the virtues and faults of its reflection through Twentieth-century ears.

Introduction

If, amongst those who have any kind of sympathy towards so-called "serious" music, a ballot were to be held to find the most universally popular composer, it is probable that two names would emerge as contenders for the title: Beethoven and Tchaikovsky. The appeal of these two giants is extremely strong because each had, amongst his other attributes, that gift most vital of all in the struggle for recognition and acceptance: the ability to direct his music unerringly at the emotional centre of his listener. It may even be suggested that the music of Tchaikovsky makes so strong an onslaught upon the emotions that many listeners feel assaulted by it and consequently over-compensate by being unwilling to admit that they enjoy his music. Tchaikovsky will not appear on the lists of those listeners.

Another name may not appear on some lists, but for a different reason. The average listener will perhaps be heard to admit to "liking music but not knowing anything about it," or "I know what I like but I can't remember the names." If he or she did "know something about it" or could "remember the names," the name of Mozart would figure on the list. Mozart's music has a power to appeal directly, but also another great quality too subtle accurately to define: it appeals subliminally. It is not intended to suggest thereby that Mozart's music is "greater" than Beethoven's or Tchaikovsky's but that its qualities are elusive, its appeal more delicate, and its recognition more difficult. Some years ago, before the days of the "Top Twenty" and the million-seller single, there was a pleasant item of music often to be heard on the radio in a variety of arrangements. Its title was *In an Eighteenth Century Drawing Room*. The character of the music was so redolent of the decorous atmosphere of such a room that the music was regarded by many to be a newly-composed mood-piece in the same mould as Anthony Collins's charming *Vanity Fair* of the early Fifties. Only the better informed were aware that it was in fact the genuine article, taken from a Mozart keyboard sonata: indeed a piece to be played in an Eighteenth-century drawing room.* A little later, in an irreverent mood, the American parodist "Red" Ingle took another sonata movement and turned it into a skilful pop number. He even went so far as to announce the name of the piece with earthy directions at the start of the record:

> Bang thet pee-anner an' make her hot!
> Mister Moe Zart's Turkey Trot.†

Other pieces, too, became extremely popular even without the attention of Tin Pan Alley, and it is not uncommon to hear parts, particularly from the Finale, of *Eine kleine Nachtmusik* being whistled in a busy street; and the attention given by Michael Flanders and Donald Swann to the last movement of the Fourth Horn Concerto, K495, brought that piece to the notice of many listeners who would otherwise have ignored its existence. The name of the film *Elvira Madigan* will inevitably bring to the minds of those who saw it the throbbing string harmonies, stalking *pizzicato* and muted violin *cantilena* that characterised the title music, but it is by no means certain that they will all remember that it is a straight, untainted performance of the slow movement of Mozart's Piano Concerto in C, K467, of 1785. Mozart, clearly, "has possibilities," and, while he provides endless material for imaginative musical directors, others are less stylistically scrupulous when choosing music for transfer to, or expulsion by, musical computers and synthesisers, and, to the utter distress of all musical listeners, it has even been attacked by those who wish to plaster over his subtle pulses a layer of relentless "rhythm-pop" clatter.

Whether or not we remember his name every time we hear these various treatments, it is clear that Mozart's name must join the other

---

* It is the first movement of the Sonata in C, K545, of 1788.
† Actually, this is taken from the Finale, *Rondo alla Turca*, or "Turkish March," from the Sonata in A, KE300 I (=K331) of 1778.

two as one of the most popular, and most widely disseminated, of all composers. Nevertheless, the number of his works so treated is tiny when compared with his total lifework and, even though the great majority of his music is today accessible to the record buyer, only a very small proportion of it is well known.

Mozart himself experienced a similar situation. In the Eighteenth century the success of a composer depended not on how much music he had written but on how "correct" and up-to-date were his latest compositions. This accounts in part for the enormous quantity of music produced in that century, but in Mozart's case there was a further reason: his composing facility was so astoundingly well developed that, as we shall see in our discussion of the "Linz" Symphony, it was quicker and easier for him to compose a new work than it was to send away for an old one. A concomitant reason applies particularly to Mozart and to other travelling composers: a composition designed for, and well received in, Vienna or Milan might be totally foreign to the musical atmosphere of Paris. Composers visiting various centres, therefore, had to adapt their styles in order to be accepted by the audiences they were visiting because musical chauvinism played a major part in appreciation. We shall meet this factor when we turn, for instance, to the "Paris" Symphony.

Whatever the reasons, the fact endures: of Mozart's enormous output the Eighteenth-century music-lover was largely ignorant. Ironically, it was only after his death, when an uncaring world gradually came to realise that the genius it had so shamefully neglected was no longer there to be ignored, that moves were made to appreciate his music; and a further irony is that, by this time, the excesses of Nineteenth-century performing style were being imposed on Mozart's delicate art, excesses that even today leave their thickening influence on some performances. At first amazed, then awed, by the quality of the music reaching print in the first half of the Nineteenth century, the musical world was also embarrassed by its sheer quantity, and by the fact that "new" works were constantly emerging from obscurity. Confusion was compounded by the diversity and variety of Mozart's music: he seemed to have been an unbelievably prolific genius in every branch of music. Newly-found great works literally tumbled over each other for attention, forming a bewildering mass of music so great and diverse that it could not be conceived without some kind of catalogue to aid systematic appraisal. If a genius had written these masterpieces, it certainly required the application and persistence of another genius to sort them into manageable order.

Such a genius emerged in the person of Ludwig Alois Ferdinand Ritter von Köchel (1800–77), an Austrian botanist and natural scientist who had graduated in law in 1827. His interest in the music of Mozart, much of whose music was still not published at the time of the centenary celebrations in 1856, clashed with his sense of order and logic which had developed during his practice of law and botany, and he set himself the target of categorising known Mozart works and tracking down those that remained in manuscript, travelling throughout Austria, Germany, France and even England in the quest. His first catalogue—and, incidentally, the first ever to aim at completeness in the listing of one composer's works—was published in 1862 and has since been subjected to various revisions, corrections and additions, most notably by Alfred Einstein.*

With the problems of Mozart's cataloguing finally and successfully solved, another great step forward in Mozart research was taken by the publication in 1938 of the letters of the composer and his family in a superb translation by Emily Anderson. Mozart's letters to his friends, his publishers and associates, and above all to the members of his family, are numerous enough to build up a satisfyingly full picture of his life, his character and his idiosyncracies, and from them may be drawn dozens of fascinating side-lights on his activities. Another aid to understanding was the publication of other documents surrounding him, his family and colleagues. This was undertaken by Otto Erich Deutsch, perhaps better known for his exhaustive thematic catalogue of the works of Franz Schubert, but a tireless investigator also into Mozartiana. His "Mozart—A Documentary Biography" was published in 1965 and appeared in an English translation during the same year.

To these three sources are indebted, either directly or indirectly, all who attempt to write about Mozart.

*

The present study is primarily concerned with the symphonies of Mozart, and here again it is necessary to acknowledge with gratitude the writings of the Frenchman Georges de Saint-Foix, whose compact volume "Les Symphonies de Mozart" appeared in 1932, to be followed by an English translation by Leslie Orrey in 1947; Jens Peter Larsen, the Haydn scholar who contributed a lengthy article about Mozart's symphonies to "The Mozart Companion," edited by H. C. Robbins Landon and Donald Mitchell (1964); and Hans Keller, whose often

---

* The familiar "K" numbers appended to Mozart's works were the original identifications of Köchel's catalogue and show the order in which the then-current state of musicology believed them to have been composed. The letters "K.A," for "Köchel-Anhang" (Köchel Appendix), indicate those works which are of doubtful authenticity or known spuriousness: they are collected at the back of the Köchel catalogue as an Appendix. "KE" (=Köchel-Einstein) is the most chronologically accurate of the Köchel listings, taking into account recent researches into the ordering of Mozart's music. See Appendix.

abrasive views appeared in Volume One of "The Symphony," edited by Robert Simpson (1966). It is the intention of this new examination of the symphonies to offer fresh food for thought, and in its preparation the author has drawn certain guidelines which, although mentioned in passing throughout the examination of the symphonies, might usefully be outlined here.

In the case of Joseph Haydn the listener has to beware, even in these enlightened days, that the performance of a symphony may be of a corrupt text. These corruptions gained currency mainly during the Nineteenth century and many were of such seriousness that the nature of the work was damaged and the intended effect destroyed. They may have been partly responsible for the almost total neglect of the majority of Haydn's symphonies until recently: with the composer's striking effects muted or cancelled out by unauthentic emendations, listeners decided that the music was not of great interest and went elsewhere for their listening enjoyment. On the whole, the problem of textual authenticity in Mozart's symphonic scores is not a serious one by comparison. Reasonably reliable texts have always been available, even if concert audiences have tended to prefer only a handful of the later symphonies. The problem of actual performance practice is another matter entirely, and one which has received considerably less attention than is the case with Haydn.

To perform an Eighteenth-century symphony with any degree of stylishness it is necessary to understand the workings of an Eighteenth-century orchestra and, once certain facts and assumptions are accepted as important to the sound that was produced in Mozart's day, the modern conductor has to make adjustments to the sound he produces from his Twentieth-century orchestra. It is ridiculous to suggest that Mozart, as he travelled from country to country, would always have encountered the same orchestral sound, a sound he held in his mind constantly as he wrote each successive symphony, but it is true to say that orchestras then, just as now, possessed certain common characteristics. If we take as an example the Mannheim orchestra when Mozart visited the town in 1777, we find the following: ten or eleven first violins, the same number of second violins, and four each of violas, celli and basses ($=32$–34 string players); two each of flutes, oboes, clarinets, horns, trumpets; four bassoons, and timpani. With four celli, basses and bassoons, the bass-line would have been rich and solid as well as capable of considerable variation in intensity, while the upper woodwind, using instruments somewhat softer in tone than today's examples, would probably not have been as brilliant as the same orchestra only five years later when the total string strength had been reduced to twenty-eight, and two more flutes added along with one more oboe and one more clarinet. The number of horns had also been doubled. Elsewhere in Europe, however, the wind section was usually stronger than this in relation to the number of strings, yet a performance today in which the wind are given the sort of prominence which would have been heard in Mozart's lifetime is a rarity to be prized.

Today's horn-players are capable of producing a smooth tone from their sophisticated instruments whereas the nature of sound produced on an Eighteenth-century natural horn would have been raw and more open. It is difficult, in fact, to get a modern horn-player to produce the piercing quality that Mozart's audiences would have heard.* As a general rule for Eighteenth-century music, including Mozart's, B flat horns should be played in the *alto* octave rather than in the *basso*; on the other hand, C horns should always be played *basso* in every Mozart symphony requiring them, with the single exception of No. 18 (see page 133, where the whole question of Mozart's horns is examined). Trumpets, too, would have sounded different from today's instruments; they would have retained some of the silvery clarino tone of the late Baroque era and would have been played by experts who lived for their art and rarely considered the feelings of the rest of the orchestral players. In the case of timpani, today's plastic-headed instruments produce a "civilised," rich, resonant tone ideal for Brucknerian pedal-points, but in an Eighteenth-century orchestra their deep boom would have obliterated the fast-moving string lines and mingled very poorly with the trumpets, with which they frequently shared rhythms. Incidentally, it is certain that a number of Mozart's symphonic timpani parts have been detached from the rest of the parts and mislaid—even if they ever existed on paper. Quite often they would have been constructed *ad lib.* by the timpanists as they watched their trumpeter colleagues. It is our contention that, to play a D major or a C major symphony that includes trumpet parts without introducing a timpani part, is to misrepresent Mozart's music.†

A firm continuo bass-line is essential in Mozart's symphonies. Even when not specified in the score, a bassoon should double the string bass, and a harpsichord, although often superfluous as a harmony-filler

---

* Those audiences would have been attacked, no doubt, by some outrageous noises from the natural horns of the day when blown by any but the finest players, noises that the Twentieth-century listener rarely has to tolerate, but it is not the reliability of the players and instruments that is the point here so much as the actual tone produced by the horns—hardly more developed than hunting horns, and often thus described on the scores of the time.

† As an appendix to this book we have provided reconstructed timpani parts for those works in these keys that have trumpets. No harmonic liberties have been taken: the parts are basically simple extensions of the trumpet rhythms, but their use, it is suggested, will restore to the works involved their true martial character which has not been heard since Mozart's day. Critics who complain that, with his large string sections, romantically orientated phrasing and tempo manipulations, Sir Thomas Beecham added things to Mozart's music that detracted from its true character, may also complain

in Mozart's well-constructed string lines, still assists in etching the rhythms and supplying the right period atmosphere. It is not actually incorrect to use a harpsichord in all the symphonies, even up to and including No. 41, but it is definitely unwise to omit it in the earlier works. No hard rule need be laid down for what constitutes "early" in this context, but a convenient point would seem to be the mid-1770s, i.e. after No. 30 (May 5, 1774) and before No. 31 (June 1778). This division would seem to be supported by two well-known works: No. 29 gains from a harpsichord continuo while No. 31 does not.

*

Accessibility to the symphonies of Mozart did not come easily to the collector of gramophone records. In the days of the 78 rpm shellac disc, it was, understandably, the later and best-known symphonies that received most attention from the record companies, and surprisingly it was No. 39, with 17 recordings, rather than a symphony with a popular nickname, that was the most favoured. Among the conductors who recorded this symphony were Beecham, Karajan, Koussevitzky, Scherchen, Weingartner, Szell, Krips, Knappertsbusch and Walter. If the number of recorded performances is any guide, the next most popular symphonies during those 78 rpm days were Nos. 40 (with 16 recordings) and 41 (with 15, including two by Bruno Walter*). Next came Nos. 35 and 36 with 10 recordings each, No. 38 (8), No. 34 (6), Nos. 25 and 33 (5 each), No. 29 (4) and No. 32 (3: a convenient single-disc symphony†). One recording existed of each of some rare works: No. 31 (Beecham), No. 28 (Stein), No. 27 (Beecham), No. 26 (Koussevitzky), No. 24 (Swoboda), No. 20 (Fendler) and No. 14 (Swoboda). With the earlier symphonies interest fades sadly, with just one recording of the slow movement of No. 13.‡

Before the long-playing record arrived (in America in 1948 and two years later in Great Britain) it was Sir Thomas Beecham who showed most interest in recording Mozart symphonies. Altogether he brought

---

that the addition of these timpani parts is an unwarranted interference with Mozart's textures. Others may feel that, since it is virtually certain that drums did accompany trumpets in these works, as we know they did in many similar works for which genuine timpani parts have survived, it is useful to have available reconstructed parts so that the works may be brought into line with Mozart's—and the Eighteenth century's—known practice. In this way it is hoped to re-establish the textures Mozart would have expected.

* One with the Vienna Philharmonic Orchestra and another with the New York Philharmonic Symphony.

† But not always successfully so: Royalton Kisch's performance on Decca K 2200 suffered from acute distortion towards the loud end of the second side.

‡ Acting as a fill-up on the fourth side of Boyd Neel's recording of *Serenata notturna*.

ten to the gramophone, one of them twice: Nos. 27, 29, 31, 34,* 35, 36, 38, 39, 40 and 41. Serge Koussevitzky recorded seven symphonies: Nos. 26, 29, 33, 34, 36, 39 and 40. Hermann Scherchen recorded five: Nos. 29, 35, 36, 39 and 40; Arturo Toscanini and Richard Strauss three each—the former Nos. 35,† 40 and 41, the latter the last three symphonies. In those early years Otto Klemperer recorded only two Mozart symphonies: Nos. 25 and 36. Despite the relative lack of early symphonies on disc, it was still possible to obtain many Mozart symphonies of the period 1771 to 1788, but then, as now, the emphasis was on the most popular works, amongst which a fair choice of performances existed.‡

The long-playing record brought about a general widening of repertoire in all fields of music, and with it an incredible expansion of the Mozart symphony discography. Nos. 18, 22, 23 and 37§ were added almost immediately in performances by Henry Swoboda on the Westminster label, and a year or so later three Concert Hall discs conducted by Otto Ackermann added Nos. 1, 2 (spurious), 4, 5, 6, 10, 11 and 17, together with the first LP presentations of Nos. 14 and 26. A delightful disc of Nos. 19 and 21, conducted respectively by Hans Michael and Gustav Lund, closed two more gaps,‖ and the first recording of an unnumbered symphony, KE74G (K= Anh. 216), appeared on the American Royale label played by the Mozart Symphony Society Orchestra, unconducted.

While Otto Ackermann continued his series for Concert Hall, closing all the rest of the gaps in the numbered symphonies and extending up to and including No. 26, the French company L'Oiseau-Lyre also turned its attention to these early works. A series of seven $33\frac{1}{3}$ rpm seven-inch discs, a configuration that never caught on in England or America, ¶ brought symphonies Nos. 2–5 and 7–11 to the European public in performances played by the Oiseau-Lyre Chamber Orchestra under Louis de Froment, and Nos. 1 and 6 played by the Lamoureux Orchestra conducted by Pierre Colombo were coupled on a ten-inch disc. These

---

* Once with the London Philharmonic Orchestra and once with the Royal Philharmonic Orchestra.

† Twice, once with the New York Philharmonic Symphony Orchestra (1929) and once with the NBC Symphony Orchestra (1946). A public performance of No. 39, dating from March 1948, was only issued on LP: in the United States as RCA LM 2001 and in the U.K. as HMV ALP 1492.

‡ In the case of No. 40 it is interesting to note that eminent conductors were divided in their choice between the original version without clarinets (Furtwängler, Beecham, Koussevitzky) and the revised version with them (Toscanini, Ansermet, Kleiber, Bruno Walter, Richard Strauss, Stock, Sargeant). Today there is a similar unwelcome bias towards the clarinet version. See Recommended Recordings.

§ No. 37 is mainly by Michael Haydn; only the slow introduction is by Mozart.

‖ Issued on the American Period label and released in Great Britain on Nixa.

¶ These nine symphonies were released in England on two twelve-inch discs.

performances were enthusiastic rather than musicianly, and while it would not be correct to say that they misrepresented Mozart's music, it cannot be claimed that they won it many new friends. Nevertheless, for the first time most of Mozart's numbered symphonies were available to the English gramophone user, while in America all were on the market, including the unauthentic Nos. 2, 3, and 37 and a handful of authentic unnumbered symphonies. It was in this atmosphere of confusion, different series being available in different countries and no overall conspectus being presented by one conductor, that the American Westminster company in the mid-Fifties engaged Erich Leinsdorf to record all the numbered symphonies on twelve discs. The recordings were made in London by the Philharmonic Symphony Orchestra just at the time when studios were busy converting to stereo equipment and dealing with the problems of the new technique. Some of Leinsdorf's recordings were made in genuine stereo but it appears that others were monophonic and were remastered later for twin-channel reproduction. Some of the performances had real value, but many of the early works were ruthlessly hard-driven, and this, plus the fact that virtually no formal repeats were observed in the outer movements, gives to the works a breathless feel and reduces further the already small stature of many of the shorter symphonies. Since none of the genuine but unnumbered symphonies was included in the cycle (even though the spurious Nos. 2, 3, and 37 did find a place), Leinsdorf's series cannot be regarded as anywhere near complete.

The next conductor to tackle a substantial portion of the repertoire for the gramophone was Denis Vaughan who, in the mid-Sixties, recorded Nos. 16 to 24 inclusive, plus two Overtures in D: KE141A (=K161/163) and K196/KE207A.* Denis Vaughan was the first to have the courage to include a harpsichord continuo as a regular feature of this repertoire. (Incredibly, at a time when most Eighteenth-century music was being recorded with a properly balanced continuo line,† Mozart's symphonies were considered to be above such things.) Vaughan's performances were also amongst the first to bring out properly the tone of the horns, so often refined away in this music. In No. 24 B flat *alto* horns were employed, but more remarkable was the appearance for the first time on disc of horns in "E flat *alto*" in No. 19.‡ These lively performances, marred only by Vaughan's insistence on taking gracenotes too short, have been underrated; it is to be hoped that they will

---

* Owing to a misprint, the box containing this three-disc set reached the English market with the announcement that it included Nos. 15 to 24.
† Leslie Jones's recordings of Haydn's "London" Symphonies (1791–5) for Nonesuch, made in 1967, uses a harpsichord continuo.
‡ The terminology and practice behind this aspect of Mozart's orchestration are discussed on page 134.

reappear in due course,* and that some record company will engage Vaughan to record some more Mozart symphonies.

At about the time that Denis Vaughan was making his Mozart recordings the American Vox company was embarking on a series with Günther Kehr and the Mainz Chamber Orchestra. In the event it was not completed by that conductor: Peter Maag and the Philharmonia Hungarica supplied the last six authentic symphonies, but the Kehr/Maag series turned out to be the most complete so far, omitting the unauthentic numbered symphonies (Nos. 2, 3 and 37) but including, in addition to all the other numbered ones, eight authentic symphonies that had not been included in the original numeration. Kehr's performances of the earlier works were sturdy, showing good approach to tempo and weight, but the important matter of harpsichord and bassoon continuo was either overlooked or considered to be of no importance, and horns sometimes played in the wrong octave. Nevertheless, a complete recording of Mozart's symphonies was brought a step nearer, and another complete recording, while not contributing further to authenticity of performance, was the first to employ a world-renowned conductor in charge of a superb orchestra: Karl Böhm and the Berlin Philharmonic Orchestra. For sheer beauty of sound it would be difficult to improve upon these resplendent performances but, at the risk of sounding ungrateful, one wonders whether the weight of the Berlin Philharmonic is not just too great for the slender music of the early works. Niceties of authenticity are usually ignored, but the later works often respond magnificently to this luxury treatment.

A much firmer step towards authenticity was taken in the mid-Seventies when Neville Marriner and the Academy of St.-Martin-in-the-Fields produced lively, stylish performances of twenty-nine symphonies, extending from the earliest to No. 20 (1772) and including several of the symphonies derived by Mozart from operatic overtures. Although a harpsichord continuo is present as a rule rather than an exception in these performances, it is allowed to lapse in certain movements where its use may be regarded as an intrusion. For the rest, these performances are immensely satisfying: tempi are beautifully judged, orchestral balance is almost unfailingly ideal, and the playing has a flexibility and purpose that gives even the less-inspired works a bounce and vitality only rarely heard in other performances. As far as it goes, i.e. numerically more than half-way through Mozart's symphonic output, Marriner's is the most complete set so far, yet still one finds two gaps which, at the time of writing, are unfilled: KE Anh 223B (=K98) in F, apparently written in Milan in 1771 but by no means certainly the

---

* At the time of writing—late 1980—they are not available on either the American or the U.K. market.

work of Mozart, and KE74G (=KA216) in B flat, one of the works written in the summer of 1771 between the Italian visits, about which there is no question of doubtful authenticity.

The Philips/Marriner set of the early symphonies* presents a serious approach to authenticity within the bounds dictated by the use of modern instruments and playing techniques. A companion volume of Symphonies Nos. 21 to 41 (omitting No. 37) is conducted by Josef Krips but, although his readings are intensely musical and the Concertgebouw Orchestra plays expertly, these performances do not have the convincingly authentic sound that would suggest, as do Marriner's, that a conscious attempt has been made to approximate to Mozart's sound-textures. Therefore, the two series do not make ideal companions.† Certain other performances, however, seem to have sought this sound, and these will be found listed in the Appendix of Recommended Recordings.

Marriner's admirable series of the early symphonies, whilst a serious and often exciting attempt to remove the later excrescences that shroud the orchestral *timbres* that Mozart is likely to have heard, is yet hampered by two factors: the decision to use modern instruments, and the mixture of stylish performing practice (correct grace-notes, the use of continuo, etc.) with modern playing techniques. In many ways the results of such a mixture are praiseworthy and may be thought preferable to the ever-increasing trend towards ultra-authentic performances in which period instruments or faithful reproductions thereof are played in a manner, as closely as modern research allows, approaching that used at the time the music was written. To many listeners such authenticity requires, to use a fashionable phrase, a "quantum leap" in acceptance, and it is understandable that some will be unable or unwilling to take that leap. For those listeners the Marriner recordings go as far towards authenticity as it is necessary to go. There is, however, a case for taking advantage of the mass of research put in train by Adam Carse and others between the wars that has lead to our present

---

* An earlier disc issued by Argo coupling Nos. 13 to 16 is less authentic and is totally outclassed by the Philips recordings.

† While Marriner brings to his musicality an earnest musicological quest for enlightenment, Krips is content to hold in abeyance such matters as harpsichord and bassoon continuo, added timpani parts, stylish playing of grace-notes and other factors necessary to an attempt to reconstruct a sound approaching what Mozart might have heard. He concentrates instead upon drawing beauty of tone and playing from his orchestra in a traditional context—not in itself an undesirable quality by any means, but a totally different aim from Marriner's search for authentic textures and performing practice. While it is possible to give a blanket recommendation to Marriner's Philips series, the situation with Krips is less clear-cut. Although available at the time of writing only in a boxed set, the recommendable symphonies in Krips' series are listed in the Appendix against the time when the discs are released separately.

conception of what went on in an Eighteenth-century orchestra and what kind of sound it made.

In September 1978 the London-based Decca Record Company announced that recordings had begun for a complete series of Mozart's symphonies by the Academy of Ancient Music, directed by Christopher Hogwood, to be released on the "Florilegium" label of L'Oiseau-Lyre, under which banner many fine authentic recordings of music from Gibbons and Byrd to Beethoven and Weber had already been released. A disc containing three symphonies and a clarinet concerto by Jan Stamic had indicated some two years previously that Hogwood's approach to Eighteenth-century orchestral music was stimulating, but the Mozart project is uniquely ambitious in that standard repertory has never been tackled from the ultra-authentic viewpoint on such a scale before. Neal Zaslaw of Cornell University, New York, is the guiding musicologist for the project. He has returned to basics not only in the matter of the musical parts but also in the vitally important related matters of performing style and the number of players to each part. As mentioned earlier, Mozart would not have met identical performing conditions as he moved from one musical centre to another: it follows, therefore, that the ideal number of players per part varies from work to work, and Zaslaw and his colleagues carried out much research into these background conditions before the players of the Academy of Ancient Music were ever allowed to set period bow to Baroque violin. The last fifty years have brought to light countless features about classical performing traditions that were unknown to theorists of the early Twentieth century, and many more factors may remain to be discovered, so it may never be possible to agree with Zaslaw that "it has thus become possible for the first time to recreate the orchestral sound for which Mozart wrote." However, the painstaking care that has gone into the preparation of these recordings commands the greatest respect.

The basic guidelines for the Florilegium series are as follows: period instruments or faithful copies, including Baroque woodwind and natural horns; a continuo line of bassoons and harpsichord, the latter being replaced by a fortepiano in the later symphonies. Symphony No. 31, "Paris," is the only work in which a keyboard continuo instrument does not feature because the practice had been discontinued in that city by the time the work was composed. Timpani are added to every symphony lacking them when trumpets are present. Tempi are as considered appropriate to each movement and may disconcert listeners used to a more traditional approach. In particular, it is felt that many minuets and slow movements are played slower today than Mozart would have expected, and this has been rectified. All indicated repeats are observed, including, where appropriate, those *after* the trios in the minuets. There is no conductor: the performances are controlled by the Concert Master (leader) and the continuo player. Where available, the Bärenreiter scores in the New Mozart Edition are used; otherwise, the works are performed from edited MSS and other authentic sources.

These guidelines would seem to satisfy all the requirements for authentic performance laid out on p. 173, yet for some listeners, inevitably, Christopher Hogwood and his team have not gone far enough while for others he has gone too far. One can only applaud the clear-sighted attitude that, in Neal Zaslaw's words, construes the ensemble "in all its essential elements as an early Eighteenth-century orchestra which has evolved in time, rather than a Nineteenth-century ensemble which has been stripped of a few anachronistic excrescences."

Mozart The Man

Although Mozart's parents were musically orientated, there is nothing in their history to account for the amazing precocity of Wolfgang, his uncannily rapid development, or his later ability to hold music-lovers of the world in perpetual debt.* He had opportunities, it is true, though no more than most; indeed, it is a miracle that his fascination for music was not blunted by his early experiences as a *Wunderkind*, but whatever he felt as he was shuttled and whisked from one exalted gathering to the next it was music that his mind returned to ever and again. Music was the one thing that he held in deep respect—music, and his conventional Catholic religious beliefs—and those who did not do likewise were beneath contempt.

Wolfgang's father Leopold was made of altogether more earthly stuff. For him, music was the means by which he may support a family, and by his unexceptional musical talent he built for himself a quiet reputation as a reliable musical servant whose name might have been

---

* The obscurity of the Mozart family before Wolfgang's fame arrived to consolidate the name may be seen from the variety of spellings in textbooks and documents: Motsart, Motshard, Mozard, Mozarth, Moser, Mozhard, Mozhart, Mozzard.

forgotten today but for two facts: his excellence upon the violin, which is commemorated in a textbook he wrote upon the subject of playing that instrument; and his siring of one of the greatest of all musical geniuses. After four years as *Kammerdiener* (a kind of musical groom) with Count Johann of Thurn-Valsannia und Taxis at Salzburg, Leopold became fourth violinist at the Salzburg court of Leopold Anton von Firmian in 1743, where he encountered the colourful and often grotesque instrumental suites of Heinrich Ignaz Biber, whose son Karl Heinrich had been *Kapellmeister* at the court. The outlandish pictorial effects, often allied to folk elements and a simple story, were appreciated there, and Leopold soon fell to writing updated examples. For instance, every winter brought opportunities for musical representations of shivering ladies, sleigh-rides to a warming and energetic ball, and music for the ball itself. One such suite, written during the very month of Wolfgang's birth, contains evocative pictures of winter life at Salzburg, the representation of galloping horses in the *Schlittenfahrt* itself being touched in with sleigh-bells.* For the autumn season Leopold wrote a "Hunting Symphony" which, despite its conventional melodic lines, is worth hearing for the sake of its remarkable scoring: four horns, shotgun and string. The firearm is marked to detonate at certain points in the score, and the high horn writing, complete with the expected "hunting" triplets, lends a certain zest to the music which would have been acclaimed after a successful court chase. These suites and pictorial symphonies obviously would have been heard by the young Wolfgang in his earliest days, but when he sought similar colourful devices for inclusion in his own music† there is an element of genius in their use that Leopold could never muster.

Leopold never became *Kapellmeister*. Always another musician received the honour, and later, when he was absent for lengthy periods to accompany his children upon concert tours, his suitability for such a post must have been called into question. At home, his wife Anna Maria offered him equable company since she too came from a musical background, but also from an impoverished one since her father had died when she was only four years old and the family had known from

---

* A first-rate recording of this *Sleighride* in F was made by DG Archiv in 1956 (APM 14084). Carl Gorvin conducts the Bach Orchestra of Berlin with style and panache. The disc also offers a complete recording of Leopold's *Cassatio Berchtoldgadensis* in G in seven movements, from which three were taken to form the "Toy Symphony" for long erroneously attributed to Joseph Haydn. A more recent (1976) performance of the *Sleighride*, also on the Archiv label (2533 328), by the Eduard Melkus Ensemble has the advantage of modern recorded sound and some additional imaginative touches supplied in the studio (e.g. the barking of excited dogs as the passengers board the sleigh) but the performance as a whole does not reproduce the drive and enthusiasm of Gorvin's old disc.

† For example, *La bataille*, a Kontretanz in C, K535 (1788) and his own "Sleighride" in the Trio of the *Deutsche Tanz*, K605, No. 3 (1791).

that time acute financial stress. She had married Leopold in 1747 and they were feted as the handsomest couple in all Salzburg. A son and two daughters did not live to see half a year, but the third daughter, Maria Anna Walburga Ignata, later to be known as "Nannerl," was born on July 30, 1751, and proved to be a healthy infant, enjoying a life happier and longer than any of her siblings.* Another son and another daughter followed the three first-born to infants' graves; then on January 27, 1756, Leopold's and Anna Maria's seventh and last child was born: Joannes Chrysostomus Wolfgangus Theophilus.†

Before he could walk, his father and mother, doubtless aided by a possessive elder sister who was already showing signs of proficiency at the keyboard, played him short pieces, and by the age of four he was declaring a preference for the marches and dances of Georg Christoph Wagenseil (1715–77), learning them by heart to the amazement and delight of both family and friends. Soon after he attained the age of five, he sprang a further surprise by composing his first keyboard pieces. Unremarkable and derivative, they yet showed that young Wolfgang possessed the beginnings of a musical imagination. In September 1761, as an accompanying harpsichordist for the dancers, "Wolfgangus Mozhart" took part in a play with music, *Sigismundus Hungaricae Rex*, in Salzburg. The lad was fascinated by the dancers and it is not inconceivable that he joined them in the rehearsals, firing in him a love of dancing that remained for the rest of his life.

Leopold came to realise that his two talented children might, with a spot of exploitation, supplement the family income. He took them to play before Maximilian Joseph III, Elector of Bavaria, and there, between playing keyboard duets and responding precociously to the wonderment of the courtly audience, they met *Kapellmeister* Andrea Bernasconi (1706–84). The fast-growing musical awareness of Wolfgang would have been impressed by his racy, Italianate three-movement symphonies, so different from his father's. Leopold was thrilled with the success of the visit, and it is difficult to accuse him of being mercenary in the face of his declaration that he would be failing in his duty to God if he did not make known to the world the gifts He had lavished upon his son. Exploitation, thereby, became devout praise to Heaven, and whatever audiences, wondering or cynical, thought about it, it is plain that, in the hectic travelling years that followed, Leopold's conscience was as

---

* After her successes with her brother on their European tours, she retired somewhat from public view and later became a music teacher—as a sister of the great Mozart she would hardly have wanted for pupils—married well, and lived to the age of seventy-eight. Her final years were clouded by blindness, and she died in Salzburg on October 29, 1829.

† Theophilus = literally "Loved by God." This name translates into German as Gottlieb, but, during his travels to Italy in 1770, Mozart adopted the form Amadeo, later still favouring Amadè.

clear as his finances, despite vigorous protestations to the contrary, were healthy. The great adventure that was to deprive Wolfgang of a normal childhood and turn him into a roving showpiece was about to begin.

*

When Leopold announced at the end of summer 1762 that he had arranged a four-month tour centred upon Vienna, Wolfgang was beside himself with anticipation, especially so since his mother was to accompany them. The Mozart family left Salzburg on September 18, travelling via Linz* and arriving in Vienna on October 6. Wolfgang and his sister could hardly wait to see the court of the Empress Maria Theresia, but other noble houses were on Leopold's meticulously prepared list and they were not to visit the magnificent Schönbrunn Palace until the end of their first week. *Kapellmeister* Wagenseil was there, and it probably amused Wolfgang to relegate that worthy, whose keyboard works he so admired, to the role of page-turner in a performance of one of his own keyboard concerti while the precocious young Mozart played the solo part. Doubtless some of Wagenseil's symphonies were played and Wolfgang would have noticed how different they were from Bernasconi's: squarer, more sober and solid, similar to his father's and yet not so much fun, and with a rustic minuet tucked in between the slow movement and Finale. These impressions were stored away.

Meanwhile the children were dazzled by the splendour of Schönbrunn and by the charm of the royal residents. Wolfgang kissed the Empress, was pampered by Marie Antoinette, the future Queen of France, and performed musical tricks for the assembly, executing difficult pieces with two fingers and playing while the keyboard was covered by a cloth. Leopold, watching these antics and the favourable responses they provoked, must have realised that his days as a composer were over: his most useful role henceforth would be as business manager. His wife, on the other hand, probably drifted from one breathtaking event to the next, never quite sure what miracle had plucked her from poverty to become the mother of children special enough to be summoned to perform before royalty, while poor Nannerl played her parts in the duets dutifully. It could not have been easy for a talented eleven-year-old girl to be so totally upstaged by her little brother. And Wolfgang himself? It was, of course, a huge game to him. These people—princes, empresses and the like—were just the same as other folk: they smiled while he played upon the harpsichord and they applauded when he stopped, but their musical tastes were undistinguished. The only thing that separated

---

* The Trinity Inn, Hofgasse 14, Linz, was the place of Wolfgang's first public recital on October 1, 1762.

them from ordinary people was their money and, if they were happy to part with some of it while he played, nothing need stand in the way of universal happiness.

Unfortunately, something did intervene. After a concert at Schönbrunn a doctor was called to examine the young musician, who was packed off to bed with "a kind of scarlet fever," and during the next ten days a number of concerts had to be cancelled.* Before the family returned home Wolfgang had recovered sufficiently for a fortnight's visit to Bratislava (then Pressburg), and Leopold had received an irresistible invitation: the children would be welcome at Versailles.

To Leopold the visit to Vienna had been little more than a winter holiday. He wanted to show off his miraculous children in every musical centre from Salzburg to the Atlantic Ocean, taking in Versailles on the way, and they were to be off again "with the swallows" in spring 1763. Once again, however, Wolfgang's ill health—this time rheumatism—delayed things, and his mother understandably insisted that he should have time to recover. During the delay Wolfgang composed those items that carry the earliest numbers in the Köchel Catalogue, and Leopold bought a carriage. At last all was ready, and on June 9, 1763, Wolfgang, together with his family and a young valet, set out on his biggest adventure yet. As early as the second day they hit trouble: at Wasserburg a rear wheel of the brand-new coach succumbed to rutted roads; but they were soon under way again. Wolfgang collected musical experiences and styles at every point on their long journey via Munich, Augsburg, Ulm, Ludwigsburg,† to Schwetzingen, where they were received courteously by Duke Karl Theodor whose orchestra was still regarded as the finest in Europe. This was the fabled Mannheim orchestra, summering in Schwetzingen, and their disciplined playing, combining the secure style of Germany and the exhilarating *brio* of Italy with a touch of Austrian warmth, made a favourable effect on both father and son. The orchestra, which had been founded by the Bohemian Jan Václav Antonín Stamic‡ (1717–57), was now led by Johann Innocenz Christian Cannabich (1731–98), a pupil of both Stamic and Jommelli, who maintained the strict playing techniques which had been established by his renowned predecessor. The "Mannheim Style" evolved fresh modes of orchestral playing, and Mozart, no less than other composers of the time, was to be influenced

---

* "At the cost," reported Leopold, tight-lipped, "of at least fifty ducats."

† Meeting the composer Niccolò Jommelli (1714–74) in Ludwigsburg, Wolfgang would have been interested to find that the style of his operatic overtures was virtually identical to the symphonies of Bernasconi which he had heard in Munich. Also at Ludwigsburg he met the violinist/composer Pietro Nardini (1722–93), the memory of whose violin concerti may have rested in the young mind to emerge a dozen years later in his own.

‡ Better known even today by his Germanised name Johann Wenzel Anton Stamitz.

deeply by it. But if Wolfgang's musical experience had been widened, Leopold's coffers had been enriched by fifteen louis d'or; both must have felt their visit to have been worth the effort.

Continuing their way into Germany via Heidelberg, Mannheim and Worms, they arrived on August 3 for a stay of six weeks at Mainz, there giving a number of appearances until Leopold could resist the westerly pull of Versailles no longer. They had to go by way of the Austrian Netherlands, and at Aachen they were introduced to Princess Amalia of Prussia (1723–87), a sister of Frederick II and herself a composer, who rained kisses upon Wolfgang and invited them to visit her when she was back home in Berlin. Leopold, with endless charm and tact, did not take up the invitation. His motive was not that he had any reason to dislike Berlin—and he found the Princess herself charming—but purely because "she has no money," and a palace free of money, he felt, should better remain a palace free of Mozarts.

There were, however, obligations to fulfil before they were to see the chandelier-bedecked magnificence of Versailles: five weeks in Brussels delayed their progress, providing a breathing-space before the journey continued. The well-developed if harmonically thick symphonies of Pierre van Maldere (1729–68) were popular in Brussels at this time and Wolfgang would have recognised in them some of the fingerprints of the Mannheim school as well as the absence of a Minuet in third place. The mixture of styles would doubtless have puzzled the boy at a time when he was marshalling his own compositional strength to produce symphonies.

The travel-weary family arrived at last in Paris on November 18, 1763. Wolfgang was enthusiastically absorbed into the Parisian musical scene: his trick of playing with the keyboard covered (now a regular part of the act) was mixed with improvisations and other tricks to the delight of all, but the Mozarts had to wait until just before Christmas for the eagerly-awaited visit to Versailles. For a fortnight the Mozarts were treated like royalty by King Louis XV and his Consort, the only cloud being the overbearing attitude of Madame Pompadour who refused to let Wolfgang kiss her. Visiting the palace of the Prince de Conti, Wolfgang met Johann Schobert (c. 1720–67).* This composer's symphonies presented yet another possibility to Wolfgang since they were in fact chamber pieces in light style, two horns and a violin accompanying an important and melodious keyboard part.

Before they left the French capital, four of Wolfgang's violin sonatas were published—K6–K9 inclusive—showing a mixture of styles from Mannheim, Vienna and Paris. The publication was at Leopold's

---

* The unfortunate Schobert and most of his family were wiped out three years later when a feast of what they thought to be mushrooms proved to be something very different.

expense and may have been his way of marking his son's eighth birthday.* The hazardous two-week journey to London began on April 10, 1764, and once there the invitation to visit Buckingham House soon arrived. They were received by King George III and the German-born Queen Sophia Charlotte in a most grand and cordial fashion and were awarded twenty-four guineas for their entertainment. Leopold would have settled for less grandeur and cordiality if more guineas had been forthcoming, but a second audience, producing a similar fee, helped to placate him. Meanwhile their exploration of the rest of London's musical life took them to Hickford's Music Room in Brewer Street and other halls, and a meeting with two expatriate German composers was to have a deep influence upon Mozart's development. Early in 1764 Johann Christian Bach and Karl Friedrich Abel had combined their talents to take over a series of concerts formerly organised by Mrs. Cornelys. J. C. Bach had been in London for less than two years, Abel for five. When Bach arrived in 1762 it was as a replacement opera composer for the King's Theatre, also called The Opera House, at the lower end of the Haymarket. This establishment was regarded as the acme of fashion in a very active musical environment, but its reputation for quality was in danger due to the unimaginative pastiches being put on with laborious regularity by Gioacchino Cocchi. John Bach (he was accepted and his name Anglicised almost immediately) arrived from Milan with fresh ideas and a head full of charming melody, only to find that the singers for whom Cocchi had been writing were themselves tenth-rate. He struggled on with the available resources, producing a few pastiches of his own, but it soon became evident to him, unburdened as he was with false modesty, that the overtures he prepared for these productions were of considerably better quality than the stage productions themselves. To exploit his facility in handling the orchestra he amalgamated with his friend Abel, also a fluent writer of symphonies/overtures. The first Bach/Abel concert took place on January 23, 1765,† at Carlisle House, Soho Square, and it proved to be such a success that the centre of London's musical life soon shifted to Soho. These concerts stimulated the two composers to produce increasingly urbane music, and the young Mozart may have found one particular feature of their symphonies reminiscent of some of Handel's keyboard pieces that he had seen at King George III's residence. This was a species of smooth, graceful, *legato* minuet of considerable melodic beauty, quite different from the rougher and more rustic minuets of Vienna. He may at first have considered this to be a specifically English,

---

* Leopold was not too anxious to acknowledge that his *Wunderkind* had passed another milestone: he seems to have taken no steps at all to correct announcements made in London during their visit about "the seven-year-old" Wolfgang.

† Although a joint benefit concert had been given on Leap Year Day 1764.

or at least Anglicised-German, invention, but in fact it can be traced back to Italy, and perhaps more specifically to Milan: Giovanni Battista Sammartini (c. 1701–75), the "Milanese Sammartini," composed a number of such minuets, and Handel brought the style to England earlier in the century after a sojourn in Italy. It came to be a regular part of the musical language of native English composers, and we shall note several examples when we come to examine Mozart's own music in detail.

From Wolfgang's London visit came solo and accompanied keyboard works, vocal pieces, and, at last, his first five symphonies. The gentle and charming influence of John Bach is very strong in the two surviving works, Nos. 1 and 4, each of which is cast, like Bach's, in three movements, and the opening theme (the rest is lost) of KE19B is based on a rhythm identical to the one used over and over again by Bach, and later by Mozart himself. Wolfgang's debt did not end there: a group of three keyboard concerti (KE21B=K107) are merely expanded versions of keyboard sonatas by John Bach*; and as an exercise during the preparation of his own first symphony, Mozart copied out an E flat symphony by Abel (op. 7 no. 6), substituting clarinets for the original oboe parts.†

In May 1764 Leopold contracted a severe cold which induced him to move the family to the village of Chelsea, then outside London, for the better air. "In England," he wrote, "there is a kind of native complaint, which is called a 'cold.' That is why you hardly ever see people wearing summer clothes."

After a season and a half in London that not even Leopold regarded as unsuccessful, the time had come to leave for Paris again and then on to Milan, but the Dutch Envoy pleaded with Leopold to take his children to The Hague at the invitation of Princess Caroline of Nassau-Weilburg. Via Dover and Calais they arrived at Lille where they were forced to rest for a month owing to a recurrence of a throat infection that spread from Wolfgang to his father, and they did not arrive in The Hague until September 10, 1765. There, illness struck hard: Nannerl contracted intestinal typhus. It took so firm a hold that the family felt Nannerl's blameless life to be lost, but she gradually recovered only to see her brother fall sick with the same grave complaint. He lay critically ill for two months, but he, too, slowly recovered, and it was during his convalescence that he produced another symphony: No. 5 in B flat. The

---

* One may imagine this kindly man, fascinated by the uncanny ability of young Wolfgang, handing over a few sheets of music. "Here," he might have said, "turn these old sonatas of mine into concerti for me and we will play them at the next concert." In providing the boy with an exercise he donated to posterity Mozart's first efforts in writing keyboard concerti.

† Although the "Mozart" version with clarinets, has been recorded a number of times, the author knows of no recording of Abel's original.

Mozarts eventually moved on to Paris, arriving there on May 10, 1766.

Looking back on their stay in the Low Countries the Mozarts, despite serious health setbacks, could count a number of successful concerts and meetings with composers prominent in The Hague. The Court *Kapellmeister* was the German Christian Ernst Graf (or Graff) (c. 1726–c. 1802/4) who, a few years after his appointment there in 1762, changed the spelling of his name to the more Dutch-looking Graaf. He was a prolific composer of some forty symphonies,* concerti mainly for wind instruments, and chamber music. His assistant was Giovanni Battista Zingoni, a tenor who had worked in London with J. C. Bach in 1763. Both Graf and Zingoni composed symphonies with "singing allegros," another fingerprint of the John Bach style that Mozart had heard in London.

The second Paris sojourn, despite another visit to Versailles, was less hectic than the first. Illness and fatigue had weakened the family and homesickness was becoming a factor, but many miles yet lay between the Mozarts and Salzburg. Southward they travelled to Dijon and Lyons, and on August 20 they crossed yet another frontier, arriving at Geneva for a tour of Switzerland lasting nearly two months: Lausanne, Berne, Zürich, Winterthur and Schaffhausen were entertained.† The last part of the journey, through south Germany and back into Austria, took a further six weeks, and the family, tired and heartily grateful to be home, finally arrived in Salzburg on November 29, 1766. The first great tour was over.

*

It is said that he who knows all forgives all. We may forgive Leopold for his apparent ruthless insistence on driving his young children halfway across Europe and back again in a hectic and exhausting forty-one-month tour. As a struggling musician himself Leopold realised the precariousness of the living he had chosen and it was only by luck that he had secured a reasonably stable post. But his wife had borne him seven children, five of whom had died in infancy; it requires a lot more knowledge than we possess about Leopold for us to forgive him for risking the lives of the two survivors in this strenuous and dangerous tour. In addition to depriving them of much of their childhood through

---

* His symphony in F, op. 7 no 5, was "discovered" recently at Gniezno in Poland and mistaken for an unknown work of Joseph Haydn. Professor Jan LaRue corrected this impression in an article in the "Festskrift Jens Peter Larsen" (W. Hansen, Copenhagen, 1972), restoring the symphony to its rightful author; yet, as Professor LaRue points out, the correct attribution has been known since Breitkopf advertised the work for sale in 1768.

† Leopold was still making no effort to correct announcements that deducted a year from Wolfgang's age, but who can blame him for taking advantage of the boy's illness that had cruelly wasted his body, causing remarks in Paris that, in 1766, Wolfgang looked no bigger than he had been three years earlier?

arduous travel, he had insisted that their education should not be neglected and therefore lessons had to be crammed in whenever the necessities of eating, sleeping and concert-giving allowed. In the Netherlands he had come within an ace of losing both children through typhus. Many another father would have cut his losses and headed straight home without putting further strain on the young constitutions, a distance of some 500 miles as the crow flies. But Leopold insisted that the tour should go on, and our crow would have to traverse some 1,000 miles to track their progress from The Hague, via Paris, Switzerland and Dillengen, to Salzburg. Our residual sympathy for Leopold is drained even further since, after a rest* of less than ten months, he disrupted family life yet again to hasten them off to Vienna where a daughter of Maria Theresia was to be married to Ferdinand, King of Naples. The Mozarts stopped to visit the kindly monks at the Benedictine Abbey of Lambach, and they arrived in Vienna on September 15, only to meet a smallpox epidemic. This dread disease threw the Austrian capital into confusion and doubt. While Leopold awaited the expected invitation to court, Wolfgang put the finishing touches to another symphony, KE42A, in F. The invitation never arrived; instead came the tragic news that the seventeen-year-old bride-to-be had died of smallpox, and Leopold, realising that nothing could be gained by remaining in Vienna during the court mourning period, took his family to Olmütz—where both children were brought down by the same disease. Luckily it was a mild strain, sufficient to immunise the children so that Leopold might return safely with them to Vienna, which he did in New Year 1768, and they finally appeared at court on January 19.

During their year in Vienna the Mozarts met the composers Giuseppe Bonno (1710–88) and Johann Adolf Hasse (1699–1783), the latter the composer of over one hundred operas, and Wolfgang had completed another opera, *Bastien und Bastienne*, KE46B (=K50), the *Waisenhausmesse* (Orphanage Mass), KE47D (=K49), some vocal and instrumental works, and Symphony No. 8. During the journey home, father and son are thought to have called again at Lambach Abbey and may have presented two symphonies to their hosts, but both works remain the subject of conjecture as to their authenticity. On their return to Salzburg Leopold met with a severe shock where it hurt most: the Archbishop had suspended his salary for the last nine months. With difficulty he finally had his salary restored, but it was not so easy to

---

* This "rest" was filled for Wolfgang by intensive study of counterpoint. A number of church works date from this period, together with a group of four keyboard concerti, K37, 39, 40 and 41, based as a tribute on the sonata movements of Hermann Friedrich Raupach (1728–78), Leonzi Honauer (c. 1740–78), Schobert, Johann Gottfried Eckard (c. 1735–1809), and C. P. E. Bach (1714–88), whose music he had encountered during the first tour, and two stage works: *Die Schuldigkeit des ersten Gebotes*, K35 and a "Latin comedy" *Apollo et Hyacinthus*, K38.

settle back into the humdrum routine of court life and naturally his mind turned again to thoughts of travel. In order to cut down his expenses, he decided that his wife and daughter, being less valuable as money-makers, should this time be left at home. In preparation for the journey, to sunny Italy, Wolfgang composed a group of three symphonies, all of which are lost.

Both Leopold and his son were now on the staff of the Salzburg court, the latter, as "Concert-Maister," subordinate to Ferdinand Seidl and Michael Haydn; permission for the two Mozarts to absent themselves for an Italian tour was conditional upon Wolfgang actually returning, otherwise Leopold would receive no pay. During December father and son set off with a servant on the first Italian tour, Wolfgang giving his first concert on Italian soil at Verona on January 5, 1770. The tour embraced all the important musical centres including Mantua, Milan, Parma, Modena, Bologna, Florence and Siena, fetching up at last in Rome on April 11, where, in St. Peter's on the day they arrived, Wolfgang heard the *Miserere* by Allegri that he later wrote out from memory. Pressing on, they reached the southernmost limit of their journey at Naples on May 14, where they involved themselves deeply not only in the musical life of the area but also in its history, visiting Herculaneum, Pompeii and Vesuvius. After six weeks the Mozarts began their return journey via Rome where they were given an audience by the Pope. Also present may have been the Bishop of Gurk—Mozart's first meeting with a man who was to cause him such heartache and frustration later. Leaving Rome, the Mozarts cut across to the Adriatic coast road to take in Ancona, Senigallia, Pesaro and Rimini before turning inland back to Bologna and ultimately to Milan, arriving there on October 16, 1770. Many other centres saw the Mozarts before they turned homewards again, and the first Italian tour finished with their return to Salzburg on March 28, 1771. The opera *Mitridate, rè di Ponto*, KE74A (=K87), was commissioned for Milan, its florid style meeting general approval despite the intrigues of jealous native rivals, and a series of symphonies also dates from this visit. Among the many composers he met there, the one that left the greatest impression on him was the doyen of Italian symphonists, G. B. Sammartini. At last Mozart had met the man who was one of the chief disseminators of that smooth *legato* style of minuet-writing that he had encountered in London, admired, and subsequently taken into his own fund of devices. He had also met in Bologna the Bohemian composer Josef Mysliveček (1731–81), an immensely gifted and prolific composer of many symphonies, operas and chamber works. The Italians, yielding in the unequal battle against the pronunciation of his name, called him "Il divino boemo" and regarded him as one of the most pleasing and skilful of all composers, a description with which Mozart did not argue. In June 1770 the young traveller had been awarded the highest class of the order of the Golden Spur, an honour somewhat higher than those which had been conferred upon Dittersdorf and Gluck. When the newly-created knight was admitted to the presence of the Pope two days later, he wore the golden cross, proudly suspended from a deep red ribbon pinned to his tunic.

On August 13, 1771, father and son set off southwards again, arriving in Milan on the twenty-first of that month. Wolfgang was soon offered a libretto, *Ascanio in Alba*, K111, to follow up his earlier success with *Mitridate*, and the new opera was enthusiastically received on October 17. On the previous day Hasse's *Ruggiero* was performed and the inevitable comparisons were drawn. Old Hasse himself, at the age of seventy-two, had learned to be philosophical about the unfair competition offered by the fifteen-year-old Austrian. Prophetically and generously he remarked: "This youngster will consign us all to oblivion." *Ruggiero* was to be Hasse's last opera even though he lived for a further decade. When the Mozarts lunched with Hasse at the home of Count Firmian, the veteran composer acted with charm and respect towards Wolfgang, a generosity of spirit altogether unexpected in the prevailing atmosphere of operatic intrigue.

With hopes of a permanent position for Wolfgang in Milan, the Mozarts returned home for what they both hoped would be the last time before the young man settled down to a lucrative post. During the next months, however, three strokes of misfortune descended: Archbishop Schrattenbach, the Mozarts' employer, died; the Milanese appointment fell through; and in April the haughty and arrogant Bishop of Gurk, whom they had met in Rome two years earlier, was installed as Prince-Archbishop of Salzburg. The historic running battle between Wolfgang and Hieronymus, Count Colloredo, had begun. Wolfgang wrote *Il sogno di Scipione* to celebrate the Archbishop's accession, but any goodwill that the opera aroused in the Archbishop could not be substantiated because the two composers set out yet again for Milan on October 24, 1772. This time it was to be *Lucio Silla* that brought the young composer renewed success in Milan, but feelers for a permanent Italian post were again disappointed, and in March 1773 the Mozarts returned again to Salzburg, their interest in Italy and its dissolving prospects totally evaporated.

*

During that summer news came that Florian Leopold Gassmann (1729–74), a Viennese *Kapellmeister* of Bohemian origin and a prolific opera and symphony composer, court conductor at the Burg Theatre, was ailing after a fall from a carriage. Without ado, Leopold sped Wolfgang to Vienna in the hope (vehemently denied) that he might have the opportunity of stepping into the unfortunate Gassmann's shoes. All political moves, however, were effectively blocked by the presence in Vienna of Wolfgang's own employer, the Archbishop Colloredo, so Leopold had to be content with a normal concert-giving visit during which they renewed their acquaintance with Franz Anton Mesmer whom they had met on their previous visit. Scientist, thaumaturgist and musician, Mesmer (1734–1815) gave his name to the practice of hypnotism—mesmerism—in the relief of pain, but on this occasion he introduced Wolfgang to a miraculous instrument, the so-called glass-harmonica* for which Mozart, towards the end of his life, wrote a number of haunting pieces. For Leopold the Vienna trip had been disappointing, but Wolfgang's artistic nature had been immensely enriched. He had been brought into contact (not for the first time) with the music of a lofty and isolated composer by the name of Joseph Haydn, who was secreted away in the marshlands of Hungary in a splendid castle owned by Prince Esterházy. Only Haydn's music seemed able to escape imprisonment, which it did by its sheer force of character. His string quartets, opp. 17 and 20 (1771; 1772), had spread rapidly from their remote epicentre and were the prime talking-points in Vienna during Wolfgang's stay. Haydn's symphonies, too, were being played: works of enormous emotional power and depth such as Nos. 39, 49, 44 and 45, in gaunt minor keys, and Nos. 42, 46, and 47 in which major keys were strangely coloured by dark infusions of minor tonality. Even some of the keyboard music displayed this bleaker side.† So powerful was the impression of this music upon Wolfgang that he looked upon one of his colleagues at the Salzburg court with new interest: Joseph Haydn's younger brother Michael might himself have some of this strange power. In particular he paid attention to a monumental recent *Requiem* that the introspective Michael had written: an intense, moving C minor work of rich emotional appeal.

In December 1774 Mozart father and son set off for a three-month visit to Munich. *La finta giardiniera* (K196) was performed during the carnival there in January. A gentleman called Unger from the French Legation in the city attended this performance and should enter the history books as one of the most perceptive of all critics. He wrote: "Mozart, if he has not been forced like a hothouse flower, will certainly become one of the greatest composers who ever lived." Posterity has agreed less with Christian Daniel Friedrich Schubart who reported a

---

* In appearance this is an oblong box partly filled with water. A central rod fixed at a gentle slope above the water carries a series of glass discs of reducing size, the lower edges of which are revolved in the water by means of a foot pedal driving the rod. Notes are produced by the friction of wetted fingertips on the rims of the glass discs.

† The so-called "Sturm and Drang" movement in music, of which these works form an important part, is discussed more fully in Chapter Two.

musical contest between Wolfgang and Ignaz von Beecke (1733–1803), finding the latter far superior. Nevertheless, the Mozarts returned home on March 7, 1775, aglow with success and in good time to prepare a performance of *Il rè pastore*, K208, in honour of the visiting Archduke Maximilian. Caught again in the routine of Salzburg court music-making, it seemed that Wolfgang was finished with, perhaps even bored with, the flurry and panic of concert-giving tours and being displayed to sundry royal gatherings as if he were some miraculous performing dog. During the ensuing static period an incredible amount of music issued from his racing brain, including some of the greatest of all repertoire works: the Violin Concerti in D, K211; in G, K216; in D, K218; and in A, K219; the keyboard concerti in B flat, K238; in C, K246; and in E flat, K271; the Triple Concerto, K242; five masses, including the pretty little "Organ Solo Mass," K259; seven wind-band divertimenti; two flute quartets; and a host of arias, church sonatas, marches and other miscellaneous works. If no symphonies appeared during this period, there was still a great deal of orchestral activity: some nine divertimenti or serenades were produced, among them the big *Haffner* Serenade, KE248B (=K250), composed for the wedding of Elisabeth Haffner.

Least appreciative of all men, Archbishop Colloredo made no secret of the fact that he regarded the Mozarts as an expensive incumbrance. Wolfgang, in desperation, had written to his old friend Padre Martini in Bologna to test the musical temperature in Italy, but this probe was parried gently and cleverly. Meanwhile, in March 1777, Leopold applied for leave to take Wolfgang on another tour, but the Archbishop played dog-in-the-manger: how was he expected to maintain a musical establishment and provide entertainment for the Emperor Joseph II, due for a visit shortly, if his irresponsible music suppliers were to detach themselves and go off across Europe like beggars? For a few more months Wolfgang tolerated the jibes of his "Most Worthy Prince of the Holy Roman Empire, Most Gracious Sovereign and Lord," but the poison he had received rankled in his soul and he reached breaking-point at the end of August. The letter he wrote to the Archbishop vented with amazing restraint a fraction of his wrath: "I trust that Your Grace will not take my humble request amiss, bearing in mind that, three years ago, when I applied for leave to visit Vienna, Your Grace graciously said that I should certainly be well advised to seek my future elsewhere since I could hope for nothing here." Wolfgang pointed out that he owed much of his education to his father and that, in seeking to establish a better living elsewhere he was merely fulfilling an obligation to God in attempting to provide for his father's later years. The Archbishop was fully up to such verbal subtleties. He wrote to the Court Chamber that father and son, in accordance with the Gospel, have permission to seek their fortunes elsewhere.

This was not at all what Leopold had in mind. At the age of fifty-eight he felt that his days of unemployment should be over and, in what must have been a humiliating meeting for Leopold but a profoundly satisfying one for the Archbishop, he was granted permission to stay. For Wolfgang, however, the time had come to part. Plans were made for him to travel with his mother to Paris. The parting was painful, but least of all perhaps for Wolfgang whose drive to leave Salzburg was a consuming thought. His joy at being away flows out of his letters at this time. The trip to Paris was to take in other centres along the way, the first being Munich, where Wolfgang's mind worried upon the possibility of obtaining regular employment. Sanguine at first, his encounters with various contacts proved disappointing. One suspects that missives had passed from certain high places in Salzburg to lay down more poison for the self-possessed Mozart in his efforts to establish himself in Munich. Wolfgang renewed his friendship with Josef Mysliveček, "il divino boemo," who had undergone a bizarre operation that had removed his nose, the doctors asserting that this action would cure his venereal disease. Generously Mysliveček offered to share with Wolfgang a commission he had secured for two operas for the next Naples carnival, giving the young composer the more important part of the contract; but when it came to it there was a cold silence from Naples. With his Italian contacts, had the spiteful Colloredo effectively blocked this scheme, too?

Deflated, Wolfgang took his mother to Augsburg. A meeting with a Catholic nobleman Jakob Wilhelm Langenmantel generated neither money nor goodwill, but an association with the piano-maker Andreas Stein was much happier, even though the concert arranged to present three of his pianos in the Triple Concerto, K242, brought in less money than had been spent on it. A cordial welcome awaited Wolfgang at the Heiligkreuz Monastery where he gave a dazzling display of improvisation. At one point a sonata was placed before him to sight-read. It was chosen specially to stump the young pianist with its polyphonic complexities. For a moment Wolfgang looked at the music, then shook his head and admitted that it was too much for him to play without preparation. Embarassed, Father Zöshinger made to remove the offending sonata, fearing that he had upset his guest, but Wolfgang restrained him and, with a twinkle in his eye, played it through perfectly. The monks were delighted by this prank, and their delight was immeasurably increased by the musical gifts that Mozart left with them: two *Missae breves* (KE186F=K192, and KE196B=K220) and other sacred compositions.

Leopold heard of the expensive Stein concert and instantly forbade further "tomfoolery," insisting that his wife and son seek more remunerative opportunities. This they did, Wolfgang regretfully, for he was in the process of losing his heart to his cousin Maria Anna Thekla Mozart, a vivacious young lady with spirited manners and a sense of fun that matched his own.* During their stay at Augsburg Wolfgang's mother had suffered from a depressing and persistent chill, but unwisely her retiring nature had made light of it. They moved to the more musically stimulating atmosphere of Mannheim where things had changed since their last visit in 1763. Cannabich was still head of the musical establishment, but the pioneering spirit of the orchestra was gone, the enormous library containing some 500 trail-breaking symphonies by Jan Stamic, Antonín Fils, Ignaz Holzbauer, Frantisek Xaver Richter and others was considered to have fulfilled its purpose and was becoming old-fashioned. Preferred now were the smoother works of Cannabich, Ignaz Fränzl and Innocenz Danzi, occupying a plateau that had grown on the steep experimental slopes of the earlier, now dead or vanished, masters. The Mannheim orchestra still considered that it led the world in discipline and polish, seemingly unaware that the lessons it had taught had been well learned and expert orchestras were springing up elsewhere, particularly in France and the Low Countries. Nevertheless, enough musical perceptiveness remained for Wolfgang to be well appreciated by musicians and Elector alike, and for a time it looked as though an appointment might come his way. For weeks the matter hung in the balance, Leopold's letters accusing Mozart of not trying hard enough to secure a post and Wolfgang's replies refusing to take life seriously. Soon the correspondence was bringing pain to both sides: the maturing son was fighting against the steadying experience of the father, and matters were not helped by Leopold's suspicion of deeper motives behind the friendliness of Cannabich towards Wolfgang. Did not Cannabich have a nubile unmarried daughter, and was not Wolfgang, if only he would adopt a responsible attitude to life, a most eligible bachelor?

Gradually the reason for the courtly procrastination became apparent. The appearance of Wolfgang, presentable, wordly and skilful, fired in the Elector an acquisitive spark. He liked to have him around, but to make it permanent would be to alienate his second *Kapellmeister*, Georg Joseph Vogler, into whom the Elector had sunk a great deal of money in sending him to study intensively in Italy. Perhaps some politically acceptable compromise might arise if the two were to meet. The opportunity came in December upon the occasion of the completion of a new organ in the Protestant Church. Vogler was to play; Wolfgang was to join the listening tests. History does not record the result of this trial from the viewpoint of the organ, but the meeting between

---

* Wolfgang's letters to her are full of coarse humour that, if it did not make her laugh, would certainly have made her blush.

Wolfgang and Vogler was a disaster: instant dislike on both sides brought the Elector's plan tumbling down. Wolfgang's opinion of Vogler was duly relayed to his father, and we may picture Leopold spreading his hands in despair at the apparent intransigence of his son and deciding once and for all to put a stop to the Mannheim fiasco. He laid plans for his recalcitrant son to go forthwith to Paris with the Mannheim instrumentalists Wendling, Ramm and Ritter, now that the Elector of Mannheim had closed his court and rushed off to seek his succession at Munich subsequent to the death of Maxmilian Joseph of Bavaria. It was a sad time in Mannheim. The famous orchestra, Europe's finest for more than thirty years, Burney's "Army of generals," was at an end, and although the band eventually followed the Elector to Munich, the spell of Mannheim was broken for ever. What could Wolfgang do in the circumstances but take his mother to Paris? He soon found a reason to flout his father's demands. He wrote to say that he was going to visit the Princess of Orange, none other than Princess Caroline of Nassau-Weilburg, who had invited the Mozart family to The Hague in 1765. "She loves singing and has a nice little orchestra," he wrote. "I shall be accompanied on the journey by Herr Weber whose sixteen-year-old daughter has a beautiful, pure singing voice." The daughter referred to, Aloysia, was the second of Fridolin Weber's four daughters. What Wolfgang did not admit was that he had fallen blindly in love with Aloysia, which is why he did not want to go to Paris. Leopold was furious. He renewed attempts to get Wolfgang to Paris, but Wolfgang rebounded with a madcap scheme to take Aloysia and her father to Italy where, he felt, her voice would make the Webers rich. In any case, he asked his father when detailing these plans, who would wish to travel to Paris or anywhere else with Wendling and his Godless friends?

"Enough! You will not go to Italy with the Webers. You will go to Paris without delay, and your mother will accompany you to make sure you get no more hare-brained ideas." Such was the essence of an immensely long letter Leopold fired off, and it did the trick. Wolfgang, bowing to the blast, retained his pride by pretending that he did not really mean that the Italian trip should take place *before* the Paris one. In any event, the decision was made and the Mozarts—mother and son—left at last for Paris in March 1778. It was an ill-starred trip.

*

Musical Paris was a very different city from the one Mozart had known as a boy. Joseph le Gros, Director of the Concert Spirituel, dominated the intrigue-ridden scene, and the contents of those concerts was centred upon a new craze, the Sinfonie Concertante, an artificial style of symphony in which two or more soloists were spotlighted. It thus satisfied the Parisian taste for big orchestral sounds in the tuttis and hero-worship of famous players in the episodes. A colourful character, Giovanni Giuseppe Cambini (1746–1825)* produced a new *sinfonie concertante* every month: empty, feather-light works when compared with the *Sturm und Drang* compositions then sweeping Europe. In the presence of Wendling, Ramm and Ritter, who had preceded him to Paris, and of Punto the horn-player, Mozart immediately fulfilled Le Gros's request for a *concertante* for flute, oboe, bassoon and horn. Parisian politicians went to work and the performance of Mozart's piece was delayed again and again. It eventually sank without trace.†

More fortunate was the Symphony No. 31 in D that Mozart wrote for the Concert Spirituel, a brilliant work full of Mannheim *clichés* and pompous effects, a style eagerly appreciated by the Parisians, who were outraged that a mere visiting Austrian should dare to flout their conventions by commencing the final Allegro at a low dynamic level. "They all held their breath," wrote Mozart, "and when the *tutti* arrived they applauded loudly."

The busy composer was forced to leave his mother virtually imprisoned in dingy quarters where she was numb with boredom and discomfort, unable to read even at noon because of the poor light. Thrown back on private thoughts, she must have pictured her famous son in his social whirl and apparently careless of her well-being; and her husband and daughter fretting their lives away in Salzburg. What use was she to any of them? Neglected, and with a feeling of superfluousness, she gave up the struggle on July 3, 1778. Wracked with remorse, Mozart broke the news to his father as gently as he knew how.

A brief reunion with dear old John Christian Bach, on a visit from London, was the only thing left for Mozart in Paris, so, hearing that the musical establishment in Salzburg was being reorganised and that there would be room for him there, he made his way back home slowly, inventing dozens of reasons to dally because the prospect of working

---

* In his youth, Cambini is said to have been captured with his *fiancée* by corsairs during a voyage to Leghorn and, strapped to a mast, he witnessed the violation of this unfortuante girl, after which he was sold into slavery only to be released on account of his magical violin-playing. Once settled in Paris, Cambini was not above writing some "Boccherini" quartets for a publisher when finances pressed. Cambini's only other claim upon posterity is his invention of wind quintets for flute, oboe, clarinet, bassoon and horn which may have developed from chamber arrangements of his later *sinfonies concertantes*.

† Amid mysterious circumstances, it is supposed to have surfaced again about a hundred years later, the oboe part curiously transferred to clarinet. Some recordings have been made of this work, KE297B (=KA9), but an interesting experiment was made by the late Karl Ristenpart who re-allocated the upper parts in an attempt to reconstruct the original. A recording of this version, conducted by Ristenpart, exists on Nonesuch H 71068, coupled with the C major Concertone, for two violins and orchestra, KE166B (=K190).

again for the Archbishop was still horribly unattractive. At last he arrived in Salzburg and settled down to work under the taunts of his supercilious employer, producing many of his most famous works. For Munich he wrote *Idomeneo*, visiting that city to arrange its first performance while the Archbishop went off to Vienna leaving Leopold free to bring Nannerl to Munich for the *première*. All was going well when the Archbishop, apparently remembering his role as Mozart-tormentor, summoned Mozart to Vienna. The composer dropped everything and obeyed, arriving there on March 15, 1781, straight into the demeaning servitude he so detested. Petty annoyances, minor and unnecessary restrictions, and the feeling that Archbishop Colloredo regarded him as of hardly more importance than the lowest servant—all combined to induce a strong resentment in the twenty-five-year-old composer. The crisis came early in May as the Archbishop was preparing to leave Vienna. A package had to be escorted immediately to Salzburg and the Archbishop chose Mozart for the errand. Mozart refused; he had some money owing to him in Vienna and he had no wish to give it up for the privilege of acting as a messenger-boy. In a face-to-face altercation Colloredo called Mozart a villain, an arrogant fool, and other insults. Mozart stamped out, shouting "I will have nothing more to do with you!" In a letter to his father he encouraged him roundly to condemn his son's precipitate action and thereby avoid prejudicing his own position, but at the same time he pleaded for his father to sympathise privately with his decision. He was disappointed. Leopold was heartily tired of his son's tantrums, no matter how caused.

It is from Mozart's correspondence that we learn the story of the celebrated kick. A few days after his verbal collision, the composer arrived at the House of the Teutonic Knights, the Archbishop's Viennese residence, to hand in his formal resignation. Upon his arrival he met the good-natured Court Chamberlain Count Arco. By this time the Count's conciliatory nature had been worn thin by Mozart's wronged attitude and at last it gave way, an immaculately shod foot being applied to the proud Mozartean posterior.

*

Out of work yet again, Mozart lived as a paying guest with the Weber family, now resident in Vienna. Aloysia meantime had married, old Fridolin had died, and the mother, Marie Cäcilia, saw in Mozart the opportunity to marry off her other daughter Constanze, now eighteen years old. By accepting pupils and writing easily-sold short pieces,*

---

* Including the eight variations on a march from Grétry's opera *Les mariages samnites*, that Cambini had previously taken for treatment by string quartet.

Mozart began to make his freelance position pay, entering into, and winning, a keyboard contest with Muzio Clementi (1752–1832), associating with Antonio Salieri (1750–1825), whose name was to be linked so fatefully with Mozart's later, and at last, in the winter of 1781, meeting Joseph Haydn. Already familiar with the older composer's music, perhaps even the forthright and assured Mozart may have been overawed by that first meeting, for a certain reserve prevented the acquaintanceship from ripening then into friendship. Haydn could visit Vienna only rarely each winter when his Prince's demanding schedule allowed it, but gradually these meetings built a friendship that was to count as one of the most mutually respectful in musical history.*

The following August Mozart and Constanze were married, a marriage which Mozart saw as the rescue of a girl from hard usage by her mother. They settled in Vienna to a happy if precarious life, Wolfgang fighting along the untrodden path of self-employment and his timid but loving wife trailing after him in trusting confusion. From the start she seemed intent on disproving the theory that two can live as cheaply as one: controlling the uneven cash flow proved completely beyond her and poverty was an ever-present spectre. During a visit to Salzburg in July 1783 to present Constanze to his father, Wolfgang's first son died of dysentery, aged only two months. While there, Wolfgang renewed his acquaintance with Michael Haydn and wrote for him two duets for violin and viola that the older composer had been unable to supply for the Archbishop.

On the return journey to Vienna the Mozarts called on Count Thun at Linz. He was preparing a concert and asked Mozart to contribute a symphony, no less. "As I have no symphony here, I am having to write one at top speed," he wrote to his father. The result was the "Linz" Symphony, No. 36, K425, not a short and lightly-scored piece as one might expect from a composer in a great hurry but a full-length, four-movement work, complete with a slow introduction, the first Mozart had written for a symphony, for large orchestra including trumpets and drums. Also performed at Linz was a symphony that Michael Haydn had written the previous May,† Perger No. 16. Perhaps the Count expressed a liking for slow introductions, for Mozart added one to Michael Haydn's work, and it is because of this that the whole work was at one time attributed to Mozart: Symphony No. 37, in G, KE425A (=K444).

---

* Mozart's study of Haydn's music enriched his imagination and strengthened his melodic resources. He jotted down several themes from Haydn's middle-period symphonies (Nos. 47, 62 and 75: see K387D) and the second Trio of the Minuet of Symphony No. 51 may have suggested the theme for the slow movement of Mozart's Horn Quintet in E flat, KE386C (=K407), written for Joseph Leutgeb.

† Did Michael Haydn make a gift of the work of Mozart as an acknowledgement for rescuing him over the matter of the duos?

46 / mozart: the symphonies

Back in Vienna, Mozart once again threw himself into strenuous composition. Amongst his new works was a third concerto for the aforementioned horn-player Leutgeb.* It appears that this musician, also a cheese merchant from 1777, was either a fun-loving and carefree fellow who took Mozart's jokes in good part, or a humourless dullard only dimly aware but perhaps resentful that Mozart was making fun of him in his scores. "Ass, ox, fool," he writes on one of them, "I have taken pity on you!" "Ass, idiot, pig," he scrawls elsewhere. One may imagine Leutgeb coming across the obscure "musical" indications *Oh che stonatura* and *ohine*, and going to a fellow musician to ask about their meaning, only to discover another of Mozart's petty insults: "Oh what a noise" and "alas!"

Mozart's busy life in Vienna hurtled past. Domestic events, concerts, dealings with publishers and teaching were all slotted in with his own personal heaven of composing. Piano concerti occupied 1784 (he produced six in that year), but other works tumbled out so fast that he at last found it necessary to keep a catalogue of his music, a document that has proved invaluable in the dating of his later pieces. The following year found an interest in freemasonry reflected in his music, and he joined the Grand Lodge of True Concord, setting the seal on his friendship with fellow mason Joseph Haydn. For some time Mozart had been suffering from vomiting and fever and had had to take an enforced rest from composing for some three months in 1784. This unexplained symptom stalked him for the rest of his life and may well have been a contributing factor to his death seven years later.

Nannerl had married in the August of that year; Mozart invited his lonely father to visit him in the New Year and, although the old man suffered miserably with the cold, his heart was warmed by a spontaneous remark from Joseph Haydn: "As an honest man, I tell you before God that your son is the greatest composer I know personally or by reputation." After so many years of worry and exasperation over his son's erratic behaviour and wild ideas, these words spoken by

---

* It is possible that Michael Haydn had written a piece for his friend Leutgeb (or perhaps for the Salzburg cornist Franz Drasil) and had asked Mozart to convey it to him when he returned to Vienna, but it seems that the little work underwent transformation before being handed over to the cheese merchant. The piece in question is a Romance in A flat, for horn and strings, listed as by Michael Haydn in the Rettensteiner Katalogue (Bayerische Staatbibliothek) and dated "Salisb. 30 Aug. 795" (i.e. 1795) but, as Mary Rasmussen suggests in a fascinating article in "Brass and Woodwind Quarterly." Winter 1966/67, not only is this Romance built on a theme identical to the Romance, *larghetto*, of Mozart's Third Horn Concerto No. 3, K447, of 1783, with other close similarities, even identicalities, carried through to the ends of the movements, but internal evidence also suggests that, despite the late date given for Michael Haydn's piece, it was in fact written before Mozart's. Whatever the truth of the matter, the coincidence of the works illustrates the close ties between Mozart and the younger brother of Joseph Haydn.

a great figure of the day swelled his spirit with pride as he joined in with his son's activities and was inducted as an apprentice freemason. In this mood of satisfaction he returned to his lonely duties at Salzburg, carrying with him golden memories of string quartet evenings at his son's fine apartment, the parts played respectively by Joseph Haydn, Karl Ditters von Dittersdorf, Mozart on viola, and Jan Křtitel Vaňhal on cello. Both Dittersdorf and Vaňhal were extremely prolific symphonists, the latter offering considerably more in the way of originality than the former.

The year 1785 saw the production of *Der Schauspieldirektor*, K486, and *Le nozze di Figaro*, K492, followed in May 1786. These and other works brought money flowing into the Mozart household, but it flowed out again with depressing ease. Mozart never learned from his father the trick of frugality. Vienna literally buzzed with tunes from *Figaro*, much to the jealousy of Vincenzo Righini (1756–1812) and Salieri, both of whom had unperformed operas awaiting performance, but it was Martín y Soler's *Una cosa rara* that forced *Figaro* off the Viennese boards after only nine performances. *Figaro* nevertheless took root in Prague and, rejecting temptations to go to London and Italy, Mozart followed his opera to the Bohemian capital. He had felt for some time that Vienna, so full of music and friends, did not offer the opportunities he desired. He arrived in Prague to find the city ringing with melodies from the new opera. Delightedly he reported that the Bohemians "talk of nothing but *Figaro*, play, sing, scrape, blow nothing but *Figaro*!" While in Prague he renewed his friendship with another prolific symphonist, František Dušek (1731–99) who was instrumental in securing for Mozart a valuable commission: another opera. Anxious to start work immediately Mozart took Constanze home to Vienna without delay and, back in Prague nine months later, *Don Giovanni* was completed. One day in April 1787, while still formulating the preliminary sketches for the opera, Mozart was puzzled, perplexed and possibly angry when a lad of seventeen, but claiming to be fifteen (a genuine mistake, caused by his father's desire to sensationalise the sensational), slouched into his apartment. His appearance was the cause of derision, if not alarm: short, sallow, stooping, with a heavy head and a squat nose. His manner was surly, his language a succession of coarse grunts, and he bore a letter of introduction from Archduke Maximilian, the Elector of Cologne. In the youth's stubby fingers it seemed an incongruous document, but those same fingers held a surprise for Mozart when they were loosed upon a keyboard. Here was a strange sound indeed, one which we now know was urging music impatiently into the next century, towards the *Pathètique*, the *Appassionata* and the *Emperor*. Despite his other commitments Mozart spared some time for the boy from Bonn, and we may conjecture that he showed him some old serenades* for two clarinets or two basset horns and one bassoon, perhaps simply to illustrate the use of wind instruments in ensemble.†

The strange youth was soon driven from Mozart's mind by a return of the stomach fever that had so debilitated him in August 1784. This may have been aggravated by worry over the health of his father, now sixty-eight years old. A sensitive letter to his father at this time shows some of the philosophy of freemasonry: "Death is the greatest friend of mankind," he wrote, "and I find its inevitability reassuring and consoling." Leopold departed this life on May 28, 1787, and the news was conveyed to Mozart by a family friend, Franz D'Yppold.

Finances were again bringing worried frowns to the Mozarts' foreheads, yet the reason was certainly not lack of industry on the composer's part. An endless succession of compositions large and small, but invariably great, was entered into the catalogue. After the usual delays *Don Giovanni* was given on October 29, 1787, once again to enthusiastic applause, and it was repeated three times in five days. Those evenings at home with the Dušeks after the intoxicating performances and acclamations must have been amongst Mozart's happiest memories. Full of success, he returned home with Constanze in mid-November. Why did he not stay in Prague? It seems that, just as the imminent death of Gassmann in 1774 would leave a void which Mozart had hoped to fill, so now the famous Gluck, seventy-three years old, was seriously ill. He died on November 15, 1787, and this time Mozart was in the right place at the right time. On December 7, 1787, after seven years of freelance freedom, Mozart's appointment was promulgated: *Kammermusikus* to Joseph II, His Apostolic Majesty, Emperor of the Holy Roman Empire, King of Hungary and Bohemia, Archduke of Austria, etc. His annual salary was 800 gulden; Gluck's had been 2,000. His duties were to provide dance music each year for the court masked balls.

Apart from the D major Piano Concerto, K537, few works appeared in 1788 until the great enigmas of the summer months. Beset with financial worries, Mozart also seems to have been artistically frustrated.

---

* The five divertimenti, KE439B (=K229 and 229A).

† It is possible that he told Beethoven to take them back to his room to study them at leisure, but when he did so the boy found a message saying that his mother was seriously ill in Bonn. In the rush to pack up and leave, Ludwig would have stuffed Mozart's manuscripts into a bag along with his shirts, and they were never seen again. Let us stretch the surmise further still: once back in Bonn, Beethoven studied the divertimenti closely and then produced a set of three duos for one clarinet and bassoon, perhaps as an exercise, but in any case very much in his own personal idiom. Then, in the tumult following his mother's death and the subsequent moves, Mozart's old serenades were stored away amid other papers, to be discovered years later and sold off to a Bonn music dealer. In any event, they were published for the first time in the last years of the century by none other than the Bonn firm of Simrock!

Working with incredible rapidity, his genius gushed forth in three works which are quite simply the most perfectly fashioned symphonies of the Eighteenth, and perhaps of any other, century: Nos. 39, 40, and 41, completed respectively on June 26, July 25, and August 10. No outside commission has come to light, and the death of Theresa, the Mozarts' fourth child, on June 29 seems to have been the only concrete stimulus for the anger, despair and frustration of No. 40 in G minor. Temporarily satisfied artistically, he fell to the production of canons often of a ribald nature and, as the 1788/89 winter season approached, another large batch of *Deutsche* and minuets for the court balls. One more masterpiece came in September: the noble Divertimento in E flat, for string trio, K563.

Lack of money may have dictated another move to a cheaper district outside Vienna, but the comparative isolation may have assisted Mozart's intense concentration during that summer. He made friends with Johann Michael Puchberg, a freemason and a member of a wealthy family of wine-merchants: in this friendship he saw the possibility of resolving some of his financial vexations. His letters to Puchberg, in which he frequently begs for money, make acutely embarrassing reading. There is no doubt that Puchburg went out of his way to help, and he must have realised that the money he contributed was dead and buried despite Mozart's promises of speedy repayment. Other acquaintances were to help the struggling composer, too, but all was in vain as Wolfgang's marriage drifted aimlessly among the sharp rocks of their creditors.

Early in 1789 Prince Lichnowsky invited Mozart to join him on a visit to Berlin, leaving Constanze behind. In Berlin he met King Friedrich Wilhelm II and Queen Frederike, but financially the trip was not worth the effort and he brought home no promises to lighten the future.

Now it was Constanze's turn to fall ill. She was packed off to the baths at Baden for the cure, throwing yet another strain upon Mozart's income. Another baby daughter, Anna, was born, and died, on November 16, and sad though the parents must have been, with a healthily growing four-year-old boy in the family, one wonders how they would have clothed and fed another child. The revival in August of *Figaro* did little to ease their poverty but a commission for a new opera held out some hope. *Così fan tutte* was successfully received in Vienna on January 26, 1790, and later in Prague, Leipzig and Dresden, but Mozart's expected financial breakthrough did not take place and again and again we find him writing pathetic letters to the good-hearted Puchberg. When wondering at the endless benevolence of this young man whose fortune Mozart seemed determined to demolish, we also wonder at the depth of the well down which the composer poured his funds. Is there some hidden factor about which we know nothing?

How had he managed in his earlier lean years without the Puchberg crutch, and how would he have fared if Puchberg had refused to take the responsibility of his debts? Constanze's continued poor health demanded that she move ever and again to Baden—so often, in fact, that one begins to wonder whether it was only the cures that attracted her. During her frequent absences Mozart consoled himself with his good friends, but it is likely that when they visited him they were doubly welcome if they brought a loaf, a round of cheese or a bottle of wine to make the evening less empty and arid.

Thus, in dire financial trouble, fighting a mysterious illness which would come and go like a shadow, frequently deprived of the company of a wife he loved deeply, and pressed to seek new but ever more flimsy excuses to beg money, one of the greatest composers of all time passed his final months. There was excitement still to come, further hopes to be smashed, and much good companionship of friends and pupils, but those who know his music of the last two years may hear in it a mellow, tragic, almost willing acceptance that the inevitable end was drawing close. The quality is all the more poignant in that the composer was still only in his mid-thirties.

*

On October 9, 1790, in Frankfurt, Leopold II was to be crowned Holy Roman Emperor; Salieri and Pater Ignaz Umlauf (1746–96) were to accompany fifteen court musicians there from Vienna for the festivities, but Mozart was not to be among them. He decided to attend in any case, pawned his silver and bought a carriage. He gave a concert after the coronation but the audience was pitifully small and Mozart's remuneration smaller still. From Frankfurt Mozart travelled to Mainz, then to Mannheim, in an attempt to find a better post, and from Mannheim, via Augsburg, he went to Munich to give a concert for the King of Naples who had recently taken delivery of some music by Joseph Haydn. Back in Vienna, Wolfgang received two invitations to go to London: one was from Salomon, who promised to come back for Mozart when his first tour with Haydn was over. So Haydn, at the age of fifty-eight, was off to London! He will never survive the journey, thought Mozart. Tearfully, he bid his friend goodbye with the prophecy that they would never meet again. Haydn was to remember these words in London when, surrounded by honours and success, he heard of Mozart's death. As a tribute he introduced into the slow movement of his Symphony No. 98 in B flat a passage which unmistakably evokes the brooding Andante of Mozart's last symphony.

With the reappearance of an old friend, Emanuel Schikaneder, hope grew again, for his proposal was for a fairy-tale opera, *The Magic Flute*, to be performed in Vienna before Salomon returned from London. Mozart set about the task with his customary alacrity. Money from a new opera would help pay for the new baby and for Constanze's continuing cures at Baden. The opera and the new Mozart were both produced in the summer of 1791 in Vienna, and both were successful. Franz Xaver Wolfgang appeared first, on July 26, and was to grow into a professional pianist and composer, changing his name along the way to Wolfgang Amadeus Mozart. He wrote some fifty works and died in 1844 in Carlsbad. The other offspring, Die Zauberflöte, was completed on September 28, and played twenty-four times to full houses. Meanwhile, another operatic commission had been received from Prague, where Leopold II, the monarch Mozart had seen crowned in Frankfurt, was to be proclaimed King of Bohemia. All was to be carried out in an unconscionable rush, and the music for La clemenza di Tito was assembled with care and punctiliousness by the ailing Mozart in two-and-a-half weeks. He and Constanze dashed off to Prague for the première, but as the opera was disappointingly received they returned home in time for the opening of Die Zauberflöte.

Mozart's lifework was almost complete but there remained yet one further incident which could have come from the lurid pages of a romantic novel. In July 1791 a messenger presented himself to Mozart. He was tall, of forbidding appearance, and dressed in unrelieved sober grey. He brought a commission for a Requiem, but appended to it were strange conditions: no one must know of the grey man's visit, or of the commission itself. The Requiem must be delivered by a certain date whereupon handsome payment would be made.* The effect of these circumstances upon the mind of the sick, over-worked and poverty-depressed composer may well be imagined. His masonic teachings had given him the courage to look at death without fear, but the conviction that his health was failing, coupled to this sinister secret commission for a mass for the dead, was altogether too much. Fatalistically he set about composing the required work, but the weight of Die Zauberflöte, and later of La clemenza di Tito, was too much and he was forced to take a short cut. His mind travelled back to the noble C minor Requiem of Michael Haydn, written in 1771, and his incredible memory served him well: Mozart's D minor Requiem is like Michael Haydn's C minor Requiem remembered. But even this labour-saving procedure did not entirely solve his problem, for the work was never completed by Mozart himself.

At last success and substantial financial reward seemed within reach, with an almost certain bright future in England, but with

---

* It is now known that the "mysterious stranger" was Anton Leitgeb, a messenger from Count Franz Walsegg-Stuppach whose wife had died that February. The Count hoped to pass off the Requiem as his own composition.

crushing inevitability Mozart's health gradually slipped away. Fainting fits became frequent and prolonged, vomiting continued, and he was to complain of numbness of the extremities, weakness, depression and exhaustion. The *Requiem* still occupied his mind, but he was too weak to give it his whole attention. His hands and legs swelled painfully, making it impossible for him to work or walk, his body grew stiff and his forehead hot, and ever and again he was unable to retain what little food he had eaten. The body that had been so abused in early life took revenge and refused to support his teeming brain. On December 4, 1791, he became partially paralysed, yet still fragments of the *Requiem* escaped from his fevered lips, and he drifted in and out of a coma with the noble melodies circling inside his head like the swirling snowflakes outside the window. At five minutes to one o'clock on the morning of December 5 his soul finally escaped the trials and vexations of life. His thirty-sixth birthday was still nearly two month distant.

*

The true nature of Mozart's last illness has exercised minds and pens for nearly two centuries and will doubtless continue to do so because there is no way of knowing the whole truth. A favourite diagnosis is uraemia, a condition in which waste matter is passed into the blood and not expelled properly due to the breakdown of kidney function. The effect is a form of blood-poisoning, and it is noteworthy that Mozart himself intermittently believed that he had been poisoned while at other times dismissing the idea as preposterous. The poisoning of one person by another in Eighteenth-century Vienna was entirely possible and we should be unwise entirely to discount the likelihood that Mozart was a victim. On the other hand, if we embrace it, who are the suspects? Closest to Mozart was his wife, who had ample chance to poison him if she had wished to do so. Did she in fact have a lover in Baden who encouraged her? Certainly not Georg Nikolaus Nissen, whom she married in 1809, an official at the Danish Embassy whom she did not meet until six years after the death of Mozart, and no one else presents himself as a possibility. Despite Constanze's shrewish mother and self-first upbringing, the whole idea seems ridiculous and may be dismissed as, at the very least, unlikely. But there were many others who had access to Mozart's food during those last months while Constanze was away at Baden: his circle of friends, although not large, contains some possibilities. The first name to come forward is Salieri's. Pushkin suspected him strongly enough to write a poem on the subject, and Rimsky-Korsakov agreed with him enough to write an opera about it. Yet what motive could he have had? That Mozart's operas were too successful? A moment's thought demolishes that: operatic success was at that time a flickering thing—one flame burned brightly before being outshone by another. A successful opera by Mozart would last a few months at most before being pushed off the stage by an opera by somoene else and Salieri was well positioned to take his turn in the musical chairs. Unless he was prepared to poison all the other operatic composers in Vienna, the removal of Mozart would not have done him much good. Puchberg? Again, what motive? He was a gentle and kindly man who thought enough of Mozart never to press for credit, even to waive all rights to the money he had lent, and furthermore to help Constanze financially, unasked, after she had become a widow. If Puchberg was ever embarrassed by Mozart's importuning letters he need only have said "No." Süssmayer, Mozart's young pupil? By all accounts he was not an over-bright pupil and his ambitions to become a composer would have only been helped by his continued association with the master. Other composers, inside or out of Mozart's immediate circle, can be ruled out simply because they did not stand to gain appreciably from Mozart's death. A suggestion has been put forward that Mozart in some way transgressed a rule of his masonic lodge and for this he was required to suffer the ultimate penalty. It may be left as a suggestion until some proof of so drastic a measure comes to light.

One name remains to be considered: Joseph Leutgeb, the cheesemonger and horn player. Mozart admitted that he found it difficult to control his urge to play tricks on the poor man, and some of those we know about go beyond the limits of practical jokery. What of those we know nothing about? Is it possible that, one day, in a fit of particularly inventive foolery, Mozart went a stage too far? History reports that the two men remained companions right up to Mozart's death, but it is certainly suspicious that the first onset of serious vomiting occurred shortly after Mozart became reacquainted with Leutgeb in Vienna, and his symptoms are consistent with gradual, prolonged and regular poisoning.

*

How does one judge a character as complex as Mozart's? Examination reveals some of his motives and that, no less than the rest of us, he was subject to the thrust, pull and bruising of the time in which he lived. It is said that life is what one makes it, but this never has been true: life is what others make it for us. The old adage should be amended to read: life is what one makes *of* it, or, happiness depends upon one's attitudes. Mozart grew up with the mental attitude that his life was, if not predestined, then certainly largely in the hands of outside influences. As a member of a devout Catholic family he had been taught that God provides our happiness, like a kindly uncle dispensing sweets, and that if we transgress then God will remove our means of happiness. The Mozarts' letters show that they regarded the gift of good health or of a safe journey as if it were a prize graciously handed out for good, or in spite of bad, behaviour. What chance, then, has the individual of shaping his own life, with God and his fellow men by turns blocking and guiding his progress?

Mozart survived the monstrous burden of his own genius with resilience, humour and courage. His family bonds were strong and his gradual disillusionment with his father (and vice versa) no more acute than in most similar relationships. There are dishonourable episodes in Mozart's life that it is the duty of a biographer to report. A severe lack of self-discipline and restraint has been noted: one may argue on this evidence, backed up by a childish sense of humour that frequently descended to the lavatorial, that he never "grew up" to face the responsibilities of life, yet could this trait not equally be a result of a fatalistic nature that resigned itself to the pull of outside forces and the belief that God was at the helm?

In 1787 we note what seems to be an unpardonably disloyal act on Mozart's part upon the death of his father. For the demise of a pet starling he had written an ode, but for the passing of the man who honestly believed that he had had Mozart's well-being at heart for nearly a quarter of a century he produced *Ein musikalischer Spass* (A Musical Joke). Who can guess whether there were motives behind this apparent lack of respect? Even more embarrassing are the letters to fellow-freemason Michael Puchberg begging for money in a tone that seems to suggest Puchberg's deep and unending indebtedness to Mozart, and becoming more blatantly cringing and desperate as the sad correspondence progresses: "I make so bold as to implore you to lend me a hundred gulden for a week ..." (June 1788); "If you value our friendship will you send one or two thousand gulden for a year or two?" (the same month; Puchberg could not raise the requested amount and told Mozart so, whereupon the composer asked Puchberg to raise the money from some other source!); "I offer you, not thanks, but new demands ... can you and will you lend me 500 gulden ... ?" (July 1789; three days later Mozart wrote again: "I fear that I have angered you, since you have not replied!"); "I am due to receive next month 200 ducats for my opera. Will you rescue your friend from embarrassment until then by lending him 400 gulden?" (December 1789); "Once more, but I assure you for the last time, I call upon you to assist ..." (April 1790, and, as no reply was received, another demand was sent off a few days later); "If you will send me anything, even if it is only the small amount you sent last time, you will greatly oblige ..." (the same month); "Can you not send me something?" (August 1790); "I shall receive my quarterly salary next month but I need about 20 gulden until then ...

I am anxiously awaiting the money" (April 1791); "If you, most dear friend, can send me a small sum I shall be exceedingly obliged" (June 1791).

The Mozartean pride was strong, so we may only guess at the straits to which he had been reduced before writing such letters; it must have been with acute pain that he recalled his father's words warning him to steer clear of a certain Parisian harpist: *"Have nothing to do with him. He has a very bad reputation as a dissolute fellow. Furthermore,"* adds Leopold darkly, *"he runs up debts."*

Leaving aside the sad tale of Mozart's financial stresses, we find a charming and vivacious young man. His sister Nannerl described him as a sociable person, rarely dispirited until the combined weights of poverty and illness brought him down during the final months. As would be expected of an intelligent and carefully educated man, he was personable and always ready with a smile and a witty retort. He allowed his education to show in his letters: he was a fluent and accurate writer, and he loved to pun in different languages since he had at his command a working knowledge of Italian, French, English and Latin in addition to his own tongue. He delighted in all sorts of other games in his letter writing: highly-ornamented initial letters, transposed words, nonsensical dates (e.g. 50 October), alternate lines upside-down, and many others. When not composing or writing letters he was never happier than when in the company of a good book.

Much of his composing seems to have been done in his head. He would be preoccupied for a period, perhaps while appearing to concentrate on a game of billiards or skittles, or upon a meal, working out in his mind a compositional sequence as a master chess-player might consider the course of a game, then, the problems solved, Mozart would be content to transfer the results to paper while surrounded by idle family chatter. His remarkable musical memory would allow him to fix in his mind perhaps an entire movement (or certainly an extensive portion of one) and then go through the exercise of writing it down merely for the benefit of others. It is impossible to guess just how long the intricate details of a work remained in Mozart's mind before fading away to make room for more, but it is probable that he could recall at the very least the broad outlines, and possibly many of the finer intricacies, of virtually all his compositions.

Mozart was slightly below average in stature, but his thin figure made him seem unusually small, and his pale complexion would have given him the appearance of an ailing man, perhaps even of a consumptive. Neither unduly vain nor careless in his dress, he would have made an elegant figure when engaged in his favourite pastime of dancing; he was, however, proud of his fine head of natural fair hair and seems to have worn a wig only when convention demanded. His voice was soft and well modulated but, in excitement or anger, it could be forcefully projected, though never raucous. In short, despite his slight stature, he had presence, poise in his bearing, and breeding in his manner.

1: Youthful Works: Symphonies Nos. 1-14 (1764-71)

First Movements

Although this chapter promises a discussion of "Symphonies Nos. 1–14," there are no less than thirty-four works to be considered in this first incredible eight-year burst of symphonic activity.* The first is an E flat symphony from 1764, KE Anh109 1=K18, known as Mozart's SYMPHONY NO. 3, which we now know was not composed by Mozart but merely

---

* In deciding what to include in our survey of the symphonies the net has been cast wide to include a number of "symphonies" which have been taken from operatic overtures. The precedent for this is the fact that several symphonies which are part of the standard numeration are, in effect, overtures (Nos. 23 in D and 24 in B flat, for example) and one is even described as such (No. 32 in G: *Overture in the Italian Style*). On a number of occasions Mozart plucked the overture out of an operatic score, tacked on a slow movement and Finale (or perhaps *only* a Finale) and used the work as a symphony. In this way several viable concert symphonies have been added to Mozart's total and have been included in our discussion. Single-movement overtures, although often displaying symphonic characteristics, have been omitted because they were really conceived with the opera house in mind, but the symphonies which the composer himself extracted from three of his big serenades are included.

The numbering of Mozart's symphonies can never be described as simple: for

copied out by him. It is in fact one of forty-two symphonies by Carl Friedrich Abel*: op. 7 no. 6, possibly a recent work when Mozart was visiting London but not published until 1770 in Amsterdam and 1780 in London. Scored for two oboes, two horns, bassoon and strings, it was presumably lent to the young composer as an exercise in composition and transposition, since the two oboes have been replaced by two B flat clarinets. Thematically the first movement shows the bold style which was one of the elements so admired at the Bach/Abel concerts, but in particular the device of a detached quaver arpeggio in bar 4, giving strength plus lightness to the music, must have caught Mozart's attention since it became one of his favourite tricks:

The second subject is an irresistible trio for two clarinets over a running bassoon accompaniment that would have sounded even more pungent in Abel's original scoring:

---

example, three of the works included in the forty-one numbered symphonies are unauthentic (Nos. 2, 3 and 37). The original Köchel catalogue gave each symphony known at that time a "K" number as a matter of course, but subsequent research has amended the dates of some, throwing the original chronology awry, and others have since been discovered, so that more than thirty symphonies now bear alternative "KE" numbers. The policy adopted in this book is to retain the original and well-known *genre* numbers for symphonies Nos. 1 to 41. For the symphonies not included in that system the Köchel numbers are given in full on their first appearance only, the "KE" number first and the original "K" number afterwards in brackets; thereafter, the "KE" number only is given. The purpose is to convey the order of composition: whereas the original "K" numbers cannot do this, the "KE" numbers reflect a truer chronology. The appendix contains a complete list of all applicable numbers.

* Abel was particularly plagued by cross-attributions: two of his op. 1 symphonies published in London in 1761 are alternatively ascribed to Toeschi in "Denkmäler der Tonkunst in Bayern," Vol. IIIi; three of his marches and some of his flute quartets were credited to J. C. Bach; and all six of his Trios, op. 3 (London, 1770), appear elsewhere as by Mozart's friend F. X. Dušek.

Even though there is no evidence that Mozart was fascinated enough with this wind trio to emulate it in his own works, there are other features in this music (by no means peculiar to Abel or to London) that he apparently regarded as necessary in the writing of a symphony since he used them frequently in his earlier years: the lithe, energetic string passage-work contrasting with gentle phrases, and the almost constant rapid chatter of quavers in the inner and/or lower parts. This example from Abel's development section illustrates these points:

Another feature Mozart would have noticed is the lack of a formal exposition repeat, probably a convention left over from the time when these symphonies of J. C. Bach and Abel were transferred unchanged as overtures from the opera theatre. The scoring of Abel's work is completely typical of the time except for the unusual freedom allowed the bassoon, usually employed merely as a member of the continuo group.

Considerable space has been spent on the first movement of this little E flat symphony since it is evident that Mozart, on the threshold of his own symphonic career, also gave it close attention. Less space need be allowed a B flat symphony from this period because it is obviously spurious: KE Anh223A=K17, once called Mozart's SYMPHONY NO. 2. Scored similarly to the Abel work but without an independent bassoon part, it is a rustic, rather awkward four-movement work that the Mozarts may have brought with them from Salzburg. There is no evidence that it is a work of Leopold's; neither is there any evidence that the young Wolfgang studied it. We may therefore put it on one side and proceed to the first genuine Wolfgang Amadeus Mozart Symphony: SYMPHONY NO. 1, K16, begun in Chelsea and finished in Soho.

How bold an opening, arresting the attention for a succession of melting chords lasting eight bars. The sequence is repeated, complete with an attention-grabbing horn dissonance (E flat against F), and the movement is then under way with the devices Abel has taught:

The momentum is maintained through the second subject by judicious syncopation, upbeat to the half-bar:

and violin semiquavers over repeatedly rising bass figures. A light codetta brings the double-bar marked for exposition repeat. "I don't care what they do in England," one can almost hear Leopold saying, "in Austria we *repeat* both halves of a first movement." Taking the first theme, Mozart commences the second half of the movement in B flat; but he modifies the repeat of the opening by shifting upwards into C minor and pass through F minor to arrive expectantly in E flat by bar 93. The second subject is then sounded in the tonic and the recapitulation is clearly half-completed already. Mozart is evidently wrestling with form in this movement.

The fight continues in SYMPHONY NO. 4, K19, composed early in 1765 in London. A strong and imposing dotted unison opening leads to the expected balancing passage in light, detached notes, the whole repeated. Busy semiquavers on violins accompany a leaping bass phrase thrice placed as the music gathers impetus. Although the material is more varied than that of the first symphony, there are signs that Mozart is already learning economy—less notes are being utilised to produce more effect, particularly in the second subject, and in the following section there is a hint of the mature composer to come as a fragmentary syncopated violin melody is floated over syncopated violas and unsyncopated bass crotchets, producing an oddly loping effect. At what should be the end of the exposition there is a sudden shocking drop to a unison on A sharp *(fp)*. The music soon recovers but neither the first subject nor the loping idea returns as the movement prepares to wind

62 / mozart: the symphonies

up. At the end of the movement, however, we find to our consternation the first repeat mark in the symphony: in a conventional work with a conventional repeat scheme we would hear the first part (exposition) twice, but here the straight-through design is heard twice on end. The method is unusual: possibly unique in the first movement of a symphony.

A group of problematical symphonies comes from this same London period: KE19A (=KA223) in F is lost and possibly also spurious, KE19B (=K Anh222) in C major and KE16A (= K Anh220) in A minor are also lost, and KE16B in C major exists only in sketches. The incipit of the A minor work suggests a promisingly independent movement while that of the symphony in C, KE19B shows strong reliance upon the opening rhythmic pattern used extensively by J. C. Bach and others and later also by Mozart.

SYMPHONY NO. 5, K22, in B flat was written in The Hague and indicates that Mozart had remembered a trick he learned from the Mannheim-influenced composers in Paris: the effective use of a repeated phrase treated to a *crescendo* (the lost A minor Symphony, KE16A, after the initial flourish, also calls for a *crescendo* over a pattern of repeated quavers). The phrase concerned (marked *a* in the example below) winds its way upwards for an octave-and-a-half as it makes for the second subject: classical *crescendo* material designed to heighten tension. Note once again, at the start of the symphony, the almost immediate recourse to the lightening effect of separated quavers, and the characteristic use of the *fp* dynamic.

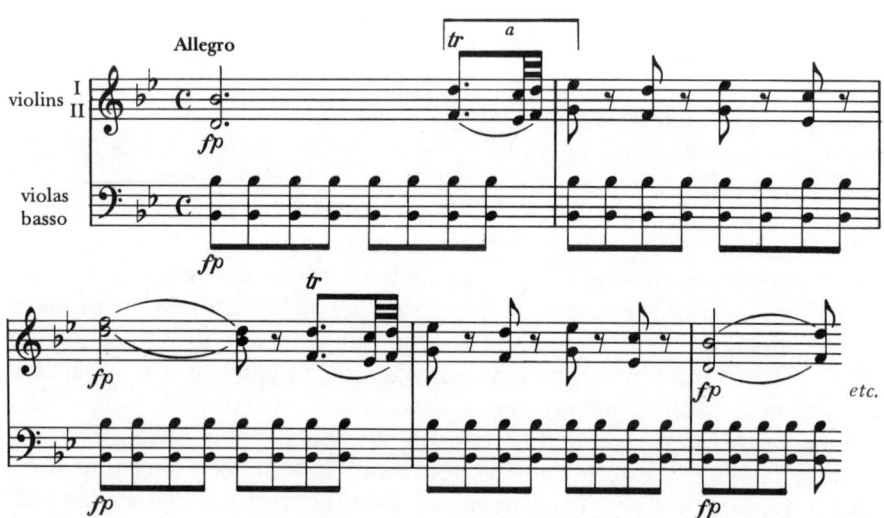

In comparison with the first movement of No. 4, that of No. 5 is briefer, more breathlessly urgent, even though the bipartite second subject has an expansive quality about it, partly dispelled by the canonic imitations of the second part; the use of B flat as a central tonality means that the horns (which should be played in the *alto* octave for music of this date) have a commanding and well-defined voice, their frequent top sounding Fs and Gs imparting a hectic mood which is intensified by the bass-line's non-stop pounding quavers, Formally, the movement is the most satisfying so far. There is no double-bar, the codetta rushing headlong into the development, welding the one to the other, and the recapitulation is tightened by the omission of the long *crescendo* section. Even in these earliest days no-one could accuse Mozart of recapitulations that mechanically followed the progress of the expositions. A restatement of the brief opening subject serves as a coda.

SYMPHONY IN F, KE42A=K76 did not follow until some eighteen months later, possibly completed in Vienna in autumn 1767. It is Mozart's first four-movement symphony. Gone is the urgency of the English and Dutch symphonies; replacing it is a leisureliness allied to a spaciousness of scoring that shows an incredible advance. To the previously constituted orchestra of two oboes, two horns and strings, Mozart adds two bassoon parts, used to build a substantial bass-line but also to bring colouristic relief to this first movement. The previous accompanying quavers are found again here, but their insistence is reduced by frequent breaks and by the dynamic being kept low. The first subject unfolds gracefully amid rich wind chords, the rhythm being marked gently by the middle strings. Tension mounts slightly as violins indulge in a little syncopation, but the second subject restores the laziness of the first with a pastoral interchange between oboes and bassoons immediately followed by another device that is to become a regular feature of the symphonies: the "Scotch snap." After the repeat of the exposition the first theme is restated at length in C major (its formal recapitulation, being redundant, is omitted) before a completely new fragment featuring a triplet figure slips disturbingly amidst minor keys, ultimately alighting decisively upon three unexpected chords. The second subject is then heard starting in D minor. Tonal clouds drift across the music for several further bars before, with a sigh of relief, the minor tonality is dismissed, the remainder of the movement seemingly all the brighter for having been threatened. Both halves of this first movement are marked for repeat, but in view of Mozart's dramatic tonal stroke it would be a mistake to observe the *da capo* of the second half.

Shortly after KE42A came another symphony in F: SYMPHONY NO. 6, K43, composed in Olmütz and Vienna at the end of 1767. The first movement could hardly be more different from that of its predecessor. Bassoons are not specified as independent voices, the scoring being restricted to the usual oboes and horns with strings, but the violas are sometimes divided. The formula employed at the beginning of Symphony No. 4 is used here again almost intact,

No. 4
violins (supported by octave unisons on wind and lower strings)

No. 6
violins (supported by octave unisons on wind and lower strings)

and the urgency of No. 5 has returned in the pounding rhythmic quavers, but the rarer imagination of KE42A is absent as much play is made with the opening phrase by lower strings. The contrast provided by the second subject, a wistful affair on undulating second violins and violas answered by the first violins, is soon dispelled by a return to rather conventional and repetitive passage-work. The development, after the exposition repeat, puts the opening phrase again in the bass. This serves as its restatement since it does not occur in the recapitulation. Bright and energetic though this movement is, the appearance of KE42A has led us to expect something considerably more developed.

At the beginning of 1768 there emerged a SYMPHONY IN G in three movements which has come to be called "Lambach" Symphony (KE45A=KA221), or to differentiate it from another symphony in the same key (see below), the *Alte Lambacher*. Larsen thinks that the work looks back to Wagenseil, and there are certainly things about it that seem to put it at odds with the surrounding works, yet when one examines the details of the first movement it appears considerably closer in style to Mozart's preceding symphonies than to Wagenseil's essentially static, more provincial, style of writing. If we assume for a moment that the work is a genuine product of Mozart's pen, let us first look at the new devices he used: the horn parts in G are written with boldness, but not necessarily more so than in the case of the B flat horns in Symphony No. 5, although in this G major work the first horn ascends to a top sounding G (written C above the stave), the highest horn note

youthful works: symphonies nos. 1–14 / 65

Mozart had yet written, and towards the end there is a completely untypical octave fanfare. The oboe parts are rather more developed and independent of one another than we have so far encountered, but Symphony No. 7 will show similar characteristics. Several points, however, will be no surprise to the student of Mozart's style at this period. At the start, under the violins' rapid Alberti-like accompaniment, the celli and basses in unison have a leaping figure that is first cousin to the violins' openings in Symphonies No. 4 and 6, quoted above (see page 64), and the whole scheme is mirrored in bars 24–27 of Symphony No. 7—see below. True, Mozart has not previously *commenced* a symphony with the theme in the bass, but we have seen how he would transfer a melody from upper strings to the basses, and to begin a work in this way was a logical progression of thought. Later in the movement the composer allows the theme to cavort in the bass under violin semiquavers in a way closely allied to a passage in Symphony No. 6:

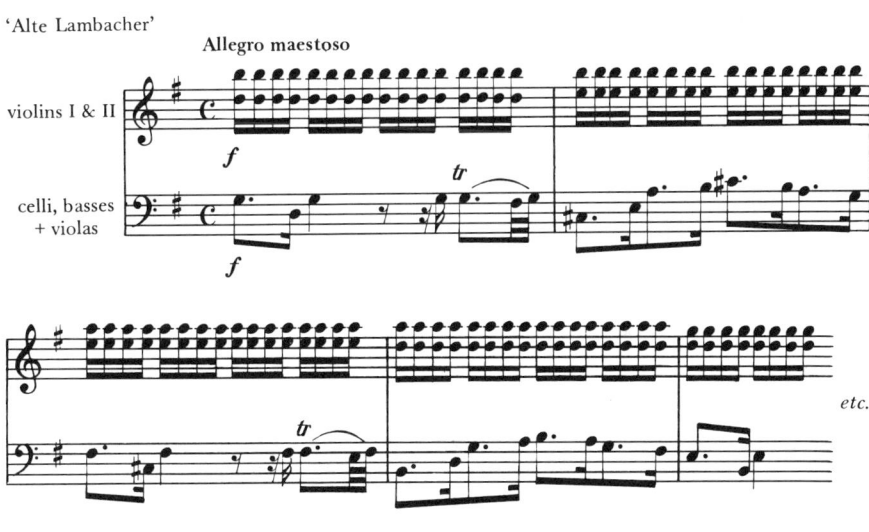

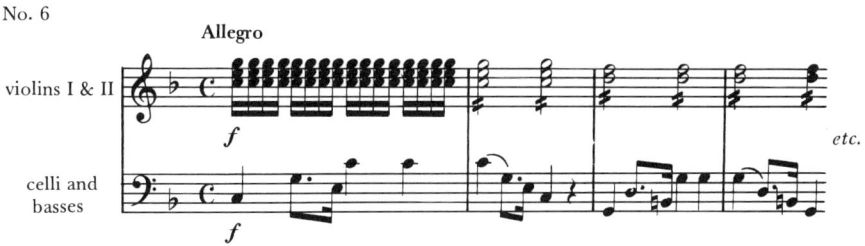

The development section commences with the main theme in the key of the end of the exposition, as has been done before, but previously, where the second subject has taken a large share of the recapitulation to the virtual exclusion of the first theme, here the second subject is neither strong nor well defined enough to take the responsibility. Instead, the first theme is transferred to violins for a proper formal recapitulation. Typically Mozartean is the use of the *fp* dynamic and the alternate slur-*staccato* phrasing:

It will probably never be proved whether or not the *Alte Lambacher Symphony* is *echt*-Mozart; perhaps Leopold had a hand it it; perhaps an entirely different author composed it. Whatever the truth, it is an exciting work with notable horn writing and some splendid ideas.

At about the same time another B flat work appeared: the SYMPHONY, KE45B=KA214, composed in Vienna. Its first movement possesses the pounding quaver bass we are coming to expect, while over it the violins have a most athletic part crammed with rapid figurations and swiftly ascending scales. The first of these scales ends with a tiny detail that seems to be a fingerprint of all composers who worked in Vienna: a falling (or rising) syncopated figure* marked *a* in the following example:

This is the first Mozart symphonic first movement in 3/4 time— in fact, apart from the lost (spurious?) KE19A which is in duple time, it is the first not to be in common time. The triple time lends to the work an operatic bustle and pace which, with its "welded" form (i.e. no double-

---

* Although we have identified this species of syncopation as specifically Viennese, it must be made clear that it was by no means practised exclusively in that city at the time. Prominent use was made of it by Joseph Haydn well before his "Viennese period," for instance, and both J. C. Bach and Abel found it a valuable device.

bar, the exposition running straight into the development without a pause), would suggest some kind of stage origin. The second theme is, in embryo, what so many later rocking Mozart passages were to become: a swaying, almost waltz-like rhythm supporting a delicate sighing melody.

Contemporary with KE45B is Mozart's first smyphony to include trumpets and drums: NO. 7 IN D, K45, completed on January 16, 1768. The rest of the orchestra consists of the usual strings with oboes and horns, but when Mozart decided to use the symphony as an overture to *La finta semplice* he omitted the trumpets and timpani and added two flutes and two bassoons, also removing the third movement Minuet. Apart from Symphony No. 4, three years earlier, Mozart had largely avoided the Eighteenth-century's favourite symphonic key of D major. So common was this key that one will frequently find the majority of the symphonies and overtures of lesser-known composers resorting to it in order to give brilliance to the strings and to make the work playable for trumpeters and drummers. All seven of Andrea Bernasconi's symphonies are in D, as are all four of Giuseppe Gazzaniga's (1743–1818), sixteen of Giovanni Pietro Maria Crispi's (1737–97) eighteen, and twenty of Pasquale Anfossi's (1727–97) twenty-two. By contrast, as we shall see later, composers such as Vaňhal seemed to go to extreme lengths to avoid the key of D. Following the example of countless previous symphonies in D with trumpets and drums, Mozart's opens with three sharp *tutti* chords. A confident, spiky, violin theme ensues, *piano*, its quaver rhythm interrupted by a splash of *forte* semiquavers and then by a descending phrase of Mozart's favourite detached quavers. The three chords are repeated and a pause brings the teasing second subject, abruptly ousted by the bass melody against Alberti violin accompaniment that was mentioned above in connection with the *Alte Lambacher* Symphony. Being once again in "welded" form, Mozart joins the exposition to the development with a sighing string passage (marked, exceptionally, *pp*), quickly taken up by oboes. A series of strenuous syncopated violin arpeggios brings a whirling string and oboe unison driving into the recapitulation, which begins with oboes weaving a delicate web around a suggestion of the first theme. Otherwise the reprise is unusually regular.

The first movement of SYMPHONY NO. 8, K48, completed on December 13, 1768, is in the same key and has the same scoring, but there is little further resemblance between the two. Whereas No. 7 had held an aloof stance, No. 8 is informal and friendly, notwithstanding a surface brilliance imparted by brass and percussion. The first theme ranges widely across more than two octaves: top D, dropping to A, then completing the octave to D, then down to a totally unexpected C natural, whereupon the first violins become enmeshed in a knot of confused passage-work, finally sorting themselves into a triumphant two-octave interval:

After further unexpected intervals, a set of detached quaver chords is greeted with a joyous roulade of recognition from oboes. Finding itself in A major, the music pauses as if surprised, then bustles through to the end of the exposition without bothering about a second subject. The development is pre-ocupied with those wide intervals, and the recapitulation extends them even further like a newly-awakening person idly stretching. Both halves of this movement are marked to be repeated and such is the delightful humour of the piece that it seems a sin not to obey this simple request.

Three symphonies, KE66C, KE66D and KE66E, dating from this period are regrettably lost (see page 36), but one other has survived: the SYMPHONY IN G MAJOR, known as the *Neuer Lambacher* since it was found in the Lambach monastery that Mozart and his father visited on their way from Vienna to Salzburg in January 1769. Like its companion, KE45A,, it is scored for two oboes, two horns and strings, but unlike that work it is in four movements. Anna Amalie Abert in her sleeve-note for the first recording of this work (Archiv 198 409, 1967) implies that this four-movement format is proof *for* Mozart's composition as strong as the three-movement format of KE45A is proof *against*, and she elects to dismiss KE45A from his list of works. In view of the similarities enumerated above, we should be wary of taking such a course, particulary since the "missing" Minuet of KE45A may very well have been removed by the Benedictine monks at Lambach as being unsuitable for concert performance there. Turning to the *Neuer Lambacher*, Miss Abert is inclined to accept it as genuine Mozart, finding the "faults" of KE45A ("laborious stringing together of motifs, short-winded repetitions") entirely absent. At first sight it would seem that different composers wrote the two symphonies. On the other hand, we have already discovered when discussing the identically-scored D major works, Nos. 7 and 8, how different two adjacent Mozart symphonies can be. Surely it is no more out of the question that Mozart wrote both Lambach symphonies with or without assistance from his father, than it is that the Mozarts brought with them from Vienna a work in which neither had had a hand. The *Neuer Lambacher* is a typical Viennese symphony: the first movement bristles with Vienna-isms. The first subject makes much use of the gentle syncopated figure noted above in connection with KE45B, accompanied by the broken-chord Alberti backing found in KE45A and in No. 7, both common Viennese devices. The contrasting *tutti* and three rising chords followed by a springing bass and a stretch of syncopated connecting tissue leads again to the gently syncopated figure. The second subject is similar to that in No. 6 and brings the codetta via yet another touch of syncopation. Unusually for Mozart at this period the development section is rather long. It commences with the three rising chords from the middle of the first subject, and later there is play with an attractive descending chromatic phrase which might be regarded as typically Mozartean had the work been written half-a-dozen years later. The recapitulation is unexpectedly regular. Use of the horns in this work is restricted to unspectacular harmonic supporting lines and differs dramatically from their use in KE45A, although it is not unlike Mozart's employment of these instruments in many symphonies of the period. All in all, however, the *Neuer Lambacher* Symphony does not seem to tie in too well with the genuine Mozart line of development, and incontrovertible proof of its authorship by Dittersdorf* or Vanhal would be considerably less of a surprise than similar proof of Mozart's authorship.

A bold, ceremonial air informs the first movement of the SYMPHONY IN D, KE73M=K97, written in Rome in April 1770. It is one of four symphonies, all in D, that Mozart composed in Italy during the first half of that year, two of them ceremonial works and two rather more domestic in character. KE73M sets off chordally with detached quavers over a constant quaver bass-line, alternating between violas and basses. The melodic content is fragmentary and undistinguished, the movement relying upon momentum and brilliance of orchestration for effect. The second subject is even more fragmentary, the main melodic interest coming in a new theme first announced at the start of the development section over a syncopated violin accompaniment after an unexpected *tutti* unison C. Violas also etch in the theme in contrary motion.

Also very public in style is the SYMPHONY IN D, KE73N=K95. The two first movements, right from the outset, are clearly from the same mould:

---

*The family resemblance between this symphony and Dittersdorf's Symphony in C major, Krebs No. 1 (c. 1765), a very popular work throughout Europe in the Eighteenth century, is remarkable.

70 / mozart: the symphonies

The contrasting material in KE73N comprises merely a long section of detached quavers over a rhythmic quaver bass-line. All is brilliance and empty effect, there being virtually no thematic interest in the movement. In this respect it offers no more musical value than some of the operatic overtures of J. C. Bach, Bernasconi, Jommelli, and countless other Italianate composers, and its use as an operatic overture is substantially confirmed by the employment of a device soon to become one of Mozart's favourites: a harmonic bridge to the Andante. The scoring of this work is unusual in that two trumpets replace the horns, and timpani are absent. The non-use of timpani in a D major work of this period when trumpets are present, whether inside or outside of Mozart's output, is very much the exception. From the time of the French military music of the Sixteenth century, trumpets and drums were virtually inseparable.* They provided the staple tone-colours of military musical establishments throughout Europe, and it was upon these establishments that impresarios would call when trumpets and timpani were required on the concert platform. A convention grew up during the first half of the Eighteenth century by which composers would automatically write for one voice when writing for the other. A score of the Seventeenth or Eighteenth centuries that includes trumpets but omits timpani should therefore be regarded with suspicion. Would timpani

---

* Adam Carse, in "The History of Orchestration" remarks: "Timpani are associated with trumpets in the scores of Lully and other French composers. The constant and intimate association of trumpets and drums in the 16th and 17th centuries strongly suggests the view that drums would be used in conjunction with trumpets even though no specific parts were written for the former." Musical evidence suggests that this practice held sway into the Eighteenth century also, but the question then arises: if no parts exist, what did the players play? The answer is that these military timpanists were adept at improvisation—scores they knew by heart would be treated to variations on successive performances, and unfamiliar music would still fall into clearly understood patterns so that improvisation would be a relatively easy matter with players who were so well acquainted with the tiny actions and expressions of their trumpet-playing colleagues that they could "follow" them adequately through any score.

youthful works: symphonies nos. 1–14

have been used in Mozart's Symphony KE73N? The answer is almost certainly "yes." If the parts were actually written down rather than improvised on the spot, they may well have become detached from the rest of the music just as countless other percussion parts were separated when the works were played by organisations that did not boast a timpanist (see also footnote on page 18).

The two other D major symphonies from early 1770 present no such problems since neither employs trumpets: merely the standard classical orchestra of two oboes, two horns and strings. They are SYMPHONY NO. 11, KE73Q=K84, and KE73L=K81. The former, as has been pointed out by Jan LaRue ("Mozart Jahrbuch" 1971/1972), is attributed to Dittersdorf in a set of parts in the Prague National Museum, while the latter was listed as by Leopold Mozart in the Breitkopf Catalogue Supplement in 1775. Professor LaRue has scrutinised the exposition of the first movement of No. 11 according to a "style analysis" so intricate that one receives the uncomfortable feeling that he is probing deep into the unconscious psyche of the composer. Three other Mozart symphonies and four Dittersdorf symphonies of approximately similar date are analysed according to the same principles, the exercise revealing differences and similarities that "considerably strengthen the possibility of excluding Dittersdorf as the composer of K–V.73q," an impression also given by any fairly superficial perusal of the score. The attribution of KE73L to Leopold Mozart is also mistaken since both first movements have points in common that indicate that the same composer wrote both works, that composer being Wolfgang Mozart. Each has a very clear-cut "welded" form, the recapitulations following closely the course of the expositions after a short token development, and each has a breezy, theatrical flavour. Thereafter the similarities cease; it may be instructive to examine schematically the totally different proportions of the movements, each of which has four distinct subjects:

A→B→Link→C→D (Codetta)→Dev.→A→B→Link→C→D (Coda)
27 8   7   13   7   10   27 8   7   13   8

A → B → C → D → Dev. → A → B → C → D → Coda
14   14   8   10   12   14   14   8   10   2

72 / mozart: the symphonies

These differences do not weaken the argument that the works were written by the same composer. In fact, stylistically the movements adopt the same thematic and harmonic language, and it is fascinating to see how far the young Mozart could modify formal moulds while adhering to the same basic design. Of the two movements, that of No. 11 is the more interesting. After the initial *tutti* in which one hears yet again the familiar detached quavers, the long first group (A) has in its second half a whip-like rising figure contrasted with a descending run in semiquavers, while the pretty, rocking, second subject (B) proves, with the benefit of hindsight, that the true author of the work is the one who went on to compose the most delicate sections in the later violin sonatas and keyboard concerti. This graceful filigree creation is floated over Mozart's favourite accompaniment of alternating pairs of slurred and *staccato* quavers.

The second part of the third theme (C) is really a bridge passage of alternating *forte* and *piano* fluttering violins over a striding crotchet bass-line.

The first movement of KE73L largely ignores the detached quaver device until the development section, when it is interspersed with heavy A major chords which lead precipitately into a regular recapitulation. Earlier, the second subject (B) uses the same technique as the equivalent section of KE73Q, complete with rocking second violin and viola accompaniment, but the first violins' melody here lacks a similar piquancy.

The end of 1770 saw Wolfgang in Milan, where his opera *Mitridate, rè di Ponto* (KE74A=K87) was completed. The three-movement overture is a SYMPHONY IN D with many of the traits of the concert symphonies discussed so far, but its first movement betrays its theatrical ambitions by breathless, headlong passage-work and driving quaver rhythms. As a prelude to an opera it is ideal, but the only really memorable moment is a sudden brief prominent duet for the oboes. Very much the same breathless character informs the SYMPHONY NO. 10 IN G, K74, written during the same month. As in the *Mitridate* overture, the opening yet again displays the detached quaver arpeggios which are threatening to become a mannerism, but in other respects the first movement has passage-work of considerably greater imagination: the second subject group is divided into two parts, and the two oboes extend their moment of glory, so grudgingly allowed in the overture, into a delicious duet occupying the whole of the short (six-bar) development section.

One other symphony may have been written in Milan at this time: the SYMPHONY IN F, KE ANH 223B=K98, but there are doubts as to its authenticity. There is a superficial similarity between the equally doubtful *Neuer Lambacher* Symphony in the opening of the first movement —in particular the Viennese lilting syncopation—but later there is a completely untypical insistence upon strings of triplets: untypical themselves in a genuine Mozart first movement, and also in the reliance the composer places upon them in the melodic line. These triplets invade every one of the eleven bars that comprise the development section; they re-appear of course in the recapitulation and are stamped out by bass strings in the tiny coda. When a blizzard of triplets re-appears in the 2/4-time Finale, turning that movement's rhythm into 6/8,* the drive of the music is exciting but there is no differentiation in pulse between first and last movement. One may doubt that Mozart would have been so unimaginative.

No doubts surround the authenticity of three of the four symphonies that Mozart is said to have written in Salzburg in the summer of 1771, between the two Italian visits: SYMPHONY NO. 9 IN C, KE75A (=K73); SYMPHONY IN B FLAT, KE74G (=KA216); SYMPHONY IN F, K75; and SYMPHONY NO. 12 IN G, KE75B (=K110). Of these, the work in B flat for two oboes, two horns and strings is not regarded as genuine enough to be included by Larsen in his essay, and no recording is known to the author. The incipit of the first movement bears a relationship to that of Symphony No. 8 (see page 68)

* Joseph Haydn had adopted the same device in the Finale of his Symphony No. 41 two years earlier.

even to the quaver bass-line, while the use of the *fp* dynamic is characteristic, but this evidence is not heavy enough to enable a decision to be given about its authenticity.

Symphony No. 9 has a slight but open-hearted first movement in common-time: what little melodic interest exists is carried by the bass-line under an accompaniment of violin semiquavers. The orchestration includes trumpets and timpani, but these and the usual wind complement of oboes and horns play an insignificant part, and the whole movement is, if anything, a step backwards in Mozart's development. There are signs that the movement was composed in even greater haste than usual, and there is heavy reliance on detached quavers in the development. These appear yet again in the opening movement of the Symphony in F, K75, but they are beautifully welded into the fabric, appearing in the codetta and coda: in the former position they actually heighten the contrast brought by the development section. This section, introduced by a chord of the last inversion of the dominant seventh with a B flat in the bass—a jolting call to attention—brings a Mozart surprise: a strangely *legato* development that bears no apparent relation to the rest of the movement. This first movement is much more advanced than that of Symphony No. 9, and the scoring at times recalls the Mannheim composers: the oboes have independent parts virtually throughout and join with the horns to produce considerable freedom and attractive harmonic colouring. Outwardly similar in scoring and time-signature (3/4), the first movement of Symphony No. 12 is in fact a totally different matter. The opening theme drives the music breathlessly, the abrupt descent at the end of our example leading back to a precise restatement which then brings some whip-like descending figures that propel the music even more urgently:

The insistent bass quavers in the first subject at last cease as the second theme appears: a waltz-like song for oboes in thirds, lightly accompanied by strings and punctuated gently by horns; but this is only an episode, a lull, before the running bass quavers return to lead unexpectedly to a restatement of the driving first theme in the dominant. The exposition, which is marked to be repeated, disintegrates in a riot of syncopation. The development is divided into two parts: the first, of sixteen bars, takes the mood of the second theme and examines it almost sadly, but the excitement of violin semiquavers and running basses occupies the second part (six bars) to herald the recapitulation. Now the whip-like first violin figure is echoed by seconds as part of an imitative sequence that resolves itself before the re-appearance of the second subject. From this point, surprisingly perhaps, the recapitulation runs a regular course. This movement shows a distinct advance in Mozart's writing: there is a cohesion in the widely-contrasting material that is not always evident in earlier works, and a sense of purpose and direction that grips the listener from first note to last. It is worth mentioning, too, that the composer has finally mastered the 3/4 metre for use as a forward-moving rhythm without loss of first movement dignity, something that Haydn had discovered rather sooner in his symphonic experience with the first movements of Symphonies Nos. 3, 14 and 23 (1759–64).

In the late summer of 1771 in Milan Mozart presented his opera *Ascanio in Alba*, K111, the OVERTURE (*Allegro assai*) and opening Andante Grazioso of which were turned into a symphony by the addition of a *presto* Finale, KE111A (=K120). The work is written to the Italian formula: the key in D major, the orchestra somewhat larger than for the usual concert symphony of the period (two flutes *and* two oboes as in the *Mitridate* overture, plus two horns, two trumpets, and timpani, with the usual strings), and the thematic material is brilliant without being illuminating, spirited without being inspired. The opening three-octave flourish echoes countless similar Italian overtures and all the expected tricks are included: detached quavers, alternately pounding and melodic bass-lines, and so on. The only ingredient one might expect to find which is absent is a more brilliant deployment of trumpets and timpani, but here, amid the empty-headed bustle, these instruments are treated with remarkable restraint. Along with a slightly more prominent use of trumpets and timpani, virtually all these characteristics, transferred to another festive key, are to be found in the SYMPHONY IN C, KE111B (=K96), composed in Milan in the late autumn of 1771. The two flutes are omitted, but otherwise all the signs are that this is another operatic overture to which, in this case, a Minuet has been added in addition to the Finale. The emptiness of the themes obviously appealed to the audience for whom this work was written, for we find time and again that the most routine of Mozart's symphonies were written for Italian audiences.* Before he left Milan Mozart produced another symphony which bears hardly a trace of the mindless brilliance of the two

---

* Even though these Italian symphonies may bring disappointment after the achievements of works such as Symphony No. 12, there is about their content a gaiety and

works just discussed. It is the SYMPHONY NO. 13 IN F, K112, completed on November 2, 1771. Scored only for oboes, horns and strings, it displays some of the delightful humour of No. 8. A falling *tutti* triad brings an unexpected rhythm, that of the first movements of Haydn's Symphony No. 28 and Beethoven's 5th, but this is only a trick to spring the rhythm forward; it has neither the heavy melodic responsibility of its forerunner nor the fateful import of its successor. Second violins, joyfully independent, set to with a will to enliven the music still further with a series of briskly ascending scale-figures. A subsidiary idea consists of a gentle bow by oboes and violas answered by an oddly non-committal, static, violin phrase that seems intent on holding back the progress of the music:

but suddenly and furiously repentant at their own inertia, the violins burst into life, remembering at last to introduce a courteous second theme in octaves just before the end of the repeated exposition. The development takes this second theme for a moment, examining it to see if it will turn into something else, but the movement is impatient to progress with the material of the first theme, the courteous little fragment is cast aside rudely and the end of the section not so much enters the recapitulation as collides with it. One spirited horn flourish adds colour to the regular reprise.

At the very end of 1771, after Mozart had returned to Salzburg, he composed the SYMPHONY NO. 14 IN A, K114, the first movement of which must be considered as another major step towards complete maturity. The scoring has not been used before by Mozart unless we count the lost Symphony in B flat, KE66D, of 1769; two flutes, two

---

verve which carries the music along irresistibly, and the scoring is often more interesting than one would expect—for instance, the horn suspensions at bar 34 of KE111B—but too often today these subtleties are not heard in performance as they doubtless would have been heard when the music was new. In addition, possibly in an effort to tone down the primary colours of a C major or D major work with its over-obvious triadic melodic flourishes, performers will insist on "shaping" or "moulding." Such tactics are applied to the opening of the C major Symphony, KE111B, by Neville Marriner, each of the identical flourishes being played as if it were a *decrescendo*. The unashamed boldness of the music is thereby destroyed.

horns and strings. The combination of high horns in A and flutes gives to the music a freshness and innocence that was discovered by the Mannheim symphonists some years earlier, and it is significant that this was the scoring selected by Jan Stamic for his "Spring" Symphony in A major. It was also chosen for three symphonies in A by Antonín Fils, for two by Toeschi, and for a number by Christian Cannabich and Ernst Eichner; and earlier in the year in which Mozart completed his Symphony No. 14, Luigi Boccherini in Madrid had scored his A major Symphony, the last of the set of six of op. 12 (Gérard No. 508) for the same combination.* Mozart himself was to return to this scoring in Symphony No. 21 the following year. It seems that the slightly raw tone of A horns mixed with the softness of flutes in an A major work was a standard colouristic effect to which composers and their audiences were attracted. At the start of the first movement of Symphony No. 14 we realise that we are back in Vienna-influenced Salzburg: the gentle *piano* opening, with its cool syncopation in the melody, is something the hot-blooded Italians would never have tolerated. The initial statement for violins alone, *piano*, is then repeated, *forte*, clothed in gorgeous wind colours, and soon the two flutes and two horns are holding a stately dialogue in strutting tones, a dialogue that might have been written by Jan Stamic himself. A polite second subject is announced in three-part imitation—first violins, seconds, then violas—but the music is not in scholarly mood and a fermata circumvents a threatened technical *cul-de-sac*. The exposition ends with an independent second violin part rushing from one B to another before settling upon E. The development section opens with another interchange between the wind groups, again in a proud strutting rhythm, the horns tactfully supported by violas (presumably because Mozart was not too certain of his cornists),

---

* Leopold Koželuh, later to be a great rival of Mozart in Vienna, produced an A major Symphony "A la française" (1780–90), which adds two oboes to the flutes, horns and strings.

and the section ends with yet another example of independent writing for second violins. The recapitulation is regular, the material presented in the same way and in the same order as before, but in such an eventful stretch of music this never brings a trace of superfluity.

Slow Movements

The slow movements of these early symphonies are apt to congeal in the mind of the casual listener into a single featureless mass of music in 2/4 time, in the key of the subdominant of the first movement, marked *andante*. First, then, some statistics. Of the twenty-five surviving symphonic slow movements from the period 1764–1771, the following depart from the composer's favourite 2/4 time-signature: KE42A, KE73N and Symphony No. 14 are in 3/4; Symphonies Nos. 7 and 12 are in 4/4; Symphonies Nos. 10 and 11, and K111 are in 3/8; and KE111B is in 6/8. While subdominant is by far the preferred tonality, the following departures may be noted: Symphonies Nos. 6 and 11, and KE75A are in the dominant; Symphonies Nos. 1 and 5 the relative minor; KE 111B the tonic minor. The marking *andante*, or a qualified version of it, is indeed universal, the qualifications being *andante un poco allegretto* (Neuer Lambacher Symphony), *andante grazioso* (the two operatic overtures: *Mitridate* and *Ascanio in Alba*), and *andantino* (K75). In the last-named symphony the two central movements exchange places: it is, incidentally, the only Mozart symphony in which the slow movement *follows* the minuet and trio.

In the matter of scoring, most of these Andantes include at least two wind instruments in addition to the strings, the only exceptions being No. 7 (*La finta semplice*), No. 8, the *Neuer Lambacher* Symphony, KE73M, and Symphony No. 13, all for strings only. In only four of the slow movements are the strings muted: No. 6; KE45A; KE Anh223B; and K75. All are in two-part rudimentary sonata form with the exception of the following: No. 5 (the whole movement is to be played through from beginning to end twice—see the first movement of No. 4); KE45B; No. 11; and KE74A (all through-composed without repeats).

The above cold facts give no idea of the nature or quality of the music, so matters should be rectified by a brief discussion of some of the outstanding Andantes from this period. That of SYMPHONY NO. 1 attains a depth of expression only rarely heard again in the slow movements of this period: against triplets on upper strings, the oboes and horns intone a chant-like melody based on a progression that forecasts the dynamic use to which the composer put such four-note *motifs* in his

youthful works: symphonies nos. 1–14 / 79

Symphonies Nos. 33 and 41: it heralds the "Jupiter" theme, in fact. In the bass a scrap of melody appears again and again, twisting this way and that as if searching for an answer:

The mood of this C minor piece is not one of personal suffering but more of ecclesiastical commitment, but we may ask what prompted this sombre tone picture so early in Mozart's career. It is extremely unlikely that he was aware of the somewhat similar mood of the first movement (*adagio*) of Haydn's "Der Philosoph" Symphony, No. 22 in E flat, since that work was only months old and would not so quickly have travelled as far as Paris or London; and Leopold's instruction is hardly likely to have inspired it. The most likely source would be his London friend and prime musical contact John Christian Bach. That composer's first published symphonies in London were the six Italianate overtures of op. 3, which appeared in 1765 but were certainly played in the Bach/Abel/Mozart circle before then. All six are in major keys, and two of them (No. 2 in C and No. 6 in G) have Andantes in the minor, but in the *tonic* minor, not the relative. On the other hand, two symphonies from op. 6 (Nos. 3 and 5, both in E flat) have Andantes in the relative minor, C minor, and these works certainly circulated before Terry's suggested publication date of "? 1770." No. 5, in fact, had travelled as far as Leipzig by 1766, in which year it was included in Breitkopf's catalogue there. But the characters of the J. C. Bach slow movements differ markedly from that in Mozart's work: even the impassioned C minor Andante Più Tosto Adagio of Bach's G minor Symphony, op. 6 no. 6, has moments of light relief not found in Mozart's Andante. It is necessary to dig deeper into Mozart's brief experience for other possible influences—to his stay in Paris in 1763/64. Amongst the works heard there at about that time are to be found several that could have left their mark on the young eclectic: a number of E flat symphonies with C minor slow movements by François Martin (op. 4 no. 6, published in 1746), Pierre Talon (op. 1 no. 3, 1753), Frank Beck* (op. 1

---

* Although resident in Bordeaux, Beck had his symphonies published by the Paris firms of Bayard, Chevardière, Huberti, and Venier.

no. 4, 1758; op. 2 no. 4, 1760; op. 3 no. 4,* 1762), Pierre Vachon (op. 2 no. 6, 1761), Jean-Baptiste Miroglio (op. 10 no. 3, 1764), H. Leemans (op. 1 no. 3, 1765) and Charles-Guillaume Alexandre† (op. 6 no. 1, 1765). All the dates given above are of the Paris publications and do not necessarily reflect composition dates, which may in some cases have been many years earlier. Wherever the inspiration came from, it is interesting to note that the young Mozart's movement did itself provide inspiration for an unknown Russian composer in about 1800: a symphony based on Ukrainian themes has an Andante which, near the start, strongly recalls the lowest line of its predecessor on *pizzicati* basses.‡

The second movement of SYMPHONY NO. 5 is in G minor and is scored for two oboes, two horns and strings. It is interesting to note that the composer does not require his horn players to change crooks; rather does he construct his odd little movement in a way that allows the horns to be heard in the central bars in more varied music than the simple sustained D octaves with which they begin. After the opening section the music moves to B flat for a passage that foreshadows the overlapping entries at the start of the Andante of No. 40

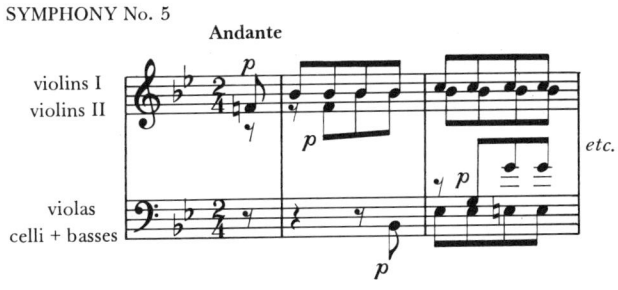

---

* The Un poco Adagio of this symphony is in 6/8: Mozart's movement is in 2/4 but with constant triplets giving the effect of 6/8.
† In the Presto Allegro first movement of Alexandre's Symphony in F, op. 6 no. 1, Mozart may have first encountered the device of detached quavers that we had occasion to remark upon so frequently when discussing his first movements.
‡ This Russian symphony is recorded by the Moscow Radio Great Symphony Orchestra conducted by V. Esipov on Melodiya D 018241-2.

and the arrival of the music in this key brings the opportunity for some telling horn punctuation that is lost in the lower parts if the players do not crook their instruments in B flat alto. As in the first movement of Symphony No. 4, Mozart requires the whole movement to be played through again from beginning to end.

Horns play an even more telling part in the Andante of the SYMPHONY IN F, KE42A, joining with two bassoons to bring an unusual colour to the music. For the first time, as far as we know, Mozart sets a symphonic slow movement in 3/4 rhythm and takes the opportunity to copy the slow graceful minuets that he heard in London. Gone are the introspective sounds of the two earlier minor-keyed movements; instead, there is a gentle melody enhanced by all of the wind and made irresistible by the use of *pizzicato*, violas twice finding themselves out of synchronisation. Close imitation of J. C. Bach's flowing minuet style is still in the future; meanwhile, Mozart's experimental scoring may be noted for the sometimes strange combinations it produces.

For the Andante of SYMPHONY NO. 6 Mozart asks his oboists to change to flutes* for a gem-like movement full of rocking charm (divided violas accompanying in semiquavers) and melodic repose amid muted strings. Two years later, in the sixth movement of the Serenade in D, KE62A=K100, this idea had crystallised, the two flutes holding their melody more firmly. Similar characteristics are to be found in the Andante of the ALTE LAMBACHER SYMPHONY, KE45A, the rocking accompaniment now on second violins and violas, but the wind section is confined to two horns in G which become melodically active only in the second subject (in the dominant of G); their parts in the reprise, which they would have found impossible to play now that the music is back in the tonic key of C, are taken by violas, celli and basses. In the Andante of the Overture *La finta semplice*, SYMPHONY NO. 7, Mozart opens with a ringing bottom G on violins, marked f, and in the second half he teasingly misplaces this note so that the bemused listener is never quite sure where it will appear next. The progression from G follows the line to G sharp, then up nearly an octave to F sharp, down to C, then B natural again after a feint at G, and finally back to C.

Such subtle moulding of material can be noticed throughout these early slow movements, subtleties that cannot be enumerated here without going to unjustifiable lengths. The listener, with or without a score, will delight in discovering them for himself. Attention is drawn, however, to the delicious oboe solos in the Andante of the SYMPHONY IN D, KE73L, which, in the second subject, hold a dialogue with the strings that extends, clause by clause, until a final acid touch of dis-

---

* The movement was originally composed as a duet for Melia and Oebalus, *Natus cadit, atque Deus*, in the "Latin Comedy" *Apollo et Hyacinthus*, K38.

sonance by way of conclusion at the double-bar. One hears here the opera composer in the concert hall.

The slow "London" (or "Milan") minuet style of Andante is heard again in SYMPHONY NO. 11, in SYMPHONY NO. 10, in the SYMPHONY IN D, KE73N, and in the richly-scored ASCANIO IN ALBA OVERTURE (two flutes, two oboes, two horns, with strings), which is perhaps the closest yet to the J. C. Bach and Sammartini model that Mozart has come. The Andante of SYMPHONY NO. 14 is in 3/4 but does not come into the same category since its bass-line lacks the firmness and smoothness of the best of these examples. On the other hand this Andante has qualities that we expect from a much more mature Mozart slow movement: infinite grace and delicacy combined with a miraculous melodic sense that in the second subject displays a superbly-judged hint of chromaticism. The development section assumes unusual importance, too, the four undulating string lines woven with surprising skill. Finally, mention must be made of the extraordinary C minor Andante of the SYMPHONY IN C, KE111B. The overture-like first movement may well point to the work having connections with the stage but the Andante makes this link even stronger: surely this strangely dark movement, with its amazing alternations of *p* and *f*, was an entr'acte or a scene-setting interlude in some tragedy? Over a pulsating 6/8 rhythm on lower strings, violins and oboes intone a withdrawn melody which seems to search for tranquillity, while in the second half sombre horn chords reinforce the restless alternation of *piano* and *forte*.

Minuets and Trios

Mozart was never convinced of the necessity of the Minuet and Trio in his symphonic schemes, unlike Haydn, only ten of whose symphonies, and none of them later than 1763, omit a dance movement. As late as 1783 Mozart "borrowed" a symphony from Michael Haydn for use in Linz and, while he evidently considered it necessary to add a slow introduction, he did not add a Minuet despite the fact that his own "Linz" Symphony, K425, of that year, does include such a movement. Three years later he composed the "Prague" Symphony, omitting the Minuet. On the other hand, he converted quickly to the four-movement layout in his earlier years, possibly due to the pressure of fashion from Vienna, Mannheim and Paris. When composing sets of minuets for festive balls, Mozart took care to provide variations of mood, style and instrumentation for consecutive listening. His symphonic minuets of this early period do not offer such variety but, taken separately, with other music between them, they serve their purpose admirably, and it is in that context that they should be heard, even though, for convenience, they are considered here as a group.

In comparison with Haydn's symphonic minuets, Mozart's do not show the same imagination in matters of phrase lengths and proportions. "This," we can almost hear Leopold telling his nine-year-old son in the autumn of 1767 when they were in "minuet country" (Vienna), "is how a minuet should go," and under that watchful stare Wolfgang produced his first symphonic minuet (for the SYMPHONY IN F, KE42A) with nicely balanced proportions: twelve bars in the first part and sixteen in the second. After the minuet-like pulse of the preceding Andante the composer evidently felt obliged to introduce a more robust movement, which he did by employing a firm, clearly-defined melodic line and a strong bass in which bassoon, violas, celli and basses span a decisive octave on the downbeat of each of the first four bars. But surprises are already in store: with a touch of chromaticism Mozart introduces a hint of exotic Turkish colour in the next eight bars, violas supporting second violins in the lower octave:

When the second half has followed a similar course, bassoon and all the strings in octave unison seize this Turkish phrase, put it into the relative minor and subject it to repeated scrutiny in a disproportionately long (thirty-six-bar) Trio which alternates disconcertingly between f and p.

As in his first symphonic slow movement, so too in his first symphonic Minuet and Trio Mozart produced something special and memorable before proceeding to more conventional music. The description "conventional" serves for the Minuet of SYMPHONY NO. 6 which follows that work's meltingly beautiful Andante. Once again the Trio uses a phrase from the Minuet as a starting point, a trick he eschews in the next

Minuet (from the SYMPHONY IN B FLAT, KE45B) so that the contrast between this lightly-scored Trio and the main Minuet, with its ringing fanfares for the horns, might be all the greater.

The third movements of the two 1768 D major works, SYMPHONY NO. 7 and SYMPHONY NO. 8, show the contrast Mozart was capable of putting into outwardly similar movements. The former, though, is somewhat characterless, with too much reliance on a triplet upbeat and a Trio for strings alone that borders on dullness, while the latter is a splendidly pompous piece with a headlong semiquaver string figure that drives the music forward, and a Trio (like its companion, in the subdominant) that includes oboes and horns and introduces dynamic light and shade, even extending to two tiny *crescendi*. Much the same comparisons may be drawn between the next two surviving symphonic minuets: that in the NEUER LAMBACHER SYMPHONY is an undistinguished movement in the conventional proportions of 8+16 bars with a mild central C major Trio of identical layout, while that in the SYMPHONY IN D, KE73M, possibly composed for some grand celebration in Rome, has a muscular heartiness once again impelled forward by string semi-quavers. In performance these grand movements should be played with exaggerated pomp and a staid tempo to heighten their ceremonial character and, where the scoring includes trumpets and timpani, as in KE73M, these instruments should be allowed to cut through the rest of the orchestra in a manner all too rarely heard today. Mozart would have been astonished at the modesty of mid-Twentieth-century trumpeters and timpanists (or at least by the modesty forced upon them by conductors imbued with a love of late Nineteenth-century orchestral balance); he was used to players who were determined to be heard no matter what the feelings of the rest of the orchestra, and he scored his music accordingly, allowing the noisiest instruments only brief notes amid liberal rests but bringing them in at cardinal points. The next Minuet, in the SYMPHONY IN D, KE73N, is another such pompous piece for which the author has provided a timpani part (see Appendix) to complement the trumpets and provide a rhythmic foundation somewhat firmer than Mozart's running quavers. It is the rhythmic stability of the Minuet in the SYMPHONY IN F, KE ANH223B, that the composer, whoever he was, seeks to undermine with a touch of disturbing syncopation at the beginning of the second half and with a curious across-the-bar wind answer in the Trio.

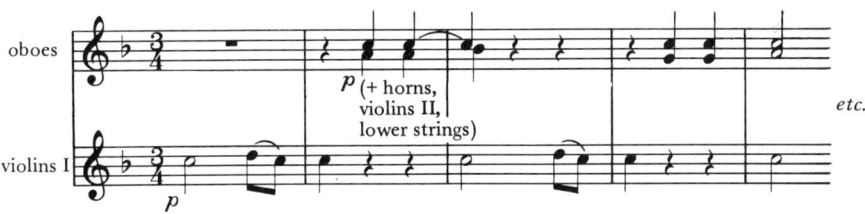

Exceptionally, this Trio is in the tonic key of the Minuet, an indication, perhaps, although not a strong one, that the symphony is not a genuine work of Mozart's. No doubt, though, concerning SYMPHONY NO. 9, whose Minuet is another in the ceremonial series with trumpets and drums, a graceful strings-only Trio providing contrast. In fact, each one of the Trios in the Minuets of the four symphonies composed in Salzburg in the summer of 1771 between the Italian visits—NO. 9 IN D, the SYMPHONY IN B FLAT, KE74G, the SYMPHONY IN F, K75, and SYMPHONY NO. 12—displays this lightening of texture amid the more robust Minuets. The main Minuet of K75 is based on the kind of melody that would bring confusion to dancers if the movement were ever to find its way into the ballroom. In concert performance equal confusion would have met the unprepared listener by the positioning of this Minuet in second place, immediately after the first movement: its unassuming opening would have allowed the audience to believe that a slow movement had in fact begun, only to find themselves disabused of this notion by the energetic phrasing as the movement belatedly remembers its role as a dance movement in bar 5:

Minuetto

Rustic vitality and a lop-sided approach to the balance between the two halves of a Minuet were Haydn fingerprints, and it may be that composer's influence at work in the measured beat of the Minuet in Symphony No. 12, in the unexpectedly extended second "half" of twenty-eight bars against the twelve bars of the first part, and in the teasing oboe answers at bars 14 and 16. The Trio spends most of its brief life in tonal ambiguity, settling on G major only for a moment at the central double-bar.

Contrast is again the keynote in the SYMPHONY IN C, KE111B where the theatrical gloom of the C minor Andante is swept away by another ceremonial Minuet ablaze with trumpets and drums.* In the case of SYMPHONY NO. 12, the Minuet is written out in full after the Trio, excluding the repeats. Nothing in the music seems to justify this procedure except that a horn figure in the last bar, present before the

---

* "Ablaze" is the wrong word to use when one considers modern performances. Even Marriner's reading tones down these instruments to no more than a mild garnishing of the string sound.

Trio, is now omitted. In SYMPHONY NO. 13 the Minuet is again written out after the Trio but this time retaining the repeat marks. There is no doubt that this makes a more substantial movement of a rather short and undistinguished piece designed with strict regularity in mind: eight bars plus eight in the Minuet, and the same in the Trio. Both this Trio and that in the next Minuet, to SYMPHONY NO. 14, are for strings only, the latter entering the tonic minor for a pathetic interlude in which a graceful melodic line on first violins is set against a subdued chattering from seconds. The second half of the Minuet itself is extended to eighteen bars to include a tiny development section before the return to the square-cut opening theme.

Finales

At this early stage Mozart relies, with one or two remarkable exceptions, upon Italian models for his Finales, and in this he was in the company of the majority of composers throughout Europe. Invariably fast (*allegro*) or very fast (*allegro molto*, and once, in Symphony No. 13, *molto allegro*, or *presto*), the favoured time signatures are 2/4 and 3/8, with three excursions into the latter's close relatives 6/8 (Symphony No. 6) and 12/8 (Symphony No. 8 and the *Neuer Lambacher* Symphony). Not once do we encounter 3/4 or common time, or even duple time. The purpose of this rapid movement in breathless rhythm was, in the opera house when it concluded an overture, to set the audience's pulses racing expectantly for the beginning of the action, and, in the concert hall at the end of a symphony, to leave the audience exhilarated. Formally, the movements are usually constructed like the old dances in two parts, the second of which may include rudimentary developmental material which makes it, therefore, about half as long again as the first part. Not satisfied with being restricted too severely to this plan, Mozart introduces a number of exceptions, as in Symphony No. 1 where the first repeated section of 16 bars is followed by a non-repeated section of 137, and in Symphony No. 10 where the proportions are 16/113; and a number of works in which the two sections are of almost (and in one case exactly) equal length: No. 7 (51/55), No. 8 (29/29), No. 11 (92/96), KE73N (59/61), and K75 (47/56), each half marked for repeat. In the Finale of the Symphony in D, KE73L, the proportions of the two parts are reversed: 76/47. Starting with Symphony No. 5 there are a number of through-composed Finales without any repeats: KE45B, KE73M, KE74A, KE75A and KE111, two of them operatic overtures;

and near the end of the first period (Symphonies Nos. 12 and 13) the Finales consist of several repeated sections strung together, rondo-fashion. Although in nearly every case these movements run to over 100 bars, they all seem short due to the rapid tempi and short bar lengths.

In character the earlier Finales closely follow those of John Christian Bach: in isolation it would be difficult to differentiate between them, so closely does Mozart model his style upon that of the older man. A selection of incipits in 3/8 time will illustrate the similarities:

Detailed examination of these Finales is hardly necessary: Mozart moves from the dance-like structure to something near the rondo, a move already begun as early as SYMPHONY NO. 1 where, when the movement has run its course, an additional piece, too long to be regarded as a coda, unexpectedly upturns a figure heard earlier. After that a repeat of the opening statement ties up the loose ends. Did Leopold Mozart express the fear that the Finale up to bar 122, complete though it was, was too short and advised his son to add a tiny episode? The

Finale of SYMPHONY NO. 4 allows Mozart to indulge in a little innocuous humour: first and second violins throw a scrap of melody back and forth in the first theme and in the second theme the violas and violins offer a *legato* ascending fragment to the basses who are able to answer it only in awkward *staccato* augmentation. Overcome by the basses' clumsiness, the violins dissolve into mirth:

Such high jinks* are to be heard ever and again in these early, light, carefree, often empty-headed Finales, most of which would respond unkindly to analysis but each of which contains at least one feature designed to attract attention. In SYMPHONY NO. 5 it is the rumbustious part for the B flat alto horns, reaching frequently to top A (sounding f″); in SYMPHONY NO. 8 the surprise ending to the first part: a graceful oboe-led cadence marked *p*, which comes as an even greater surprise at the very end of this pompous D major Symphony; in the SYMPHONY IN D, KE73M, the judicious placing of one slurred bar in a passage of *staccato* quavers in 3/8 rhythm (like a boy dashing away, slewing himself round a vertical post, and dashing back again);

in the SYMPHONY IN D, KE73L the whimsically off-beat second subject† which takes over the short development section, only with difficulty fighting its way from minor to major; in the MITRIDATE OVERTURE, the rushing Mannheim *crescendo* of the main theme, built up in true Stamic style with successive wind entries rising stepwise over a held horn octave; in SYMPHONY NO. 10 the bantering main theme that shows evidence of the influence of Michael Haydn, and the drop to G minor for the whole of the middle section based entirely on a new theme; in SYMPHONY NO. 9 the straightforward rondo form with written-out repeats, the fourth episode of which is also couched in the tonic minor; in the SYMPHONY IN B FLAT, KE74G, the catchy across-the-bar phrasing of the main theme; in the SYMPHONY IN F, K75, the tiny *piano* answering phrase after the first theme breaks off, the dynamics of which are reversed later; in SYMPHONY NO. 12 the central binary episode in G minor, and in the SYMPHONY IN C, KE111B, the startling foretaste in the second subject of a phrase from the Overture to *Die Entführung aus dem Serail*, showing again the composer's interest in quasi-Turkish colouring.

A thematic device used a number of times in these early Finales is the tonic-establishing trick of stamping up and down the tonic arpeggio, a feature we will have occasion to notice again in later

---

* It is "conversational" music of this type that dictates the separation of the violins in performance to left and right. Here, for instance, and in the antiphonal writing in the Finale of Symphony No. 6, Neville Marriner scores heavily over those conductors who place all the violins on the left.

† Also heard, but to less advantage, in the Finale of the *Mitridate* Overture.

symphonies.* An allied device is the alternation of tonic and dominant chords at the beginning of the Finale of the SYMPHONY IN D, KE73M; and it will be noticed that this kind of obvious "public" writing is almost invariably reserved for the pompous symphonies in C or D with trumpets and drums. It is possible that Mozart heard this kind of writing when in London: Arne's *Artaxerxes* (1762) was popular at the time and its D major Overture, a large-scale symphony-overture in three connected movements, features both triad stamping and tonic/dominant shuttling.

The most advanced Finales in this early group are those which venture furthest from the Italian style in three- or six-pulse.† The SYMPHONY IN F, KE42A possesses a more staid and Viennese character than most of its companions, while the SYMPHONY IN D, KE73N, with its frequent upward scales for second violins, has a firm sense of purpose about it; but the most astonishing achievement in these early Finales is that to the SYMPHONY IN B FLAT, KE45B. There is an urgency in the melodic lines that thrusts the music forward with intense inevitability over pounding semiquavers, the whole coloured by the hectic tone of the B flat alto horns—an amazing achievement for a twelve-year-old composer. Although the Finale of the last symphony in this group, that to SYMPHONY NO. 14 in A, with its introduction of an entirely new theme in the development section, is possibly the most mature (and incidentally, vastly more advanced than the primitive 3/8 rondo that concludes Symphony No. 13 of only two months earlier), it is the drive and vitality of the final Allegro of KE45B that offers most promise.

---

* No matter how obvious this trick may be, it is certainly wrong to refine it away with a *diminuendo* as Marriner does when the triad returns at the very end of Symphony No. 11.

† Although Mozart obviously felt obliged to put the Finale of Symphony No. 11 into 2/4 rhythm, 3/8 having been used for the preceding Andante, he almost immediately reverts to triplet motion so that the listener's initial impression is of a 6/8 movement. The same triplet pulse quickly overtakes the Finale of Symphony No. 7, co-existing with the dotted quavers of the leading theme.

2. Consolidation: Symphonies Nos. 15-34 (1772-80)

More than half of the symphonies discussed in the previous chapter do not bear a generic number and may be identified numerically only by reference to their position in the Köchel Catalogue. In the present group, too, several works do not bear a generic number, but all are easily identified without recourse to Köchel: four are overtures to operas and three are symphonies which Mozart himself, or someone else with the composer's acquiescence, extracted from large-scale serenades. All the rest have established generic numbers. The twenty-seven works take us from the period of experimentation to the time, in his early twenties, when Mozart had reached a position of assurance from which he crossed the threshold to genius.

It was earlier found convenient to group together first movements, slow movements, Minuets and Finales to show Mozart's methods of tackling given tasks and to trace in similar movements the progress of his development. We also discovered a certain differentiation between the works, arriving at a point in 1772 where several distinct parallel lines exist in the symphonic process with, nevertheless, undeniable shading off at the edges. In discussing the following works of consolidation a different approach—one that divides the works into groups—will be more helpful since it is evident that by now Mozart is writing "purpose-built" symphonies. The headings chosen for this section, therefore, are:

> Overture Symphonies
> Three-Movement Non-Overture Symphonies
> Four-Movement Symphonies
> Sturm und Drang
> Horn Symphonies
> Serenade Symphonies

Overture Symphonies

The terms "sinfonia" and "overture" were synonymous in the language of the Eighteenth century but, although the brief three-movement operatic overtures of the earlier years might readily be confused with works designed for concert symphonic use, by the 1760s and 1770s a sharp line was being drawn between the two styles. Concert symphonies tended to be more relaxed in thematic content (except in the *Sturm und Drang* strain, to be discussed below), and expansiveness was abetted by liberal use of double-bars that required the repeat of the first, and frequently also the second, half to be taken. A dance movement was often, though by no means invariably, inserted, and the Finales were beginning to move away from the breathless 3/8 and 2/4 rhythms of the operatic overtures.

Meanwhile, the true theatrical overture retained its "welded" form (i.e. no repeats in the first movement), a welding that sometimes extended to a physical connection between two or all three movements, and the Finale was likely to be written in short bars and/or short note-values. The characteristics of an operatic overture were brevity, gaiety, noise and brilliance. If the terms "sinfonia" and "overture" were still confused, then the styles at least were clear-cut by the 1770s.

The OVERTURE IN D to *Il sogno di Scipione* is almost a caricature of the overture style. It is a big piece recalling the least subtle of the Italian symphonies in D major of 1770, and heavily scored for pairs of flutes, oboes, horns, trumpets and timpani, with strings. The opening triadic flourish occurs no less than ten times, and upon the last statement the unrelieved D major is pushed aside rudely by a minor-keyed passage leading into the Andante. For contrasting material the first movement resorts to the "Scotch snap," a device of which Mozart was evidently fond in these middle years, and a second subject which is a mere shadow of his earlier charming rocking themes. Towards the end of the first movement (bars 108–113) it is as if the composer himself becomes impatient with his own empty gestures as he interrupts the Scotch snap with a moment of severe drama, but he immediately remembers his obligations to the cloth-eared Eighteenth-century theatregoers and fulfils them with eight bars of compensatory meaningless crotchets. If the tonality of D major remains unrelieved by the slow section (*andante*), the mood is certainly balm to battered senses. This could be introductory music to an idyllic pastoral scene, the wash of oboes and cooling flutes prominent in the orchestration.* The last ten bars see repeated quavers in celli and basses as the music prepares regretfully for the onslaught of the final Presto, which follows without a break. In the event it is a carefree, bustling movement of no little charm, but on the whole the Overture comes into the category of introductory music designed to be listened to on the most superficial level.

Outwardly, the OVERTURE IN D to *Lucio Silla*, completed in Milan at about the same time, falls into the same category, but there is evidence of more care in its production, more humour in its lines. Tonic and dominant posturing invades the opening bars but the vivacity of the string writing, as syncopations succeed semiquavers at the headlong *molto allegro* tempo, brings a variety lacking in the companion work. Two oboes (flutes are omitted) are prominent in the scoring. The second subject brings a sharp contrast as a skeletal violin theme over a rocking accompaniment (violins and violas) leads to a six-bar *crescendo* and to a delicate pattern that drops from E to C sharp (nearly an octave and a half) in three bars, only to recover a whole octave in the fourth. The development, as so often with Mozart, brings an entirely new idea: a melody that closely foreshadows the second main subject of Symphony No. 32 of seven years later, and one which relies upon the familiar lightening trick of detached quavers. Somewhat negative violin figuration brings the recapitulation which, although amended and abbreviated, does not forget to re-introduce the long *crescendo*—such a powerful attention-catcher in the opera house. A full close brings an Andante in A major that, if at first somewhat inconsequential, introduces an unexpected degree of passion in its central section over an unbroken chain of triplets on second violins. Like the first movement, the Finale is marked *molto allegro* but it does not share its thematic material. It looks back to the dance-like finales of J. C. Bach in its racing 3/8 pulse and occasional flashes of prominent brass.

---

* Denis Vaughan's interpretation of this movement is damaged more than most by his unstylish shortening of the grace-notes in the main melody.

SYMPHONY NO. 22 IN C was completed in Salzburg early in 1773 and, although not described as an overture, displays all the features of Mozart's most obvious theatrical writing. Its ceremonial character is furthered by the use of trumpets, without, however, a surviving timpani part.* The opening wall of sound, with horns, celli and basses sprawling over a C major triad, is interspersed with detached quavers in a kind of self-parody which extends to an urgent figure for violins that is an inversion of one heard in the Overture to *Il sogno di Scipione*:

This and the detached quavers soon combine to form a bridge to the second subject, a graceful idea on oboes and violas in thirds answered by another typical Mozartean string phrase of alternating dynamics combined with *staccato* and *legato* phrasing. The expected articulation with the development is broken by a fermata, and the expected, indeed one would have thought necessary, new subject in the development is totally absent, Mozart relying on unembellished repetitions of already-stated material. The operatic destiny of this work is confirmed by the marking of the slow movement, *andantino* grazioso. The qualifying adjective had been used only twice in the first group of slow movements, each time in an overture to a specified opera: *Mitridate* and *Ascanio in Alba*. It is indeed gracefully melodic, oboes and horns carrying themes of considerable charm in thirds with unusual freedom. An ear-catching device is the use of a bare held C on second viola as an accompaniment to the leading theme, a C which is dropped two octaves

---

* The same arguments apply as for D major works: trumpets are unlikely to have been heard without timpani. A timpani part has been reconstructed and appears in the Appendix.

and joined by first viola in the middle octave as the movement closes. The triplets that brought such passion in the Andante of the *Lucio Silla* Overture are milder here, fulfilling merely a contrasting role. The Finale in 6/8 begins with a theme that prances about the very same notes over which the horns and lower strings sprawled at the start of the first movement. The first six bars, repeated, lead to a central section featuring an urgent figure similar to that in the first movement: casual listening does not reveal close connections between the two ends of this symphony, but it is evident that Mozart was linking the two mentally in his "overture style." The repeated six-bar phrase brings a return to the central section, shortened, and a brief coda leads to what can only be the rise of a curtain.

SYMPHONY NO. 26 IN E FLAT was composed at about the same time but appears to have become attached some years later to a stage work entitled *Lanassa*, the German version of a work by the French librettist A. M. Lemierre, *La veuve de Malabar*. That it was originally designed as an overture is evident from the form and style of the music, and that the original stage work was a tragedy is strongly suggested by the character of the Andante. Yet again Mozart puts his overture-writing formula to the test in the first movement but, although the detached quavers, "walls" of violin semiquavers and rather unimaginative string and wind *tutti* are all present, the music has an earnestness and verve, almost a violence, that involves the listener in its momentum. The large orchestra consists of two flutes, two oboes, two bassoons (rarely divided in the first movement, the intention being to provide additional weight in the bass-line), two horns, two trumpets and strings. The use of trumpets without timpani is again a questionable feature, but the appearance of these instruments in a work in E flat (though also a military key in the late Eighteenth century) is less common. Clarinets were frequently employed in E flat symphonies before this date,* but trumpets appeared almost as frequently, sometimes with timpani.† Symphony No. 26 indicates that trumpets were indeed meant: nowhere along the line has an indication for "clarinets" been mistaken for

---

*Two of Jan Stamic's symphonies in the publication "La Melodica Germanica" (c. 1756) are in E flat and scored for two oboes *or* two clarinets, with horns and strings; in the early 1760s two symphonies by Gossec (op. 8 nos. 1 and 3) follow this scoring while another attributed to both Gossec and Roeser is unequivocally for two clarinets, two horns and strings; yet a symphony by Urban Hofstetter published in Nuremberg (an important centre of brass instrument manufacturers) includes two clarinets.

† Kuntz's Symphony in E flat listed in the Breitkopf Catalogue of 1762 as for two oboes, two trumpets, timpani and strings appears four years later in the same organisation's lists as by Querfurth for the same combination *without* drums, the trumpets shown as "2 cl" (=2 clarini); the 1767 listing gives a Toeschi symphony with "2 clar," this being confirmed as the abbreviation for clarinets when the work is given in "Denkmäler der Tonkunst in Bayern." Confusion follows, however, when in 1782/4 an E flat Symphony by Zimmerman is shown as being scored for two oboes, two horns, "2 clar," timpani and strings. Surely "clar" here means "clarini."

1: A resin box in ivory and gold bearing minute portraits of Mozart and his father. It was made in France at about the time of Wolfgang's visit to Paris in 1778 and may well have been presented to him in lieu of a fee for a concert appearance. The name "Baron de Trémant" is engraved within.

2: The house in the village of Chelsea, then outside London, where the Mozarts stayed in 1764. The plaque reads: "Wolfgang Amadeus Mozart, 1756-1791, composed his first symphony here in 1764.") In fact, that work was begun here but completed after the family had moved to Soho.

3: *The Lambach Monastery in western Austria. Since this photograph was taken the roof has been extensively restored. (Photo by courtesy of the Austrian National Tourist Office. [Otto Simler])*

4: The Stiftskirche of the Lambach Monastery. Mozart and his father were received hospitably by the monks in 1769 and in turn presented them with some church music and two symphonies. (Photo: Bundesdenkmalamt, Vienna, Archive. By courtesy of the Austrian Institute)

"clarini." A number of slightly later E flat works are scored for trumpets *with timpani* (Holzbauer's Overture to the *Singspiel: Günther in Schwarzburg*, published by Götz in Mannheim in 1776) and *without* (e.g. a Wagenseil symphony listed in Breitkopf in 1775), and an oddity occurs later still: Montillot's Symphony for two oboes, two bassoons, two horns, *with timpani*, and strings. Clearly the whole picture is fluid and references to trumpets "invariably associated with," or "inseparable from," timpani did not apply when the key of E flat was employed. It appears also that this key was more woodwind orientated in military music, the use of clarinets, bassoons, serpents and horns, sometimes with oboes, producing a smoother result than the trumpet-orientated band in C or D, and if percussion were employed it was more likely to have been the cavalry drum or the side drum than timpani. For these reasons it is felt less necessary to supply a reconstructed timpani part for Symphony No. 26, and the character of the music itself confirms this view.

The first movement, consisting of two sharply-defined themes, neither of which is put to serious development, ends *pp* on three preparatory chords and a fermata, ushering in the extraordinarily rich and sombre C minor Andante. It inhabits a world of personal tragedy and pathos, looking forward unmistakably to the mood of the great G minor Symphony of 1788 (No. 40) and perhaps to the even more intimate language of the G minor Quintet, K516. The opening theme is withdrawn, closely wrapped in imitation and unable openly to communicate its tragedy, but gradually the melodic line opens up like an unfolding lily as flutes and horns consolingly replace the second violins:

The dialogue continues for most of the movement, the broken phrases of the second subject pointing forward to the second theme of the Andante of the G minor Symphony of later that year (No. 25). A wash of rich wind tone, flutes, oboes, bassoons and horns unsupported by strings, gently eases away the sorrow as the three repeated semiquavers of the Andante turn effortlessly into the three repeated quavers of the Finale. There can hardly be music less suited to the martial punctuation of timpani tone than this dancing Allegro in 3/8, a long sonata-form piece of 236 bars recalling the urbane music of J. C. Bach's "singing allegros" and complete with a teasing little fanfare for oboes and horns, a device very much in Bach's style (bars 109–116). Earlier the two violin bodies indulge in a playful interchange, as if anxious to report that the tragic imitations of the Andante are over and done with:

Immediately following this, the first violins seize the large intervals of each phrase-end and pull them this way and that to see how pliable they are, while the rest of the orchestra virtually marks time. At the end they nonchalantly shake them off with a careless flourish.

This writing strongly recalls Mozart's delicious treatment of the material in the first movement of Symphony No. 8 of Christmas 1768.

SYMPHONY NO. 23 IN D presents a straightforward case of a missing timpani part, and a suggested reconstruction is provided in the Appendix. In an opening flourish similar to that in No. 22 the violins insist upon the opening tonic chord while the bass-line establishes the triad. Immediately a precipitate rocketing figure is launched, ascending two whole octaves in one bar, and in theatrical style the violins sink to *piano* as basses repeatedly insist on their triad. All is brilliance and contrast as the violins spin into semiquavers *forte* and then minims *piano*, before launching into syncopations, then more ascending scales, and finally a preparatory fanfare before the second subject enters. This is answered brusquely by violins and gracefully by oboes in thirds. At last, when the recapitulation has run its course, the music modulates via Mozart's beloved detached quavers and the Andantino grazioso in G commences without a break. This is a much-needed period of respite before the almost merciless insistence of the Finale. The swaying string melody soon gives way to one of Mozart's most melting oboe solos.* Another bridge-passage returns the music to D major and the stamping 2/4 Finale in rondo form destroys the memory of that exquisite slow movement. Just as the Finale of No. 26 is surely *not* designed for the muscular tone of timpani, so the finale of No. 23 is as surely designed *for* it.

SYMPHONY NO. 24 IN B FLAT, being similar in overall layout and with consecutive numbers in the original Köchel catalogue, could be considered as a twin of Symphony No. 23. They were written within a month or so of each other and both slow movements, marked *andantino grazioso*, have about them a child-like melodiousness and innocence designed to attract the least sensitive ear. Thereafter the similarities end, for they could hardly show greater differences in character. The opening of the Allegro spiritoso once again establishes the tonic triad and soon introduces syncopations as in No. 23, but the whole tone of the music is more domestic and friendly, less breathless and crude, than the previous overture-symphony. The walls of semiquaver violins are less impenetrable because they tend to be melodically orientated, and the ascending scales, so prominent in No. 23, are reduced to one example in the development section which has the effect of pulling together the music in preparation for the recapitulation. The second subject once again makes play with the Scotch snap. At the end of the movement a cleverly constructed *crescendo* ushers in a coda in which chords on weak beats are whimsically stressed—two diverse influences, one from Mannheim and the other from Eszterháza, juxtaposed and made pure Mozart by the seventeen-year-old genius. His genius is evident again in

---

* Denis Vaughan's short grace-notes detract seriously from the serenity of this melody.

the slow movement: outwardly simple and based on an almost ubiquitous figure of two slurred and two *staccato* semiquavers, it is a gem of pristine beauty, scored simply for two flutes and muted violins with gentle support from the horns. The lower strings are not muted but in the main *motif* the celli and basses play *pizzicato*.* Prior to the last appearance of the main theme flutes and horns join in an unsupported statement, once again showing, as Mozart did at the end of the Andante of No. 26, a new-found independence for the wind instruments. The last movement is another J. C. Bach-like 3/8 Finale in rather primitive form, much less extensive than that in No. 26 and in fact little more than a typical Italianate curtain-raiser.

In the early months of 1775 two more operas appeared, each with its Italian Overture. The OVERTURE IN D, to *La finta giardiniera* is, frankly, an inferior pot-boiler, much too reliant on its opening dotted posturing and subsequent repetitive sequences to add up to more than an episodic and unsatisfying piece. In common with many of the overture-symphonies, the slow movement is marked *andantino grazioso* and, although it possesses more character than the first movement, it compares unfavourably with the central sections of Nos. 23 and 24. Not even the colouristic relief of wind instruments is to be heard. To these two movements is usually added a 3/8 Allegro in D with the same scoring as the first movement (two oboes, two horns and strings). This Allegro, KE207A (=K121), is described as a Finale to a symphony or a divertimento and, having been written at about the same time as the Overture, it makes an appropriate tailpiece of 217 bars. Its primitive 3/8 pulse notwithstanding, the gliding main theme, the frequent whole-bar pauses and the rhythmic leads of the horns give to the piece rather more zest than is to be found in the Overture itself.

The OVERTURE IN C to *Il rè pastore* is another in the series of C major works scored for trumpets without timpani: a suggested timpani part is included in the Appendix. The rest of the scoring is for pairs of oboes and horns with strings. A totally different approach from the Overture to *La finta giardiniera* is adopted in this work. Three chords establish both rhythm and tonality and urgent running pairs of slurred quavers gradually fragment as they wind higher and higher over a pounding bass-line. It is of such stuff that *crescendi* are made, and the influence of the Mannheim composers is indeed unusually strong here, the oboe and horn writing thickening the texture with sustained chords. All the brilliance is in the violin lines as whirling semiquavers alternate with sudden disruptive dynamic changes. The second subject is again

---

* In the main theme the important grace-note in bar 2 should be read at the indicated value so that the pulse of the melody is maintained: Denis Vaughan unexpectedly does so, and his performance, with its subtle phrasing and dynamic moulding, is most pleasing, if not always strictly in accordance with the score.

reliant upon the Scotch snap: a graceful episode in an otherwise headlong movement. As a codetta the bass-line takes over the *crescendo* idea which is then omitted from the recapitulation (there is no real development section), and an alternating low and high, *forte* and *piano*, fragment borrowed from the *crescendo* theme and first heard in the exposition is developed and extended. The rest of the Overture runs its expected course until the *crescendo* brings a break in the mood, oboes switch to flutes, horns intone a pastoral melody, and the first scene of the opera follows without a break.* This first aria, *Intendo, amico*, for Arminta (soprano), is an Andantino in C and it was turned into an instrumental slow movement, with solo oboe taking the vocal part, by the editors of the Bärenreiter edition of the Overture (1957).† In concert performance its provenance is somewhat obvious, especially when, in bar 33, the soloist is called upon to provide an impromptu cadenza, and the lack of key contrast makes it untypical of Mozart's "genuine" three-movement overtures, yet the aria is a charming piece and its unauthentic use here brings it (and the Finale which follows) to a wider audience, justifying such "symphony making." An extension from the end of the aria leads without a break into the Finale, a Rondo in C, KE213C (=K102), written in August 1775 (four months after the rest of the Overture) and scored for an identical orchestra. It is a disproportionately long movement of 316 bars, the first two sections of 16 bars each repeated to make a total of 348, but its nature and the use of wind chords to enrich the harmony make it a suitable addition even if the Mannheim mannerisms of the first movement are otherwise lacking.

Finally we come to the greatest of all the overture-symphonies, a work so vibrant with inspiration that it deserves a place alongside the greatest of the last symphonies: SYMPHONY NO. 32 IN G, known as the *Overture in the Italian Style*, completed on April 26, 1779, in Salzburg, and scored for a large orchestra of two flutes, two oboes, two bassoons, two trumpets, timpani, four horns and strings. Unusually for a work specifically designated "overture" it is in neither of the "theatrical" keys of C or D but in G major, and this is the first time that Mozart had included trumpets and drums in a G major symphony. Even so the trumpets are in C; two of the horns are pitched in D and two in G, and the wide range of brass tone available to the composer is put to sonorous use.

At one time the work was thought to have been written as the Overture to Francesco Bianchi's (1752–1810) opera *La villanella rapita* a pastiche of arias and set-pieces by Bianchi himself, Guglielmi, Sarti,

---

* Most recorded performances of the Overture are of the single-movement version, a concert ending rounding off the first movement in typical style.
† Marriner's recording includes this movement and the Finale, KE213C.

Martin, Paisiello and Ferrari which eventually boasted an Overture in D by one or other of the two last-named; alternatively it may have been used to introduce *Das Serail, oder Die Unvermutete Zusammenkunft in der Sklaverei zwischen Vater, Tochter und Sohn* (The Seraglio, or The Unexpected Meeting in Slavery of Father, Daughter and Son), K344, a *Singspiel* whose title was later mercifully shortened to *Zaide*.

Strictly speaking, this G major work should be called "Overture in the Italian Format" or "Overture in the Mannheim Style." Mozart's visits to Mannheim had left a deep impression upon his composing habits, impressions which he turned to advantage in the symphonies of the late 1770s, but his recent visit to Paris had also influenced him to the extent that Symphony No. 32 opens with an exceedingly bold *premier coup d'archet*, joined rhythmically by two of the horns, the trumpets and timpani, and melodically by all six of the woodwind instruments. A brief, quiet reply for first violins and celli, enriched harmonically by middle strings, brings a repeat of the opening statement, again answered by quiet strings. The music sets off to a flying start and, amid grand rising figures on two horns, flutes and lower strings strengthened by bassoons, the music launches into an exciting passage that maintains its momentum by constantly varying note lengths and by switching the argument from treble to bass and back again. Soon is heard a typical spinning *motif* that brings the first group to an end and establishes D major in time for the second subject. This looks back seven years to the equivalent section in the Overture to *Lucio Silla*:

SYMPHONY No. 32

'Lucio Silla' Overture

but the new version is more varied and less sequential, and it is set against a slow harmonic comment from violas and celli which moves to celli, basses and bassoons and finally to horns. A classic Mannheim *crescendo* of eight bars, *pp* to *ff*, incorporating a long timpani roll, brings a combination of both themes in a passage of high excitement.

A new idea is heard in the development, a sweetly ingratiating violin melody interrupted by impatient wind fanfares. This leads to a static violin passage of *staccato* quavers while violas mark time in regular crotchets, but this is an unsatisfactory role for the normally unassuming violas and they prematurely re-introduce the first theme, immediately finding an ally in the second violins, who toss the *motif* back to them. The whole orchestra is caught up in the urgency and there is an incontinent rush to five commanding, whip-like statements of the opening upward flourish to the dominant and a short pause as resolution is awaited from dominant to tonic. The resolution comes, but it brings with it an unexpected change of tempo to *andante* and a movement in 3/8 of great lyrical beauty. The fluidity of the main melody is untypical of Mozart who, at this period, usually composed in a more rhythmically rigid style. This is as near to a real slow movement as he ever came in his middle-period symphonies, its melting lines recalling the slow movements of some of the Mannheim composers and in particular Antonín Fils, whose rich vein of melodic beauty has been only rarely captured on disc.* This is not to imply that Mozart here is composing "like" Fils, but the relaxed, somewhat wistful, nature of the melody is certainly closer to him than it is to, say, the *legato* minuet style of J. C. Bach and Sammartini. Higher woodwind are given great freedom while both bassoons support the lower strings. In both codetta and coda the oboes and two of the horns play a gentle, unsupported pastoral call. Suddenly the strings quiver with expectancy, alternating from *forte* to *piano*, and the spinning *motif* from the first movement returns. By-passing the opening flourish, the music drops straight into the detached quavers of the second subject, now in the home key. The recapitulation has arrived, complete with the long hard *crescendo*, and the Overture drives towards its conclusion until brought to an abrupt halt by a restraining fanfare that for a moment releases the tension. A short coda rounds off this dazzling orchestral showpiece.

---

* Three of his symphonies have been recorded: in A (Saar Chamber Orchestra under Karl Ristenpart, on German Electrola STC 91103); in E flat (Vienna Radio Orchestra under Gayor Otvós,, on Westminster WST 17128); and in G minor (Prague Chamber Orchestra, unconducted, on Supraphon SUA 19148). A more enthusiastic attack on Fils's riches is long overdue.

Three-Movement Non-Overture Symphonies

An arbitrary sub-section, perhaps, since the similarities between these five works and the following group of four-movement symphonies are much stronger than the mere difference of the missing minuets, but it is felt advisable to pinpoint these works in order to differentiate them clearly from the three-movement overture-symphonies discussed above. In the early- and mid-1770s the different style can be recognised immediately by Mozart's employment of the double-bar and repeated exposition in the first movement (and in Nos. 17 and 27 by the repeat of the second half also), although in the two later works (Nos. 31 and 34) he dispenses with this device.

SYMPHONY NO. 16 IN D, K 128, of May 1772, opens with a divertimento-like 3/4 Allegro maestoso modestly scored for oboes, horns and strings. Two distinct themes are heard: the first opens with two crotchets a fourth apart, a gambit that Mozart pared down from the five-note phrase of No. 15 (see below), repeated in No. 28, and widened to an octave for No. 29,

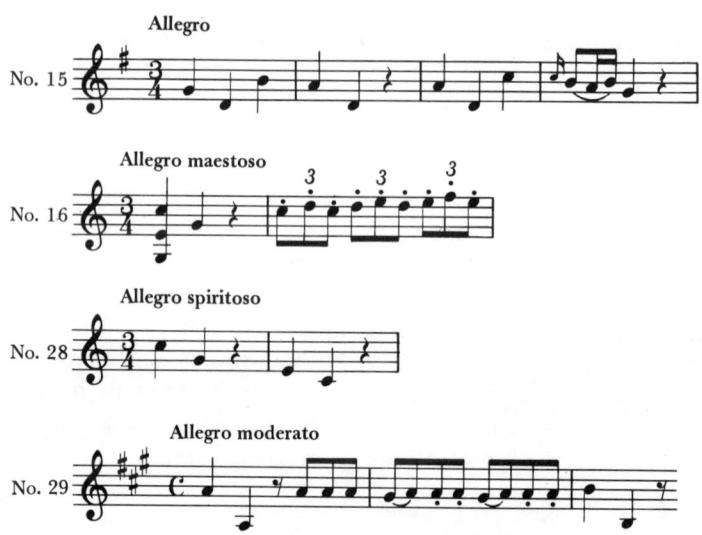

and is concerned with a rather verbose triplet rhythm. The second idea takes an initial octave leap and stretches it progressively to a ninth, a tenth, and even a thirteenth in what is for Mozart unusually boisterous writing, while the bass-line becomes most argumentative. The triplets are totally ignored in the development section, as is the second subject;

instead, a smooth melody is played twice, simply providing a moment of contrast before the recapitulation. Here, though, two abrupt changes of tonal direction* catch the attention before the reprise is allowed to run its course. Perhaps borrowing an idea from the first movement, the Andante Grazioso includes a comically argumentative bass-line in its second subject that is taken up by violins in the second half. Altogether, this movement, both halves of which are marked for repeat, is rather superficial and, scored for strings alone, gives the impression of having strayed in from one of the contemporary "Salzburg Symphonies" (i.e. the three Divertimenti, KE125A–C [K136–8]). A joyful 6/8 *allegro* movement concludes the work without disturbing the equanimity of the symphony—except that the unusually long coda includes an episode in which horns are brought to the fore in a hunting *motif*, very nearly the only opportunity in which these instruments are allowed to shine in the whole work. Formally, the Finale of Symphony No. 1, with its strange extra section, is recalled.

From the same month comes SYMPHONY NO. 17 IN G, the first movement of which commences in a more business-like manner than its companion, with pounding quavers in the lower strings and a sustained octave in the horns supporting an onward-pressing first subject built on Scotch snaps and detached quavers. Soon the second violins, whose furious semiquaver activity at length demands attention, force the first violins to join them in a dizzy upward D major scale that disconcerts the oboes into startled imitation, and the Scotch snap then returns to prepare for the second subject. The long-note harmonies of the horns, frequently joined by oboes, show that Mozart is again shamelessly paying tribute to Mannheim, as the succeeding *crescendo* confirms.† For a moment the development recalls Vienna as first violins introduce the characteristic gentle syncopation, but the questioning Scotch snaps enter and force the music into their home ground for the recapitulation. The "disconcerted oboes" effect is extended here into a little canon, and other minor changes also bring variety to the reprise.

Innocent charm pervades the Andante in C, constructed in two repeated halves. It is so simple and yet so perfect a miniature that one once more remembers the divertimenti that Mozart composed at this time.‡ Diverting also is the 3/8 *allegro* Finale, yet in the development

---

* The similarity to the false recapitulation in the first movement of Haydn's Symphony No. 41, which Mozart almost certainly knew, is noteworthy.

† Although a harpsichord continuo is desirable in these early works, the player in Denis Vaughan's recording makes a decidedly fussy effect at this point.

‡ Again Denis Vaughan's performance calls for specific comment. His shortening of the grace-notes in bars 1, 3, etc., is apparently justified by the composer's decision to write out in full the complementary phrase in bars 5, 6, 7, etc., yet it *sounds* ungainly, as do the majority of Eighteenth-century grace-notes if taken according to more recent convention.

section there is a moment of dramatic harmonic conflict—a stark and unexpected effect in an otherwise carefree movement.

Less than a year later came SYMPHONY NO. 27 IN G in which flutes replace oboes to join the high-lying horn-parts in G to produce a cool wind-dominated sound recalling Symphonies Nos. 14 and 21 in A. Despite the opening chords, which call the audience to attention, this is not an overture-like symphony. The "walls" of piercing violin semiquavers are absent, and even the detached quavers play only a subsidiary role in the development. Stylistically, the music is typical of countless other composers but, in common with Symphonies Nos. 16 and 17, it looks back a decade or so—the first movements of Joseph Haydn's own Symphonies Nos. 17 and 27, together with No. 36, are recalled in the sequences and the distribution of parts, but the second subject, for strings also at first, yet again shows a strong family likeness to the famous Salzburg divertimenti. Both halves are marked to be repeated, another retrogressive step.*

The Andantino Grazioso in D begins with an almost inconsequentially pretty violin melody over a *pizzicato* bass, and many a composer would have been content to let it run uninterrupted to its end. Mozart thought differently. A second theme, having been announced on first violins over triplets in the seconds, disturbingly makes for E minor as divided violas, flutes and horns hold a menacing chord and bass strings stalk ominously. On broken octaves the violins collapse, dismayed, at the double bar. In agitated canon the violins maintain the minor key in the development section, at the end of which it is the bass strings' turn to collapse questioningly on A octaves, making way for the recapitulation. Here, the strange episode seeks D minor, lightening just before the end, but the last sounds heard are the broken, troubled violin octaves.

At first sight the 3/8 *presto* Finale falls into a regular mould, but examination reveals a hint of glories yet to come. Unusually for Mozart, it is a monothematic movement, and this concentration on one theme is a guide to the importance the composer attached to the principle of thematic construction based on four long notes. We have already met this principle in Nos. 1 and 8, and it will be encountered again in Nos 33 and 41. Mozart was not alone, however, in realising the satisfying formal balance and dramatic possibilities of four prominent notes. The technique runs like a thread through the history of music: Bach, Haydn, Beethoven, Schumann, Brahms, and Shostakovich, to name only a selection, put the device to dramatic use, but here Mozart almost throws

---

* The Ricordi score, whilst inviting the players, once they have reached the end of the movement, to return to the central point marked in the score, does not repeat the invitation at the last bar. This fault is corrected in the New Mozart Edition, published by Bärenreiter.

away its possibilities by allotting it a lightweight movement and clothing it in joyous rhythms. The first theme, with its bare contrapuntal running accompaniment, is poker-faced

and the restatement for two horns (immediately following our example) has an imperious ring, but with the second subject the melody breaks into the broadest of smiles:

Yet another pointer to the future comes in the recapitulation when the four-note figure is passed back and forth between orchestral groups, unmistakably foreshadowing the stern fugal treatment in the Finale of the "Jupiter" Symphony. An extensive coda, however, completely eschews such academic writing, and Symphony No. 27 closes in dance-like joy.

The next three-movement symphony, following our terms of reference, came five years later when Mozart was engaged in his fateful mission to Paris. The so-called PARIS SYMPHONY, NO. 31 IN D, indeed pays lip-service to French taste with its *premier coup d'archet* in the first movement and exciting string sequences, but its true style is no closer to that of the French than is the *Overture in the Italian Style* to that of the Italians. Both owe an immense debt to Mannheim. Some critics consider that the cold glitter of the first movement reflects Mozart's distaste for the musical scene he found in Paris: a despicable lowering of standards dictating that the most admired musical quality was an empty-headed sheen. Consequently he wrote his "Paris Symphony" in the same style, as a caricature of what was expected of him. If so, it is to the least consequential and most scintillating of Mannheim tricks that he resorted, wrapping them in an unusually thick orchestral cloak: two flutes, two oboes, two clarinets, two horns, two trumpets, timpani, with bassoons and strings. The first movement is enormously long (nearly 300 bars), but the length is attained by the artificial spinning-out of *motifs* and repetitions that are neither necessary nor particularly attractive. The symphonies of the Mannheim composers were popular in Paris at this time, and it is amusing to see how Mozart copied both the Mannheimers and the Parisians who were copying *them*. The first notes of a symphony were required to be bold, fearless and strikingly rhythmic. This is what Christian Cannabich and others had provided, this is what native composers copied, and consequently Mozart obliged too, neatly outdoing them all in grandeur:

consolidation: symphonies nos. 15–34 / 109

If we dissect the movement we find a twice-stated pompous octave opening terminated by a typical Mannheim rocketing figure and separated by a quiet violin link; theatrical double-dotted fragments; thick wind harmonies, almost endless triads; "walls" of violin *tremoli*; and at the end a double statement of a long *crescendo* abetted by detached quavers in woodwind and brass. All the ingredients, in fact, of a soulless overture-like work, and set, moreover, in the unsubtle key of D major. Yet somehow Mozart assembles these unpromising materials into a movement that, if it is not actually great, bears the unmistakable mark of genius. The crashing and banging of interminable octaves may assail the ear but the mind registers that a worthwhile symphony is unfolding.

Trumpets, timpani and clarinets are omitted in the Andantino, an eventful piece of a length and substance to match the first movement. Solo octaves from horns punctuate the first subject and there is a delicious answering flute roulade later, two further examples of the growing independence Mozart was allowing the wind instruments in a movement in which violins dominate the melodic line. This is a second attempt at a slow movement for this symphony. The first, an Andante in 3/4 for *one* flute, *one* oboe, horns and strings, was considered too artistic for the superficial Paris audience and Mozart was obliged to replace it with the familiar elaborate Rondo. Doubtless the Paris organisers shook their heads gravely at the opening of the Finale, but Mozart was not so ready to compromise here. Instead of the lusty opening unison that was expected of him, he dared to commence with a quiet running second violin accompaniment over which the first violins sigh Mannheim-ishly. Only in bar nine does the full orchestra enter, and then only for three bars. Nevertheless, reported Mozart, the audience stopped holding its breath and applauded the entrance of the *tutti*.* Thereafter he pampered these unmusical sensation-seekers with a full quota of brilliant passage-work, the violins leaping up as far as two octaves and a half at one point. The development seizes upon the ascending interval of a fourth with which the second theme had commenced and subjects it to quasi-fugal examination, passing it around the orchestral groups in a manner similar to the treatment of the Finale of Symphony No. 27. For his Paris audience Mozart produced a Finale of a length to match the first two movements, and its closing gestures are suitably grandiose.

Just over two years later, after his sad return to Salzburg, Mozart wrote a very different work, the SYMPHONY NO. 34 IN C, dated August 29, 1780. It received its first performance on April 3, 1781, in Vienna, conducted by Giuseppe Bonno, and it must have made a considerable effect since the orchestra consisted of four oboes, six bassoons, four horns, four trumpets, timpani, forty violins, ten violas, eight celli and ten basses. Doubtless the music triumphantly survived such inflated treatment, for the first movement has a strength and sinew that looks forward unmistakably to the "Linz" and "Jupiter" Symphonies and compares in lustre with the "festival" symphonies of Joseph Haydn (Nos. 63, 69 and 82), except that Mozart's horns are crooked in C *basso* rather than C *alto*. It opens in Mannheim style once again, with a powerful two-octave statement to establish without a shadow of a doubt the tonality of C major. The fanfare *motif* heard in bar three is rarely absent from the first theme, and the music is driven even more urgently by an up-beat *grupetto*, a brisk Scotch snap, syncopations, excitable semiquavers, and a magnificent double rocketing figure that heralds the second subject. This opening paragraph, supported by a pounding bass-line of unbroken quavers and scintillating wind writing, is amongst the most brilliant that Mozart had composed up to that time.

The long second subject group opens with a chromatic violin figure echoed by a bassoon and later by an oboe, and proceeds to a theme of prominent Scotch snaps against a rocking bass-line of alternating viola

---

* That the start on two violins was not invented perversely to twit the French audience will be evident from the fact that three earlier symphonies, Nos. 21, 27 and 28, start their finales similarly.

and celli/bass crotchets. The second statement of this theme finds an oboe answering each detached snap. A *crescendo* of ten bars leads to a totally characteristic section of detached quavers, marked by *sf* stresses on the third beat. Suddenly the violins sound a fast, loud, repeated octave D and the music hurtles towards the development section, an abrupt drop in dynamic level announcing its arrival. This section would yield countless subtleties if there were but space to examine them; it will have to suffice now to draw attention to the disturbed double-octave figure (two oboes and two bassoons) that is answered conciliatingly by violins, the latter each time trying a different argument to soothe the winds until eventually, with a heart-wrenching chromatic quest, the bass-line descends through A flat to G. The recapitulation is now due, but the music little by little fades to nothing, a mere whisper of violins answered by echoing oboes. Now the recapitulation can enter, *forte*, with tremendous effect, and Mozart outdoes even the exposition in the vividness of his writing as the previous material is restated and fanfares build a stunning coda.

The Andante di molto is in F major (the subdominant) and is scored for strings in five parts with bassoons doubling the bass-line throughout (these wind parts are not given in the Ricordi score). It is in simple sonata form without development: since the recapitulation joins the exposition without any mediating material, and that recapitulation is considerably varied in detail, the effect is of a C. P. E. Bach varied reprise on a large scale. The first theme, marked *sotto voce*, is graced by ornamental turns and its first two statements are answered by swelling divided violas in thirds, but soon the second violins and first violas are entrusted with the melody. A feature of this movement is the gentle "Viennese" syncopation which occurs in both first and second themes and reappears in the second of two subsidiary subjects. It is altogether a reposeful movement of simple melodic delight that could have been written by no one but Mozart.

It was apparently the composer's original intention to include a minuet and trio in the scheme, but no such movement survives that was unequivocally composed for the purpose. The C major Minuet and Trio, KE383F (=K409), is sometimes inserted in third place, but its suitability is in question since its scoring differs in two particulars: there are two flutes but only one viola line (except for one bar towards the end of the Trio) whereas the symphony has no flutes and the violas are frequently divided. In the Finale Mozart returns to a species of jig that was first heard in the *Neuer Lambacher* Symphony of a decade or more earlier. Its rapid 6/8 pulse is to be heard also in the Finales of two C major festival symphonies of Haydn, but the older composer seemed reluctant to use the 6/8 time signature, preferring 2/4 in Symphony No. 41 of c. 1768 and common time in No. 56 of 1774, achieving the constant jig rhythm by the use of triplets. In all these works the movements only achieve their true exciting effect of unstoppable rhythmic verve in crisp performances of pinpoint accuracy. Mozart never for a moment allows the breathless rhythm to relax in the exposition, even for a second subject, but he is not in too much of a hurry to introduce playful oboe duets in the development section, along with some poignant chromaticism just before a tiny breathing-space after which the recapitulation and a brief coda complete this rhythmic *tour de force*.

Four-Movement Symphonies

Of these ten "full-grown" four-movement symphonies, the first five date from a single year, 1772; the next four were produced over the six months from November 1773 to May 1774, and the last comes from 1779.

Opening with an abrupt statement in even crotchets, SYMPHONY NO. 15 IN G condenses its first theme to a mere twelve bars. The second subject starts with a rapid-fire *staccato* duet between low strings and violins/oboes. Mozart is in playful mood: second violins slip downwards from D to B, dragging the first violins with them, until a fermata is reached. Then, furious at the unexpected lack of activity, the second violins spin into a codetta in which only they are marked at a constant *forte*. After the exposition repeat the development introduces entirely new material before encountering a false recapitulation of the first subject while horns utter a warning in octave Bs. A dissonant passage ensues, horns intoning a string of suspensions while celli and basses hunt around for the missing key (G major) by way of a chromatic bass, horns arriving again at their threatening Bs. An entirely new theme then playfully reduces the tension as the tonic is recovered in time for the recapitulation, and the rest of the movement sticks safely to a regular reprise.

In contrast to the daring first movement, the Andante in C reverts to the formula so often used earlier: a pretty theme with soft "Viennese" syncopations, garnished by subtle comments from oboes and horns. It is a pleasant but unremarkable interlude. The Minuet, notable for its frequent rests, has as its central Trio a most graceful episode in D major that contains more than a hint of waltz-time. It lies in style somewhere between the *Ländler* and the *legato* minuet-style of J. C. Bach. A Rondo, *presto* in 2/4, concludes the symphony with an air of frivolity:

hardly a piece substantial enough to balance the weight of the first movement.

Doubtless the Salzburg musical scene was aware of the music of Joseph Haydn, brother of Mozart's colleague Michael at the Archbishop's residence. By the early 1770s Joseph had produced several symphonies in C major* that included in their scoring parts for two horns crooked in C alto, i.e. sounding as written, the tube lengths being the same as for C trumpets. Acutely interested in any musical device new to him, Mozart must have studied these parts and perhaps got his Salzburg cornists to try them over. By May 1772 they were evidently coping competently, so Mozart added parts for two C alto horns in his SYMPHONY NO. 18 IN F, where they support two other horns crooked in F.† He handles the parts cautiously in the first movement, allowing the players to warm up to their brief solo in the Trio of the third, but despite this caution the piercing, almost hysterical, tone of the instruments adds a lofty imperiousness to the music.‡ Another feature that lends a distinctive colour to this symphony is the replacement of oboes by flutes. For much of the work, apart from the Minuet, these flutes are given independent parts, and first flute is to be found frequently high up—holding its breath, as it were—to give the music a sense of spaciousness and light. The Scotch snap is again prominent in the first theme, embellishing an already rather too ornate melodic line with its clumsy rhythm, but an alternative and more graceful theme enters over a syncopated accompaniment. The second subject itself is a coy, feminine little thing of trills, triplets and Alberti quavers that has the two groups of violins nodding to each other as the lower strings stalk up and down in *pizzicato* crotchets, finally settling on octave Cs. The development commences with the true first theme and much discussion takes place before it returns in its original form, holding the stage to the complete exclusion of the alternative graceful melody.

Set in B flat with a gently pulsating 3/8 rhythm and with the violins muted (another favourite device of Joseph Haydn at this time), the Andantino Grazioso is scored for the normal strings plus two flutes and four horns, two crooked in F and two in B flat alto. The delightfully melodic violin lines of this movement are set against endlessly varied inner string parts which lull the listener with a comfortable bed of

---

* Nos. 20, 32, 33, 38, 41, and possibly Nos. 30, 37, and 48.
† There is evidence that the inclusion of these C horns was an afterthought.
‡ Two years later Michael Haydn was to use C alto horns in his "Italian" Symphony in C (Perger No. 10), a work that also includes *corno 3° ò tromba*, two tamburi, two cors anglais and two *pifferi*. The last-named instruments are Italian bagpipes: where did Michael Haydn acquire these? Did Mozart bring them back with him from his Italian trip or were they already "in stock" at the palace? Some years earlier Leopold Mozart had written a concerto for hurdy-gurdy and bagpipes, but these Austrian instruments probably differed from Italian *pifferi*.

delicious harmonies and subtly prodding rhythms. When both parts of the movement have run their course (and in a stylish performance both halves will be repeated) the violins dispense with their mutes for the concluding eight bars, proudly marked "Coda."

Eight bars also suffice for each half of the Minuet, an unusually brief span for Mozart. It is as if the main part of the movement is purposely played down so that the strange Trio will make the greater effect. This latter starts severely with four long notes as if some significant utterance is about to be made (see the remarks on Symphonies Nos. 1, 27, 33 and 41) but in the second half comes the extraordinary, if momentary, use of the two C alto horns, solo but for the tactful support of flutes and violins as they borrow the opening figure from the Minuet itself.

We can only glean from the music itself any clues to the workings of Mozart's brain: in the Finale we find evidence that either his sensibilities dictated a clean break from the 2/4 and 3/8 Finales of his contemporaries and his own earlier works,* or that through some necessity the last movement of No. 18 was imported from another symphony. So substantial is its material that the movement runs the risk of outbalancing the first. Would the composer have been so careless? Knowing his concern for symmetry it seems doubtful, and it is therefore much more likely that the Finale of No. 18 is, in fact, the first movement of a different symphony, the remainder of which is either lost or was never written. It opens with a bold drop of a fourth similar to those found at the starts of Symphonies Nos. 15, 16, and 28 (see p. 104) and continues with a pounding quaver bass-line that is often to be found in his most earnest movements. Other fingerprints tumble over

---

* A "break" is not indicated since he returned frequently to 2/4, 3/8 and related rhythms in later Finales.

each other: alternately slurred and *staccato* pairs of quavers, "walls" of *tremolo* violins, detached quavers, whip-like upward gestures, ascending scales, and a stalking bass-line, but the elaborate and prominent horn writing imparts to the movement a new, more intense sound, and its melodic construction is notable for both economy and fecundity:

The second theme (B) is reshaped from the slurred-*staccato* segment of the first, but there are two subsidiary themes. Note the use in the second subject of a chain of triplets just two bars long: a judicious breaking of the basic common-time pulse to prevent any possibility that that pulse might become wearing. The first subsidiary idea (C) is wistful in mood, the second (D) assured and swaggering, and it is this swaggering Stamic-like theme that prevails in the development section, amid fragments of violin "walls" and detached quavers, and the bass-line repeats the theme sequentially as the music runs into the regular recapitulation.

Wisdom, if such it is, after the event indicates the possibility, submitted as an alternative to the ones just given, that Mozart exchanged the positions of first and last movements. Certainly this elaborate Finale would make a good opening movement, and the first movement would be less out of place as a Finale than the piece now holding that position.

SYMPHONY NO. 19 IN E FLAT once again employs four horns: two in E flat alto and two in E flat basso. The players of the instruments marked *alto* are expected to read their parts in the upper octave while their

116 / mozart: the symphonies

colleagues read in the lower octave (see p. 134). Bars 12–14 of the first movement illustrate how this works:

Once again the deployment of brass in widely-spaced chords, sometimes spanning two octaves, lends to the work a distinctive sound that is rich but at the same time brassy and stimulating.* Oboes are retained in this work, together with strings and a bassoon in the bass-line. The opening of the first movement is impelled forward by liberal use of dotted rhythms† and violin semiquavers as an accompaniment to the striding horn figure quoted above. The second subject also relies on dotted phrasing and our old friends the detached quavers, here, as in Symphony No. 18, used with restraint as a lightening device. Unlike all except one (No. 21) of its numbered companions of 1772, the first movement of Symphony No. 19 is in welded form, the development being announced, as so often, by a full-bar chord following a brief pause. This chord (G

---

* That is, when the horn players actually play in the registers required. Neville Marriner, Denis Vaughan and Jaap Schroeder cajole their cornists to do so (the last using natural horns), and the results on their recordings are thrillingly impressive. On the other hand, when both pairs of cornists play in the same lower octave the result is dull, thick, muddy, and confused, since for much of the time one pair of horns is superfluous.

† Denis Vaughan effects this even more tightly by his stylish habit of double-dotting all singly-dotted groups.

major first inversion) brings an unsettling change of tonal centre which is held for nine bars before Mozart again disorientates his listeners with a full-bar chord of F major (first inversion), leading to a hurtling section in F minor before the dominant (B flat major) is established at the end of the development. Only now is the regular recapitulation ready to begin in the home key of E flat.

Mozart supplied two slow movements for Symphony No. 19, both in B flat. The earlier of the two, marked Andantino Grazioso, is an attractive movement in 2/4 in which oboes play a prominent part, as do two horns in the answering phrases of the main idea. The later movement is more substantial. Marked *andante* and set in 3/8 time, it is intense in mood, and the wind are used more harmonically and less melodically. There is, too, a freer use of dynamics, the violins disrupting the music with a heaving *forte* figure that is elaborated in the development section. Both movements employ horns crooked in B flat alto, a fact ignored so far by most recorded performances, basso horn tone clogging the textures damagingly.

Opening with hectic imitation between first and second violins that spreads to violas, celli and basses, the Minuetto remembers its role as a dance movement only in bar ten, but forgets it again in the middle of the second section. As in the case of Haydn's Symphony No. 29, the Trio offers bare harmonies without the complement of a melody: perhaps the continuo harpsichordist was expected to provide an improvised theme in the first half, to be answered by the extraordinary octaves of the second half.* The *allegro* Finale is a breezy Rondo based on a clear-cut melody that is an ancestor of the Finale of *Eine kleine Nachtmusik*, shorter, more epigrammatic, but just as striking.†

With three dignified chords SYMPHONY NO. 20 IN D introduces a level-headed, quietly confident theme over a repeated-quaver bass-line. A regal and ceremonial symphony has begun, a work that owes as much to similar symphonies by Mannheim composers (both Jan Stamic and Antonín Fils wrote such symphonies) as it does to the brilliant C major "festival" symphonies of Joseph Haydn (e.g. Nos. 41 and 48), all of which were almost certainly known to Mozart at this time. We await the brilliant string passage-work, the antiphonal fanfares between horns and trumpets, and the exaggerated contrast of a "feminine" second subject to bring warmth to the marble-like gloss of the rest of the movement—and sure enough, one by one, these things appear.

---

* Although Denis Vaughan's performance includes a harpsichord and the player makes a token attempt to fill the gap left by the absence of a melody, surely more could have been done here? Marriner does less.

† Once again Vaughan's performance comes into question: he crushes the grace-notes, thereby destroying the pristine grace of the recurring theme and the meaning of the first episode. On the other hand, he brings out the horn parts brilliantly.

Only one thing is missing: the weight and ictus of timpani. Here again we find that most unlikely of works: a D major ceremonial symphony that includes trumpets but excludes drums. If common-sense does not dictate that drums would have reinforced those opening hammer blows, musical considerations later certainly do. The horn fanfares at bars 14 to 16 are supported by oboes and violins against violin semiquavers, (i.e. nothing in the bass); similarly, the trumpets, horns and oboes in bars 73 and 84 are completely unsupported, as are brass only at bar 135; and several further points exist at which some bass voice is necessary. A timpani part is provided in the Appendix: perhaps its use will bring performances of this noble symphony somewhat closer to the effect the composer intended until an authentic drum part is discovered.*

The second subject again employs the Scotch snap, but it also nods towards Vienna in its mild syncopations marked by typically Mozartean *fp* stresses.

Following the example of Haydn's festive Symphony No. 41 in C, Mozart's No 20 provides a contrasting Andante in 2/4 for solo flute against muted violins, a pizzicato bass line adding the characteristic Mozartean tone colour. The similarity between this melody and that of the Finale of Symphony No. 19, despite differences of tempo, mood and key, is uncanny:

---

*Christopher Hogwood's recording with the Academy of Ancient Music includes an improvised timpani part.

Each of the two parts of the movement is marked for repeat (the first sometimes, the second seldom, taken in performance today) and there is a short coda. After this interlude the Minuet seems all the grander, its noble pace, ascending scales, and brass octaves and fifths again pleading for the support of percussion. Second violins carry the intimate melody of the Trio before relinquishing it to firsts in the second part, only to take it up again before the return of the Minuet. Cast in 12/8, the Finale once again reflects the influence of Joseph Haydn's Symphony No. 41, whose Finale, although employing 2/4 rhythm, is set throughout in triplets. Mozart wastes little of his subtlety on this movement: the chief desire seems to be to produce as exciting a close as possible to one of his grandest and most stately creations.

More modestly scored than Nos. 18, 19 or 20, SYMPHONY NO. 21 IN A, for two flutes, two horns and strings, looks back to No. 14 in its fresh, open-air instrumentation, the A horns once again brightening the texture. The opening theme on first violins stretches up an octave but has difficulty at first in stretching down as far as that until the more athletic second violins show how it is done. The whole movement has a carefree divertimento-like atmosphere similar to the group of three "Salzburg Symphonies" written earlier that same year: the glittering semiquavers of the violin lines and the high-lying flute colouration are the features that will most readily catch the ear as the bright movement runs its course, but a sudden pause leads to a coda that at first reduces the temperature, only to bring in a *crescendo* from *p* to *ff* as a final reminder that Mannheim is still prominent in Mozart's memory.

An almost unbroken ripple of demisemiquavers carries through the D major Andante, switching restlessly from second to first violins, then to violas and flutes. The main melody is pure Viennese charm, the second somewhat more disturbed. In the development the grace of the music is ruffled by a hint of the fashionable "Sturm und Drang" mood, but this is soon swept aside by the recapitulation. A steady crotchet bass-line ensures that the chattering melody of the Minuet does not obliterate the rhythm of the movement. Chattering quickly turns to bickering as second violins find that they cannot agree with the firsts over the matter of phrasing a triplet segment of the theme,

120 / mozart: the symphonies

a problem that is solved in the second strain.* Flutes and horns produce an odd effect in the second half of the Trio by juxtaposing crotchets with the violas' quavers and alternating with the violins' *pizzicato* chords: a dry description of a most magical effect. The Finale starts, like those in the "Paris" Symphony of six years later and in Symphonies Nos. 27 and 28 of the following year, with two violins completley unsupported. They announce a delicate bouncy theme answered by nervous string unisons. Initially the second idea is calmer but second violins and violas quickly introduce an impatient rhythmic figure that returns the music to its agitated mood. Both halves of this Finale are to be repeated, and when this course is followed the bar-and-a-half general pause at the start of the development is allowed to make its startling effect twice, certainly not superfluously. A brief coda features the horns and flutes in an exciting sequence of crotchets.

The next four-movement symphony followed fifteen months later, in November 1773: SYMPHONY NO. 28 IN C, for two oboes, two horns, two trumpets, timpani and strings (the timpani part is no longer extant but a reconstruction is provided in the Appendix†). Four descending notes (see p. 104) are answered by quietly-spinning violins, the dual sequence repeated, before a "Viennese" phrase confirms the identity of the composer. Much of the movement is made up of sequences and devices more familiar from the overture-symphonies of this period —whip-like figures and "walls" of semiquavers, for instance—but there is an added spaciousness not present in the theatrical works that extends in particular to the second subject, a quiet violin phrase answered insolently by oboes, the roles then being reversed. In the development the basses repeat the spinning violin fragment before a new idea eventually appears, bringing a series of Scotch snaps and a reference to

---

*Most conductors, including Stadlmair and Vaughan, prematurely solve this problem by amending the phrasing so that the seconds agree from the start with the firsts, thus destroying one of Mozart's little jokes.

† Of recorded performances, only Georg Szell's may feature a timpani part: even that is not completely certain since the timpani, if present, are so poorly balanced that it is impossible to distinguish their *timbre* in what is, in any case, a sharp-attacked and percussive reading.

the second theme before the entry of the recapitulation and a rather conventional coda.

Violins are muted throughout the Andante which, like the slow movement of No. 21, relies upon demisemiquavers for much of its rhythmic motion. Horns and oboes punctuate without providing a great deal in the way of harmonic support: so transparent is the music that it almost seems as if Mannheim had never existed. Scotch snaps appear yet again in the second group, a device that is to come into its own in the next four-movement symphony. The Minuet and Trio are unremarkable save for a stunning horn solo that echoes the end of the opening phrase on its every appearance, while the divertimento-like *presto* Finale is a study in high spirits, opening, as so often at this period, with two unsupported violin lines. The second melody is one of Mozart's most carefree inspirations, serving as a moment of sunny humanity amid the rumbustious gaiety of the rest. Perhaps feeling that his obligations to Mannheim have not been honoured elsewhere, Mozart closes his symphony with a powerful *crescendo*.

The provenance of the "Sturm und Drang" works of the 1770s is discussed below and it is necessary here only to comment on the structure and mood of Mozart's first full-scale "tragic" symphony SYMPHONY NO. 25 IN G MINOR. Composed near the end of 1773, the work is scored for two oboes, two bassoons, two horns in B flat alto and two horns in G, with strings, the viola section of which is divided for a short time in the Andante. Heard in the context of contemporary symphonies such as Nos. 28 and 29, the G minor symphony shocks with its violent and uncompromising language.

Four long notes are intoned by the oboes over strenuous syncopated violins and violas following the same line while the basses support the whole structure in even crotchets. It is a terse statement in what might be termed "broken unison":

There immediately follows a vicious violin unison played five times and descending via a hectic dotted figure to an abrupt halt. The music seems to prepare to repeat this gripping opening paragraph but instead the first oboe repeats its four-note theme quietly, as if pleading for tolerance. With a curt octave leap and a violent thrusting figure, the violins cast aside this plea and launch into a succession of semiquavers and syncopations while violas and basses reiterate the thrusting figure and the two pairs of horns hurl a fanfare back and forth in support of the lower strings. Determined to be supreme in their violence, violins suddenly flare again into prominence with descending semiquavers in preparation for the second subject. The Scotch snaps so common in the surrounding symphonies are put to earnest work here as the theme marches sequentially upwards, smoothing out at length into slurred and *staccato* quavers before terminating in two abrupt ascending figures. A restless bass-line closes the exposition, which, together with the second half of the movement, should be repeated. It seems that the development section is set to outdo even the exposition in violence as violins and lower strings enter into impetuous canonic imitation of ever-widening intervals while second violins and violas maintain a pitiless storm of repeated quavers, but eventually the oboe's four-note phrase returns like a soothing hand, to be answered by chromatically swirling violins. In a moment of despair the strings consider a pathetic fragment of melody before the vehement recapitulation takes away any hope of consolation. A coda finds the "broken unison" still unbending, and the movement ends with three sinister bars of barely-subdued violin semiquavers.

The Andante is in E flat but despite its major key it offers little relief. Scored for muted violins and a full wind complement, it is the answering phrases of the bassoons that weigh down the music with a drooping sadness that even the oddly nervous second idea, forcing a smile, is unable to shake off. The Minuet brings a return to G minor. It is a strong movement with a second section of twenty-four bars—just twice as long as the first—giving time for some slight development of the material. The Trio, like those in several of Haydn's minor-keyed symphonies, is in the major and it at last provides a moment of grace and sunshine. It could have been borrowed from one of Mozart's wind sextets: six wind instruments play totally alone. This respite from the minor key is short-lived, however. The Finale commences with an ominous *piano* unison that devolves on to violas and basses with wind support as violins re-introduce their syncopations from the first movement. A chromatic second idea soon arrives before the second subject proper (first violins and violas) brings a more confident note, but this, too, is crushed by the return of the first theme as second violins force the music onward with savage whip-like descents. Once again a new theme is employed in the development: a malevolent fragment of a theme on lower strings. A brief coda brings the symphony to an end on two *ff* chords.

Known as "the little G minor Symphony," No. 25 is "little" in neither scope nor size, except in relation to the great G minor Symphony of fifteen years later. With No. 25, the seventeen-year-old Mozart may be said to have come of age emotionally. Certainly, as we shall see below, outside influences had upon him an enormous effect, but it would take considerably more than received impressions for a composer to produce a work of such searing drama as the G minor Symphony of 1773 without the presence of a strong personal conviction that what he was doing would not sound merely fashionable. That his coming of age was also reflected in less intense music is seen by his next four-movement symphony.

For sheer polish and elegance, few works of art surpass SYMPHONY NO. 29 IN A, written within a month or two of No. 25 and scored modestly for pairs of oboes and horns with strings. The first notes are a quiet falling octave A on violins (see p. 104) from which seems to grow the self-renewing first subject against fluid harmonies. A second statement, *forte*, supported by broad wind chords, covers the same ground, and a succession of characteristic Mozartean devices (bars 17 to 32 are quoted)

follows as a link to the second subject group. This second group is in four sections. The first opens with five crotchets; the second has a prominent trill whose continuation is echoed by violas; the third curls downwards in graceful imitation and rises chromatically to the fourth, a strutting *motif* again decorated by trills under a held oboe octave. If this expenditure of material seems lavish, almost wasteful, what are we to make of the development, which ignores all these riches and treats two new ones? These are: an upward scale that terminates with the descending octave from the opening notes of the work and is passed from violins to violas and then to celli and basses (but when low strings return it to violas, the latter have meanwhile discovered that it goes just as well in the reverse direction); and an elegant theme over a rocking lower string accompaniment. When the regular recapitulation has run its course the coda takes the first theme of all and subjects it to four-part stretto in an almost casual display of amazing contrapuntal skill:)

The influence of Joseph Haydn may be felt particularly strongly in the D major Andante in which the violins are muted. The interweaving of the two muted lines is again the work of a natural contrapuntist, but such technical feats may be ignored by the listener intent on putting musical feeling first, for there is in this music a twilit beauty and a romantic atmosphere that totally belie the composer's paltry eighteen years. At the end comes an unmuted restatement of the main theme, complete with oboe and horn fanfare as if to admonish the listener that he has daydreamed long enough—other business awaits attention. This "other business" is a singular Minuet whose gawky rhythm so fascinated the composer that he included it in virtually every bar, turning it into a fanfare for oboes and horns at the end of each half and hammering it out on a unison F sharp, *fortissimo*, at the double bar. By contrast the Trio in E major is as graceful as the main Minuet is awkward.

If the first movement seems lavish in its production of thematic ideas, the Finale is rather more economical, being content with only two, yet the first, but for an upbeat, takes the very interval of a falling octave that was put to such exhaustive use in the coda of that movement. The time-signature is 6/8 and the key A; one awaits with interest to see what Mozart will do with hunting horns in such a movement. If the horns are given due prominence in performance it is not necessary to wait long before their brassy lustre is heard supporting the bass-line in an imitative passage of four notes. The second subject graces a repeated B, first from below, then from above, the last two notes being misplaced first downwards and then upwards. The comic effect is irresistible as it is also at the double bar when, doubtless through sheer high spirits, the violins rocket upwards for an octave and a half. For once, the development takes the first theme and examines it at different levels before plunging with another rocketing whoop into the reprise. With dazzling effect it is the hunting horns that dominate the coda, and with yet another joyous whoop the symphony is over.

By comparison SYMPHONY NO. 30 IN D is a work of modest inspiration. The orchestra of No. 29 is supplemented by two trumpets.* No timpani part survives, so a reconstructed one is provided in the Appendix. After the dotted opening statement the music is driven along by the popular rhythm of three upbeat quavers followed by a downbeat crotchet, a rhythm made particularly unforgettable by Beethoven. A smooth contrasting second subject, introduced by a unison trill on oboes and strings, draws on the Scotch snap to enliven its line, and later it brings in a series of unusually widely-spaced *acciaccature*. A third idea in dotted rhythm is set against the trill noticed earlier, but now it is distributed antiphonally around the orchestra, being never quite sure whether to appear on the first or the second beat of the bar. It is this third (dotted) idea that is taken for treatment in the development and, after the fascinatingly varied recapitulation, it forms the nucleus of the coda.

The Andantino con Moto is, unusually, for strings alone. Pretty enough in its own right, it is nevertheless difficult to believe that it was composed later than the slow movement of No. 29. In fact, stylistically it would not be unreasonable to place this movement several years earlier. The Minuet is much more characterful. Haydn's influence is detectable again, but there are numerous details, such as the triplet rhythm at bars 11 and 12 and the wide intervals in the second half, that mark it off from the older composer's style. The Trio, with tantalising across-the-bar phrasing, might have emanated from either composer. The opening rhythm of the first movement is extended for use in the

---

* Mozart described the instruments as *trombe lunghe*, which might be fractured Italian for "long trumpets," but whether he meant by this the straight herald trumpet or a large trumpet with an extra-long tube is not clear. The character of the parts would indicate the latter.

Finale, *presto*, a kind of *moto perpetuo* in martial rhythm that relaxes only for a brief second subject in its brassy rush. Note should be taken of the suddenly contradictory *ff* fanfares in the development—a point which, if all others fail, would indicate that percussion were expected in this work. Both halves of the movement are marked to be repeated; after which comes probably the most inspired moment of the whole work: as violins fade away on a thrice-heard fragment of melody under a spacious wind chord spanning four octaves, the symphony closes quietly and enigmatically.

Another five years were to pass before the next four-movement symphony appeared: SYMPHONY NO. 33 IN B FLAT, dated July 9, 1779. It was the last but one symphony that Mozart wrote in Salzburg, and its Minuet was not added until after he had moved to Vienna. In comparison with Symphony No. 34 of a year later, No. 33 might be by an entirely different composer. The consummate ease with which the orchestra is handled is common to both works but while the grand gestures of No. 34 require a palette enriched by trumpets and timpani, No. 33 makes its totally different effect with the almost domestic-sized orchestra of two oboes, two horns, two bassoons and strings. The exposition of the first movement is unusually extended—an expansive 138 bars. Bassoons, celli and basses, as if startled by the opening *forte* chord, break it into fragments in the first bar. Detached quavers collect the pieces and assemble them wrongly, twice, and the music shrugs off the problem as of no consequence. It is not until a new idea is reached in bar 25 that there seems to be any sense of direction in the work, and even then the device of a three-quaver upbeat to a crotchet (here dotted),

so often put to potent use by other composers and even by Mozart himself, is of only mild rhythmic urgency. Schubert's Symphony No. 5, also in B flat and *minus* trumpets and drums, may be thought of as a descendant of Mozart's No. 33, yet even that charming work has about it a greater thrust and earnestness: it is much less willing to unfold without haste. This relaxed quality is rarely encountered in Mozart's symphonies, and the character of the first movement of No. 33 is altogether unexpected. The smooth nature of the subsidiary themes abets the general languor of the music, and one in particular seems to yawn lazily before settling to a more responsible attitude:

Indeed, a certain stress, associated with the three-quaver upbeat rhythm, enters the music for a time and eventually brings a *crescendo* of triplets. Although not employing the "welded" form, there being a distinct close on F major at the end of the codetta, there is no exposition repeat, mainly because the purpose of a repeated exposition—to establish the movement's material firmly in the mind of the listener—does not apply in this case: the development deals with two entirely different matters which are announced consecutively in the first eight bars of the development:

The first, marked *a*, remains unchanged through most of the development and ushers in the recapitulation. The second, *b*, is a modified version of the lazy yawn heard earlier but now transformed into none other than the "Jupiter" theme: in bars 163–6 it is stated exactly, apart from the rhythmic change, as it will appear nine years later at the start of the Finale of No. 41. The recapitulation is subjected to some tightening of the original material, the components of the "responsible attitude" idea reversed at one point

but no further room is found for the material of the development.

The sunny well-being of the first movement is carried into the second, an Andante Moderato in 2/4 time and E flat, the subdominant. Also carried through is a personal strain of chromaticism by which Mozart so often identifies himself. It often brings a bitter-sweet pathos to his music, but here there is no bitterness in the ineffable beauty of the movement, which traverses uncomplicated sonata form in serene delight. The Minuet, added three years later, is firmly welded to the outer movements by its initial drop of an octave. It is notable for its subtle phrasing, a trick picked up, perhaps, from Joseph Haydn. The opening

stresses this point: how tempted a lesser composer would have been to phrase notes 6 and 7 in the same way as notes 1 and 2, and how commonplace would have been the result. Another instance occurs immediately after the double bar:

As a foil to the playful manner of the Minuet, the Trio is a dainty *Ländler* marked *sempre piano*.

The exposition of the Finale is a dazzling display of melodic invention, no less than five themes or ideas being offered, and being suitable, for development:

5: The Burgtheater, Vienna, today. Many of Mozart's late works were first performed here. (Photo by courtesy of the Austrian National Tourist Office [EOFVW-Markowitsch])

6: Oil painting by Gustav Klimt of the Burgtheater in 1888. Despite changing fashions, the auditorium is much as it was in Mozart's time. (Photo by courtesy of the Austrian Institute)

7: This plate from Filippo Bonanni's Gabinetto Armonico (1716, but reprinted as late as 1776) shows a player tuning the Violone, or double-bass viol. It was an essential colouring in the classical orchestra and its range descended to bottom C. (Reproduced with permission from the Dover reprint [1964])

8: Oboe by Stanesby Junior, dated 1754, typical of the type of instrument Mozart would have encountered. (Horniman Museum)

9: A hunting horn in F by Bull, dated 1699. This type of instrument was in regular use in orchestras of Mozart's day (Horniman Museum)

10: A recording session for the first complete cycle of Mozart's symphonies to be performed on period instruments played by the Academy of Ancient Music in period style, with Christopher Hogwood as Director at the harpsichord and Jaap Schröder as Concertmaster. (Photo: The Decca Record Company)

11: János Keszei playing late nineteenth century copies of timpani of Mozart's time. (By courtesy of Alan Taylor. Photo: Anthony Hodgson)

Yet Mozart, after faithfully repeating them, spurns them all and, just as in the first movement, allows his development to create its own subject. In fact, the subject commences complete

but it is reduced first to the opening four notes and then to the opening two before a woodwind and string unison based on the first four brings about the embellished recapitulation. At the very end, apparently just for the joy of it, Mozart prances up and down the scale in a manner reminiscent of his triadic flourishes in Symphonies Nos. 7, 9 and 11.

Sturm und Drang

The much-discussed "Sturm und Drang" (Storm and Stress) movement in instrumental music, to which Mozart subscribed in most branches of his art, started somewhat earlier than is usually realised. Its roots may be traced to the early years of the Eighteenth century, but not to the overtures of that time, which were mainly in major keys (almost all of Vivaldi's, for instance, are in C major), leaving any tragic developments to the events on the stage after the rise of the curtain. It seems not to have occurred to any composer before Gluck to prepare the audience for the dark mood of a drama with a suitably sombre overture, presumably because the overture served merely as an unheard background to the arrival of the audience. On the other hand, concert symphonies, with which we are primarily concerned here, did in fact often carry a strong message of tragedy, so strong in some cases* that

---

* For example, the pathetic, grief-laden tones of Vivaldi's C minor *Concerto ripieno* (i.e. concerto without soloists), RV120, P427, the crazy non-sequiturs of his B flat *Concerto ripieno*, RV163, P410, which carries the title *La conca* ("The Hollow" or "The Cave"), possibly the name of a play, and the stark violence of the amazing D minor *Concerto ripieno*, RV127, P280.

it is impossible to accept that some extra-musical stimulus was not present. This stimulus may have been the use of the works as introductions to non-vocal stage presentations, not necessarily of a religious nature, and the desire of the composer to set the dark mood at the beginning of the evening's entertainment and maintain it between the acts. That these "overtures" and "intermezzi"—what we would today call "incidental music"—have since become detached from their parent plays is entirely understandable: non-operatic stage works with optional music would frequently be given by organisations without access to live musicians, the economical necessity of the matter dictating that the words should be available without the music; and if the play might be without the music, so might the music be given without the play. These stern orchestral works gradually came to be included in concerts, and thus began a self-revitalising cycle independent of stage action.

The written word also played another part. European literature and drama in the early Eighteenth century had become largely stereotyped in an atmosphere that was ripe for the creation of new directions. Audiences were not allowed to forget that the stage action was merely make-believe, even when purporting to portray historical events. But unrest was growing in the lower strata of society, an unrest that led to the political revolutions of the second half of the century, and this new "socialist" movement found an outlet in the dramatic works of the middle years. They became crystallised in such works as "Night Thoughts on Life, Death and Immortality" (1742) by the Englishman Edward Young (1683–1765) and the works of the Frenchman Jean-Jacques Rousseau (1712–78), whose dramatic emotionalism is not reflected in his musical compositions. This new literary direction was seized upon by German authors. A succession of wasting wars had brought German drama and music to a state where it was dependent upon foreign influences: this emotionally-charged wave of drama from France, England, and perhaps also Italy, together with the revelation of Shakespeare (the first German translations appeared in 1762), struck a responsive chord in native German writers such as Johann Georg Hamann (1730–88) and Johann Gottfried Herder (1744–1803), both of whom preached the value of individual words and of poetry as producers of emotional responses. Herder's "Fragmente über die neuere deutsche Litteratur" (1767) and his friend Goethe's pamphlet "Von deutscher Art und Kunst" of a few years later set forth the principles of the new German art. Goethe presented the first important examples of the new emotionalism in his play "Götz von Berlichingen" (1773) and his novel "Die Leiden des jungen Werther" of the following year, and this vein of personal tragedy and involvement was followed by many more writers, including Jacob Michael Reinhold Lenz (1751–92) and Freidrich Maximilian von Klinger (1752–1831).*

Irresistibly the mood spread back to the art of music, and a long line of sombre minor-keyed symphonies ensued, culminating in the C minor symphonies of Beethoven and Schubert. The line also extends backwards, however, filling in the thirty years between the death of Vivaldi (1741) and the great period of concentrated interest with a fascinating series of minor-keyed symphonies from all parts of Europe. In France Louis Gabriel Guillemain, who committed suicide at the age of sixty-five in 1770, had composed a "Symphony in the Italian Style" in D minor in 1748. Sohier included D minor and F minor symphonies in his op. 2 published in Paris about 1751, and the line continues with Bailleux (C minor, 1756), Davesne (F minor, 1757), Beck (G minor, 1758; G minor, 1760; G minor and D minor, 1762), Gossec (D minor, 1758; C minor and G minor, c. 1762), Schenker (G minor, 1761), Alexandre (D minor, c. 1765), Bambini, Talon and F. X. Richter (all G minor, 1767), Maldere and Richter (D minor, c. 1769), Martini il Tedesco (G minor, 1769), Eichner (D minor, 1770) and Azais (G minor, 1770).

In Amsterdam Mahaut published symphonies in C minor and E minor in about 1750, and J. Schmitt symphonies in G minor and D minor in 1769/70, while North Germany heard C. P. E. Bach's E minor Symphony in 1756 and Hoeckh's B minor Symphony about six years later. Mannheim saw many notable minor-keyed symphonies, one of the most striking being Fils's in G minor, published in Paris in 1764 as op. 2 no. 2. Vienna produced Gassmann's symphonies in C minor (1765), G minor (1767) and B minor (1769), Dittersdorf's in E minor (before 1766), two in G minor by Wagenseil (before 1766), and Vaňhal's E minor (before 1770: also attributed to Carl Stamitz), his symphonies in A minor and C minor (before 1770) and D minor and G minor (before 1771). Incidentally, in a period when most symphonies were written in D major, Vaňhal went out of his way to avoid this key, producing one in A flat and, in 1770, a set of six in the keys A, F, A minor, C minor, E minor and B flat. Many other minor-keyed symphonies were produced in London, Nuremberg, Prague and Rome, while in Salzburg in 1773 Mozart produced the sombre Andante of Symphony No. 26 and the violently carved No. 25 in G minor, perhaps based emotionally on J. C. Bach's Symphony op. 6 no. 6 of 1766 in the same key. In this context (which includes the many minor-keyed symphonies of Joseph

---

* Klinger has received an undue share of fame in the "Sturm und Drang" movement because his play of that title (1776) provided a point of focus.

Haydn from 1768–72) Mozart's output takes on a different aspect: in a long series of major-keyed works his occasional excursions into the minor seem less incongruous, more in line with the fashion of the time. This is not to suggest that Symphony No. 25 is less valuable as a work, and certainly one cannot say that Mozart was merely following fashion. That he could be swayed by fashion is evident from the D major emptiness of many of his Italian symphonies and overtures, but the emotion contained in the G minor work undoubtedly stems from inner stresses that found an outlet through the outpourings made possible by his "Sturm und Drang" predecessors.

This "Sturm und Drang" line reached something of a crisis point in the early 1770s, with Asplmayer, Eichner, Milandre, Zimmermann, Lorenziti, Neefe, C. P. E. Bach, Reichardt, Lang, Hennig, Myslivecek, Kreusser, Mica—the list is endless—producing minor-keyed symphonies in various parts of Europe; even mild-mannered Boccherini in distant Madrid brought forth a D minor Symphony (Gérard 560, of 1771) entitled *Casa del diavolo* (House of the Devil) the Finale of which is based closely on Gluck's *Dance of the Furies* in *Orfeo ed Euridice* (Vienna, 1762), a chorus which is itself based on the last dance in Gluck's ballet *Don Juan* of the previous year. Vaňhal is prominent in the continuation of the line, but he was by no means alone: Hoffmeister's E minor Symphony was published in Lyons c. 1777, and Lachnith's in D minor in Amsterdam soon after. Also contributing were Dittersdorf (C minor, c. 1780), Beecke (D minor, c. 1781), Kraus (C minor, 1783, reshaped from a Symphony in C sharp minor!), Rigel (G minor, 1783), Michael Haydn (D minor, Perger 20, 1784), Kaffka, Ragué, Rosetti, Pleyel, Leopold Kozeluh, Dittersdorf, Boccherini, Gaetano Brunetti (all in the mid- to late-1780s) and Barthélémon, Pleyel, Schmitt and Huber (in the 1790s). Not all of these works have deserved today's neglect by artists and concert promoters.

Horn Symphonies

Common though it was, the use of minor keys threw up problems for the horn-players, whose instruments were seriously limited in the notes they could obtain cleanly. In the face of this problem, the easier solution, and one followed frequently, was simply to omit horns altogether. The other required skill, cunning, and usually access to additional instrumentalists: either crooking the two horns in different keys (Haydn calls for one horn in A and another in E in the first movement and Finale of his "Farewell" Symphony, No. 45 in F sharp minor, of 1772) or calling for supplementary horn-players. In Symphony No. 39 in G minor (c. 1768) Haydn asks for two horns in B flat alto and two in G, thus making available notes in both the tonic and the relative minor scales, and it is this neat solution that Mozart follows in his Symphony No. 25. Vaňhal's Symphony in A minor of c. 1777 calls for three horns and his D minor Symphony requires four, but another symphony in D minor (c. 1780) demands no less than five: two crooked in D, two in F and one in A. Only in a few places does he use them all at the same time and without doubling, so clearly he was determined to circumvent the restrictions which the use of minor keys impose upon brass writing.* It may be assumed that Mozart, in scoring his G major *Overture in the Italian Style* (Symphony No. 32, see p. 101) for two horns in G and two in D, was interested not so much in widening the spectrum of notes available as in enriching the sonorities of one of his grandest and most elaborately scored pieces, but he may not have resorted to this device had he not had the experience of Symphony No. 25 to call upon.

The two other symphonies with four horns raise a question that has become unavoidable in any discussion of Eighteenth-century orchestral music: whether to pitch horns in alto or basso. In our quest for an answer, here are some facts. The lowest alto crook is D. There were no D basso crooks in the Eighteenth century and composers, knowing this, called for *corni ex D*, this description leaving no room for ambiguity. The instrument they got was a horn crooked in D alto, but since there were neither basso nor altissimo crooks in D, the word *alto* was superfluous. The same principles applied to horns crooked in E, F, G, A and B flat, but later in the century the B flat basso crook began to find its way from the military band into the orchestra. This is why, in the 1770s, for Symphony No. 25 and for the slow movements in B flat of Nos. 18 and 19, Mozart could call for horns in B flat, knowing that the word *alto* was implicit in his request, but by 1788 he had to specify *alto* for a horn crooked in B flat for Symphony No. 40. From this it will be seen that alto horns are required for all Eighteenth-century orchestral music up to, say, the early 1780s, unless otherwise stated. The only exception to this rule is in the case of horns crooked in C, where *basso* was almost invariably intended. Rare indeed are works calling for C alto horns: Joseph Haydn, among others, employed the instrument tellingly in many symphonies but Mozart called for them only once, and then probably as an afterthought—in Symphony No. 18.

---

* Information kindly supplied by Professor Paul Bryan of Duke University, North Carolina, U.S.A.

Cutting uncomfortably across all the above arguments is the brass requirement for Symphony No. 19: two horns in E flat *alto* and two in E flat *basso*. The deployment of these instruments is illustrated on page 116, but here we are concerned with the use of the words *alto* and *basso*. Which of the two is implied when a composer calls for horns in E flat? If *alto*, then we must re-think the tone quality of countless E flat symphonies that have up to now sounded effective with "E flat basso" horns; and furthermore, where does this lead us in the matter of D horns? Could it be that the clogging heaviness of D horns should be replaced with the clarino wildness of horns pitched an octave higher, horns which our arguments above force us to refer to as in D *altissimo*? Doubtless this tone-colour was experimented with at the time, but the quality of the notes would have been so like trumpets, whose players could produce the same notes without the eye-watering strain suffered by their horn-playing colleagues, that composers used trumpets instead. This argument, incidentally, cannot apply to C alto horns: their tone-colour differs considerably from that of C trumpets even though the sounding notes are identical. Returning to our E flat puzzle, it seems that the answer is simply that Mozart's cornists were able to produce notes sounding either "up" or "down" by clever manipulation of the crooks available (in E flat, B flat, etc.) and subtlety in the art of "lipping" difficult notes. All those earlier E flat symphonies by Mozart and other composers remain unaffected if we realise that, in this local instance, by *alto* and *basso* Mozart meant *altissimo* and *alto* respectively.

It will be noted that the highest note for these "E flat altissimo" horns (occurring in bars 54, 56, 69 and 70 of the first movement and in the rondo-theme of the Finale) is written D", which sounds as F" (i.e. on the top line of the treble stave). For comparison, the C alto first horn I in Symphony No. 18 reaches to G" (written *and* sounding: see example on page 114), while in Haydn's "Maria Theresia" Symphony No. 48 the first horn in C alto reaches to A", as does first horn in A in Haydn's Symphony No. 5. For a higher note still, one has to look at the Trio of Jan Stamic's Symphony in G (DTB IIIi: G7), which ascends to F''', sounding a major third (C''') *above* Haydn's highest horn note. At these heights, the high horn-writing of Mozart, Haydn, and even Zelenka, seems modest by comparison.

Serenade Symphonies

In addition to the symphonies, Mozart's orchestral output includes a large number of serenades, divertimenti and cassations written for less formal occasions. They range from the short, tightly-organised three-movement divertimenti or "Salzburg Symphonies" of 1772 to the large-scale multi-movement works such as the "Haffner" and "Posthorn" Serenades. In many cases it is possible to turn these serenades into "symphonies" by the simple method of snipping out some of the movements.* This is precisely what Mozart himself did in the case of three Salzburg serenades in D, turning a leisurely evening's entertainment into something more formal.

The SYMPHONY IN D, KE213A (=K204) is made up of the first, fifth sixth and seventh movements of a seven-movement serenade completed on August 5, 1775. The missing second, third and fourth movements are, in effect, a violin concerto: it is therefore possible to separate out the serenade into a symphony and a concerto, the only drawback then being that the violin concerto will end in a key (D) different from that in which it began (A). For the remaining four movements the scoring is two oboes doubling flutes, bassoon, two trumpets and strings, to which a timpani part should be added in all except the Andante (see Appendix). In truth, these movements add nothing to our conception of Mozart as a symphonist. The opening Allegro Assai has a cold superficiality recalling the D major Italian symphonies of five years earlier but it lacks the symphonic cogency of Symphony No. 20. The Andante† in G is a showpiece for various solo wind instruments. In turn the flute, bassoon and oboe are displayed, and even the second horn (crooked in G) is allowed some prominence. This is pure serenade writing; nothing like it appears in the genuine symphonies. Much the same comment concerns the Trio: there a flute solo plays a passage that might have been taken from a flute concerto. Finally, the last movement commences with a slow introduction (*andantino grazioso*) of fifteen bars, a feature to be heard in none of the symphonies, and the rest of the movement is a 3/8 Allegro interspersed with three more appearances of the Andantino. This Finale is less symphonic than the least symphonic of those in the symphonies.

---

* Old parts exist of the Serenade in D, KE62A (=K100), minus the second, third and fourth movements, bearing the title "Sinfonia" and scored as for the Serenade but without flutes, despite the fact that flutes are so essential to the character of the retained Andante sixth movement. There seems to be no evidence that Mozart approved the abbreviated version of this early (1769) Serenade for use as a "Sinfonia," although it is unlikely, even if the flutes parts of the sixth movement had been transferred to oboes, that he would have disapproved strongly.

† This tempo indication was not supplied by Mozart.

The so-called "Haffner" Serenade was composed in July 1776 to be performed at the wedding of Elisabeth, daughter of the Salzburg ex-Burgomaster Sigmund Haffner. The scoring is for pairs of oboes doubling flutes, bassoons, horns and trumpets with strings, but when the composer removed the "violin concerto" section (the second, third and fourth movements in G) to turn the work into a five-movement (!) symphony, he or one of his associates added a timpani part,* further bearing out the contention that symphonies in D with trumpets should also, as a stylistic necessity, include drums.

What might be called the FIRST HAFFNER SYMPHONY, KE248B (=K250) is, however, no more convincing a symphony than its companion KE213A. For a start it is in five movements, including two Minuets, the second of which has two Trios, and the Finale once again commences with a slow introduction. Also untypical of his true symphonies is the opening Allegro Maestoso, an imperious, gesturing stretch of music thirty-four bars long that comes to rest on a half-close to give way to the first movement proper. This incorporates in its first-subject group the "Viennese syncopation" (marked *a*), now anything but its gentle self,

and a phrase from the majestic introduction. The second theme is divided into two parts, the first sighing quietly, while the second has about it something of a *buffo* air. As the codetta, again quoting the oboe and horn *motif* from the introduction, leads into the development, another idea from that introduction returns: a plunging *grupetto* that gradually mutates until fading out altogether. Alterations of detail take place in the recapitulation before the coda reintroduces yet again the oboe/horn figure. The last word is had by the plunging *grupetto*, angry, perhaps, at having been submerged in the development.

The second movement of our synthetic symphony is described in the score as Minuetto Galante, and its stately tread is redolent of all that description suggests. Its length of 18+32 bars is unsymphonically extended and the use of the tonic minor for the Trio is rare in the true symphonies. There follows a gentle Andante in A, in rondo form and stylistically close to the violin concerti of the previous year. As a fourth

---

* Both Münchinger and Boskovsky include this part in their recordings of the complete Serenade.

movement Mozart produced a grand and pompous Minuet, complete with the expected trumpet fanfares but with a totally unexpected questioning phrase towards the end. The first of the two Trios is in G and features a delicious *Ländler*-like duet for bassoon and flute; the second Trio, in the tonic, again features prominent wind, the two flutes remaining in thirds for most of the time against a persistent quiet trumpet fanfare. It is as if the Finale, opening at *adagio* tempo, is inviting the entry of an operatic heroine, but instead a rumbustious Allegro Assai shows itself, hoping at first as if unsure. Once established, it turns out to be full of almost Haydnesque fun and gaiety, but the second theme and a new idea in the development prove to be amongst Mozart's most characteristically carefree melodies.

The whole eight-movement "Haffner" Serenade, when all repeats are observed, would last something over an hour; similarly the extracted five-movement "Symphony" is longer than any of the genuine symphonies. It is difficult to envisage an occasion upon which it might be played today in preference to a real symphony or to a complete but shorter serenade. Less unwieldy is the SYMPHONY IN D extracted from the seven-movement "Posthorn" Serenade, K320, completed on August 3, 1779, for an as yet unknown occasion. Omitted from the serenade are both Minuets (second and sixth movements), a Concertante (third) and a Rondeau (fourth), both for wind band *concertante* with strings. An *adagio maestoso* introduction sets the mood of splendid festivity which is taken up by the ensuing Allegro con Spirito. When the second theme appears, frequently interrupted by a *forte* dotted phrase from the first theme, it proves to be unusually long, the violin melody curling and unfolding gracefully for nineteen bars before it is swept aside by a long double *crescendo* and then by an extended codetta. Much of the development is kept at a low dynamic level to give contrast to the rest of the movement. Without changing tempo, the reprise is announced by reference to the *adagio* introduction, the change in speed being accomplished almost entirely by augmentation.

—a trick carried out even more precisely by Schubert at the equivalent point in the first movement of his First Symphony:

The rest of the movement follows the expected pattern and it is rounded off with a particularly grand coda.

Marked *andantino*, the D minor slow movement once again displays unusual freedom for the wind instruments. It is one of Mozart's gently throbbing movements, neither fast nor slow, possessed of a sad peace and resignation that is intensified by subtle touches of chromaticism and by prominent use of the two bassoons. By-passing the Minuet, whose second Trio includes the posthorn that gave the serenade its name, the symphony closes with a *presto* Finale, an extended movement of nearly three hundred bars that hardly stands in need of analysis. All the expected gestures are there including a long *crescendo*, a short passage for unsupported wind, and plentiful D majoring for brass and percussion. It is, in a way, mindless music that shows in every bar the hand of a genius in boisterous but perhaps hurried mood.

None of these three serenade-symphonies makes a satisfactory symphony, a warning perhaps to other symphony-makers with sharp scissors and their eyes on the other serenades.

3: High Maturity: Symphonies Nos. 35-38 (1782-86)

Scored for piccolo doubling flute, two oboes, two clarinets, two bassoons, two horns, two trumpets, timpani and strings with "Turkish" percussion of triangle, cymbals and bass drum, the OVERTURE IN C to *Die Entführung aus dem Serail* is included here only because its layout—a fast section leading to a central Andante which is followed by a return to *tempo primo*—is similar to that of Symphony No. 32. The opera was completed after ten months' work on May 29, 1782, and was first performed in Vienna on July 16 of that year. Of basically simple design, the Overture seems to be a perfect example of the maximum effect being obtained by the expenditure of a minimum of effort, although we have no knowledge of the amount of sheer toil that went into its composition. Drawn in broad strokes of black and white, the *presto* sections are full of exotic "Eastern" turns of phrase (the action, after all, takes place in Turkey), heavy percussion strokes, unisons and octave doublings, simple scales and *tremolo* violins, and the end result is one of the most vivacious short works in the repertoire. For the Andante the piccolo changes to flute for a C minor episode that is later to be heard in the major as Belmonte's aria, the first set piece of Act I. The writing for wind is unusually free but brass and percussion are silent. The reprise of the Presto is usually extended in concert performance to make a satisfying entity.

At about the same time that he completed *Die Entführung aus dem Serail* Mozart began a SYMPHONY IN E FLAT, KE383G, but, if he completed it at all, only eighty-three bars of the Allegro and fourteen bars of an *adagio* introduction have survived.

Later in 1782 Leopold wrote to his son in Vienna to ask for another ceremonial serenade for the Haffner family: Sigmund, brother of Elisabeth, was about to be ennobled. After an impatient prodding from Salzburg Wolfgang eventually delivered the second of his "Haffner" Serenades, a grand work in five movements plus a march, KE385A (=K408, No. 2), at the beginning of August. Its scoring is for pairs of oboes, bassoons, horns, trumpets and timpani, with strings, and in this form, presumably, it celebrated Sigmund Haffner's great day in Salzburg. The following year, however, Mozart performed it in Vienna as a symphony *minus* both repeats in the first movement,* one of the minuets (which is lost), and the march, but plus two flutes and two clarinets, and, despite this considerable mutation from the format sent to the Salzburg family, it remains known as the HAFFNER SYMPHONY, NO. 35 IN D. The grandeur of his earlier Serenade is matched, if not surpassed, but one must be sure to listen to the piece as a symphony rather than as an occasional piece since it stands up well amongst its symphonic neighbours. It is even possible that Mozart originally composed the Serenade with its subsequent use as a symphony already in mind.

It is common to describe the first movement as monothematic, and indeed the main theme, with its odd five-bar shape and the descent from D, through C sharp and B, to A,

is present in whole or part, like a *motif* in a passacaglia, in most bars of the movement, sometimes in canon, sometimes almost hidden in *pianissimo* trumpets and drums. Even when absent, its shape, inverted and/or smoothed out

---

* The Ricordi score calls for both halves to be repeated, but the New Mozart Edition follows Mozart's wishes for the symphony and omits both repeats.

or subtly suggested (by what staggering process of genius can become

and remain recognisably related?), impinges upon the consciousness. But the movement is not monothematic. When the music has modulated to the dominant it comes as a shock to be greeted yet again with the first theme, *piano*, over a quiet running phrase on low strings and bassoon, but the music shakes itself violently and in doing so gives birth at last, thirteen bars later, to a true contrasting second subject, full of chromatic tints. Yet, despite the fact that it repeatedly clashes harmonically, the first theme plays along with the second, as if watching over its welfare:

A few words cannot do justice to the complexity and skill of Mozart's writing here or in any of the late symphonies; one can only hope that, in drawing attention to some points, an annotator will encourage the listener to seek out others. Subjectively it may seem that Mozart was right in deleting both repeats from the symphonic version of the work: such an over-exposed theme needs hearing only once, perhaps, but will even two hearings together really reveal all that Mozart does with it?*

By comparison, the Andante seems artless, its first theme presented neatly over a *staccato* semiquaver accompaniment, but the oboe and bassoon sighs that colour its continuation show the ability of the now fully mature composer to strike at the heart of the listener's emotions. Under, rather than over, a tantalising *staccato* line of repeated As, the second theme bows in gracefully on second violins and violas. In the development it is as if the sun has momentarily been obscured, fragments of melody being heard only fitfully through mist, but the recapitulation is the brighter for this temporary dullness, and the tantalising repeated notes accompanying the second theme are now transferred to high, ethereal Ds. Exaggerated pomp in performance is once again needed to draw the best from the Minuet, a grand gesturing piece with Scotch snaps prominent in the quiet answering phrase.

---

*Marriner in his recording omits both repeats but observes both in the Andante, a hopelessly lop-sided procedure.

Borrowing a memorable idea from the third movement of Symphony No. 18 (remember those C alto horns?), the Trio is a smiling, contrasting, episode of grace and repose.

Unison strings, *piano*, introduce the Finale, *presto*, a real operatic *buffo* movement with some rough bursts of humour. One of these is the recurring sudden *forte* drum-roll which, at first resolving on to D from A, reverses the direction as the music modulates for the second subject. A cautious affair with characteristic *fp* markings and a close on the "Viennese" syncopation, this theme is succeeded by first and second violin quavers, *forte*.* No repeat-sign marks the end of the exposition but Mozart misleads the listener by seeming to return to the opening at the start of the development, only to side-step after ten bars. Then he plays another trick and introduces the second theme in the home key: the listener is now quite certain that the music is in the middle of the recapitulation (there having been no development) until, that is, the real recapitulation arrives. Mozart's alliance, not with Mannheim, but with Haydn's sonata-rondo finales, is now established. There is a lengthy coda of pure whimsy: grace-notes play around skittishly, the first theme returns but lands up on B rather than the expected A, the false note teasingly lengthened, and the drum-rolls (now firmly A to D) force the brassy climax.

Written, as Mozart reported, at top speed for a concert in the town that bears its name, SYMPHONY NO. 36 IN C, "Linz," was completed on November 3, 1783. Hitherto the slow introduction had played little part in Mozart's symphonies: we have seen how, eighteen months earlier, he wrote one for the lost E flat Symphony, KE383G; now he not only provided one for each of his next three symphonies but also composed one specially to be added to the Symphony in G by Michael Haydn that was performed at the same concert as No. 36.

The essence of most slow introductions is a strongly dotted rhythm, a historical link to the theatrical posturing of the old Lullian *ouvertures* proving extremely difficult to break.† The *Linz* Symphony capitulates totally to the influence at first

(see example on following page)

---

* Many conductors treat these bars, 53–56, as a *crescendo*, but Mozart was in Vienna now: he did not require the transition from the *piano* second subject to the *forte* codetta smoothed out. Several stylish conductors, among them Neville Marriner, take this passage at a hearty *forte* from its first note.

† This dotted figure survives long after Mozart's death: in Haydn's "London" Symphony, No. 104, in Beethoven's Nos. 2 and 7, in Schubert's Nos. 1, 2, 3, 6, 7 and 9, and, as the slow introduction is fused into the opening Allegro, its influence can still be felt in Beethoven's Ninth Symphony. Interested readers may care to continue the line for themselves through to Dvorák and beyond.

144 / mozart: the symphonies

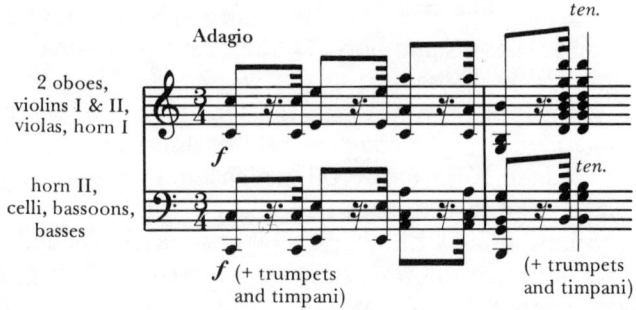

but Mozart soon re-establishes his personality in a chromatic continuation of wandering bassoon, oboe, and violin lines from under which the first subject of the Allegro Spiritoso slides with relief. Only then can the more pompous nature of the work really emerge. Yet in a movement that might be expected to follow C major precedent and resort to an undue amount of spinning-out or padding, especially considering the rush in which it was written, there is virtually none. Viable thematic ideas tumble over each other, enough to keep a lesser composer going for a year, among them a short second subject in E minor, the relative minor of the expected dominant, but this carries hardly more weight than any one of several alternative *motifs*. Fantasia-like, the development carves its way almost independently of previously heard material, all of which is restated, with minor changes, in the recapitulation. A suitably energetic coda makes light of the complexities that have gone before.

The use of brass and drums in a slow movement was still something of a rarity in 1783, mainly because the change of key (in this case to F major, the subdominant) created difficulties in performance: crooks or instruments had to be changed and drums retuned, necessitating a long gap between first and second movements. In No. 36 only the horns are re-crooked (C to F); trumpets remain in C and timpani stay tuned to C/G. Perhaps because of this, their martial tones make a striking effect in the Poco Adagio. Opening in *siciliana* rhythm, drums soon establish a kind of grim ostinato that comes and goes disturbingly. The mellow lines sung by violins and woodwind seem constantly threatened by war-like elements as off-beat *forte* chords splash across the secondary theme. Doubtfully the development presents the first theme again but brass and drums once more menace the music, so a new tack is put to the test: low strings and bassoon climb upwards and are answered with a weary sigh by violins and violas. The climbing *motif* persists and gradually finds support but, although strengthened, the music is still unable to recover; the last word is spoken amid military sonorities. In the Minuet, too, a persistent military fanfare answered by squealing violins repeatedly stretches the proportions of the movement, but the

Trio, in a nicely balanced 8+16 bar pattern, has no such problem. Its opening oboe melody is answered in part two by bassoons, and the two instruments carol it in canon at a distance of one bar.

We have noticed the slight influence of Haydn in the uneven pattern of the Minuet, and it is often said that it was at this period that Mozart was most influenced by his friendship with the older man. Particularly is this said of the finales of Symphonies Nos. 36 and 39. When we come to examine the Finale of the "Linz" Symphony we do indeed find unfamiliar elements which may well have been suggested by Haydn's music, but if so they are either taken over half digested or have been so well assimilated that they emerge totally in character with what Mozart might have done anyway. In the second subject, for instance,

we notice quavers slurred together in pairs (A), whereas Mozart might have alternated slurs with *staccati* as he had done so often before and was to do again in the Finale of No. 39; but we also notice that typical "Viennese" syncopation (B). The comically rushing violins at bars 133–141 might have been written by Haydn, but the cunningly disguised reference to the first movement at bars 120–122 is pure Mozart. In the development Mozart selects one of Haydn's favourite instruments, the bassoon, to carry the subject with which the section opens,* but this is then used imitatively in typically Mozartean style, terminating, it is true, on a deliciously Haydnesque little interchange between oboes and strings (cf. the Finale of Symphony No. 88, bars 142–158, of some four years later!) as the recapitulation sweeps in. No one can deny the daring strokes Haydn would deal at cardinal points, but when Mozart is daring, as in the oddly abrupt ending of both halves,† he is still himself.

It has for long been established that SYMPHONY NO. 37 IN G is by Michael Haydn: a three-movement work, without Minuet, that the

---

* It is almost as if Mozart had just "discovered" the bassoon; he is to put it to outstanding use in the next symphony.

† Each of which should be repeated. Incidentally, the *fortissimo* marking at long passages at the end of each half that is found in some scores is a later addition. The single f indication at bars 142 and 377 should be retained until the end of each respective section.

composer may have lent or given to Mozart when they met in Salzburg in 1783. Mozart performed it in Linz on his way back to Vienna, but he graced it with a slow introduction once again based on a dotted rhythm. This Adagio Maestoso in many performances tends to outweigh the main part of the first movement because Michael Haydn's contribution is frequently taken much too fast. The tempo marking of *allegro con spirito* does not necessarily mean that a speed faster than *allegro* should be adopted, i.e. "spirit" does not have to mean "faster." At a steady tempo the movement's driving horn fanfares are the more telling and the very rapid violin passage-work becomes unscrambled. This is not the place to examine Michael Haydn's music (although a place is certainly necessary), but the grace of the Andante Sostenuto, with its "Viennese" syncopations and independent bass-line in the minor-keyed development section should be noted.

Dispensing with a Minuet but including an enormously complex slow introduction, the SYMPHONY NO. 38 IN D, "Prague," stands on the threshold of the last three symphonies and shares some of their greatness. It was written in Vienna during December 1786 and is scored for two flutes, two oboes, two bassoons, two horns, two trumpets, timpani and strings.

The thirty-six-bar *adagio maestoso* introduction is unusually extended even by Mozart's standards.* As befits a deeply serious first movement, the mood of the introduction is sombre, the four brusque triplet flourishes giving way to woodwind sighs and a tortuously chromatic violin line. This in turn leads to a gradually mutating two-bar passage, *forte*, set against a funereal drum-beat which then gives rise to more sighs and chromaticism—the wind and strings having exchanged roles—and a linking passage in which first and second violins exchange a fragment of the *forte* passage against solo bassoon semiquavers. A dotted rhythm, *pianissimo*, brings a mysterious fermata on A from which the Allegro grows painfully on syncopated violins. Once it has made its appearance it thrusts a number of ideas at the listener, there being no apparent limit to the composer's fund of viable subjects for development,

---

* The "Linz's" is nineteen bars long, No. 39's twenty-five bars. The average length of a Haydn slow introduction is about sixteen bars, and it is not until Symphony No. 103 of nine years later that, at thirty-nine bars, Haydn surpassed the length of Mozarts' Adagio.

but it is clear that these *motifs* are meant to be heard together as one entity since no linking passages prepare the listener for each new idea. On the contrary, (A) overlaps with (B), (B) overlaps with (D), (C) joins (B) and (F) joins (E) without any intermediate material at all: these six subjects are presented all in the space of nineteen bars, and each one has the germ of development in it. Development in fact starts immediately, there being a lot of ground to cover: the first *grupetto* of (F) is combined with part of (B) and, when the music moves to the dominant, (A) and (B) join with (E) before the true "second subject" is announced:

Bassoons try over this theme while violins introduce yet another melody, or cluster of melodies. So concentrated is this exposition of 142 bars that it is vital for the repeat to be taken in performance so that the listener might have a chance to identify the various strands of material.

Nothing has been said about the colours in which Mozart clothes these strands. His scoring has an earnest and transparent sound which shows a new awareness of the potentialities of the orchestra. It is an integrated unit now, the various solos so well absorbed into the fabric that it seems as if each thematic idea and its only possible scoring occurred to Mozart simultaneously. The earnestness of the sound is intensified by the almost organic use of trumpets and timpani. The music does not smile yet it is full of intellectual wit. It is philosophers' fun, and with our musical examples before him, the listener is free to delve into the complexities of the development and the recapitulation, seeking clues like a detective, or to put his intellect into neutral and let the sheer panache of the music sweep him along.

Mozart couches his Andante in the subdominant, G major, and continues his intellectualism on a different plane. Chromaticism again has a firm place here as a succession of melodies unfolds in a shadowy procession. It is recommended that the exposition repeat be omitted because, when it is observed, the exquisite melody introduced five bars before the double bar has to be broken in the middle

before it can run on into the development. This middle section is full of pain and stress, a five-note *forte* statement answered by woodwind sighs interrupting the flow of the music and eventually marching in triumph before the equanimity of the movement is restored. The grim happenings in the slow movement of Haydn's Symphony No. 80 are recalled, and one remembers also that Mozart had been exposed to the contrapuntal processes of Handel and Bach: he brings emotionalism and intellectualism together in a unique blend of beauty, drama and skill.

In order to balance the length and complexity of the first movement it is essential that both halves of the Finale be repeated; we shall see that to do so brings rewards additional to that of improved symmetry. This racing Presto is constructed from light material that in itself seems carefree, almost gay, yet the movement does not smile. It has too much on its mind for that. Contrapuntal techniques are again prominent as the tiny fragment of theme (again cast in the rhythm of three upbeat quavers and a long downbeat, as in Symphonies Nos. 30 and 33) is examined in turn by strings and woodwind before the violins announce the lengthy second subject, the second component of which is an airy affair for unsupported woodwind, an irascible bassoon rattling out the rhythm while oboes provide a harmonic bed for the flute melody. This is as near as Mozart comes to relieving the tension in this movement. A codetta of triplets and trills brings the double bar and the first repeat. Without a pause for breath the listener is thrown into the development amid furious drums and basses. The first theme answers back but a *tutti* twice more swamps the music in a passage recalling the mutating chords of the *adagio* introduction, and unexpectedly the first theme closes ranks in tight imitation that appears to have overcome this disturbing element. It returns, however, in the recapitulation, the music eventually fighting its way clear to make for home: an unequivocal coda that, even so, still seems troubled. The second repeat, plunging from the final D back into the turmoil of A at the start of the development, brings an almost physical shock, but the movement now runs through to its hard-fought victory for a second time the end now sounding more confident.

4: The Last Symphonies: Nos. 39-41 (1788)

One encounters miracle after miracle in the study of Mozart's music and fittingly one of the greatest miracles concerns the fact that the composition of the last three symphonies, each occupying a different emotional plane, took place in a mere six weeks in the summer of 1788 in response to no known outside stimulus. Many thousands of words have been, and will continue to be, spilled over the wonder of this fact, and as we listen to the works themselves we can only stand amazed at the depth of the well from which the composer drew his inspiration.

SYMPHONY NO. 39 IN E FLAT was completed on June 26, 1788, and is scored for one flute, two clarinets, two bassoons, two horns, two trumpets and timpani with strings. The use of both clarinets and trumpets in an E flat work again illustrates the fluid state of practice that we noticed in connection with Symphony No. 26. In common with his previous two symphonies but unlike the next two, No. 39 opens with a slow introduction, and it seems that the difficulties encountered in the "Prague" Symphony are to be continued in this Adagio. Once again in strongly-dotted rhythm, the throb of drum against sombre chords, falling violin scales and misty wind writing throw us immediately into doubt, a doubt decisively shattered a few moments later when grinding discords issue from the strings. Here is bitter tragedy indeed as basses heave upwards and the inexorable rhythm is joined successively by woodwind and horns, then by trumpets and drums. This stark tone-poem lasts but a few seconds. It gives way to a painful moment of indecision before the Allegro arrives bringing open-hearted joy. Horns and bassoons immediately welcome the new mood and an intense feeling of relief travels round the orchestra as the graceful melody widens. A second idea is much more energetic, and its repeated-quaver accompaniment in lower strings and woodwind is as beautifully integrated into the texture of the music as are the violin "walls," the "Viennese" syncopation, and two subtly-placed bars of detached quavers. Mozart, in using his established tricks of language, makes each one sound new and fresh; even simple downward scales sound inevitable and right because we have heard them before in the slow introduction. As the music moves towards establishing B flat for the second subject, it uses a tiny sequence with a decisive octave drop as a means of changing key:

At last the second theme floats in on violins, is acknowledged by woodwind, and then continues briefly over a *pizzicato* bass before yielding to a codetta in which the "Viennese" syncopation is prominent. After the exposition repeat the development seizes the "key-changing" fragment and shakes it roughly, landing it uncomfortably in D flat before subjecting it to developmental scrutiny. Sighing with happiness, the woodwind reintroduce the mellow first theme and the recapitulation is ready to run a fairly regular course, providing a third opportunity to admire its subtleties, amongst which is the strange use Mozart makes of the "key-changing" figure now that it is largely superfluous.

Mozart's use of A flat for the Andante con Moto has been remarked upon with surprise, yet it follows his frequent practice of putting the slow movement into the subdominant of the first. Given this rather exotic key, however, the composer makes full use of it to make excursions into remote tonalities. Formally Mozart employs a basic rondo form but his handling of it is loose, the episodes merging into the main theme with unusual freedom. This main theme has a serene beauty that endures throughout the tonal and formal stresses put upon it later. The first episode opens with a tiny fragment that may be thought of as a link

but it gives rise later to a transcendental moment of polyphonic expertise for four woodwind lines over a horn and bass pedal.

Later still the woodwind run down three different scales as if recalling the violins' similar runs in the slow introduction to the first movement. Most subtle of all, perhaps, is the modification made to the four woodwind lines: the slurs from second to third notes in the last three bars of the above example (flutes, clarinets) are missing, as indeed are the third notes themselves, and yet the ear still recognises the reference.

the last symphonies: nos. 39–41 / 153

Mozart never wore out the minuet mould, unlike some other composers who produced great quantities of them. Neither did he seek to create a new style of minuet in Symphony No. 39, but the result is likely to remain in the memory while other, perhaps more outwardly distinguished, minuets fade away. Over relentlessly marching crotchets in woodwind, brass, percussion and lower strings, the violins play a chattering unison theme and then proceed to answer it for themselves with an elegant passage in which a grace-note is prominent:

The second half discusses the two elements, skilfully combining them into a new phrase at the end. It is for this reason that the grace note (A) sounds better when taken as a quaver rather than as a semiquaver to balance the written-out quaver later (B), because the quaver pattern into which the melody evolves is already subtly inserted into the mind of the listener. The famous Trio for two clarinets in waltz-time shows Mozart frankly enjoying the sounds of the instrument that brought from him some of his most heavenly music in the later Quintet and Concerto. Mozart compresses the form of this Trio in such a way that the answering violin melody is expected to return a third time but instead the listener is disconcerted by the return of the Minuet. Examination of this section nevertheless shows a perfect symmetry.*

The Finale, *allegro*, is invariably, inevitably, described as being Haydnesque without, however, elaboration ever being given beyond that if it is monothematic it *must* be Haydnesque. Monothematicism *was* one of Haydn's strengths, and sure enough there is only one major melodic idea in this Finale; the rather daring switches from related to unrelated keys also reflect a study of Haydn's music; and the cheery toot-toot off-beat wind punctuations in the development are found in Haydn's vocabulary as early as the late 1750s, with unexpected pauses and surprise endings almost as early. The main theme, however, with its expanding note-values and alternating slurred/*staccati grupetti*,

---

* This third movement, incidentally, is the one in which Hans Keller finds "a low degree of hidden complexity."

is the sort of idea Mozart might have stumbled on at any time, and when it is neatly divided between strings and wind

it is Mozart's smile, not Haydn's, that we hear. Who describes the second subject of the first movement of Symphony No. 40, where a similar disposition of instruments is deployed, as Haydnesque? Haydn had different, but just as fine, methods of raising a grin. The breathtaking writing for violins near the start of the movement is typical of high-spirited Mozart and the downward scales embedded therein relate back once again to the slow introduction. It may be true that the Finale of Symphony No. 39 is as close to Haydn's style as Mozart ever came, yet the comparison throws no light upon either composer. The work's chromaticism, if nothing else, demands that this Finale be listened to as Mozart and as no other composer. Let us not deny him his personality in a moment of rare spiritual freedom at a time of tense intellectual exertion. Neither should he be denied his two repeats.

SYMPHONY NO. 40 IN G MINOR was completed on July 25, 1788, when it was scored for one flute, two oboes, two bassoons, one horn in B flat alto, one horn in G, and strings. At a later date Mozart added two clarinets, modifying the oboe parts to make room for them.

Mozart's first symphonic contribution to the "Sturm und Drang" movement, Symphony No. 25, to some extent followed its predecessors in style and musical language; his last is absolutely personal. The anger and frustration of the earlier work is sublimated and absorbed, to emerge in a uniquely moving expression of grief that, for all its hidden skill and subtlety, speaks directly to the emotions. The drama commences with a rocking motion on divided violas that forms a dark backdrop to the first theme on violins in octaves. A rising and falling wind figure leads to a balancing *tutti* featuring a syncopated sliding effect stressed by prominent horns

and thence to a restatement of the main theme that modulates, bringing an angry linking *forte*, with emphatic *sf* minims supporting the violins' scales. A pause brings the heavenly second subject, basically in the relative major but given an intensely personal shade by the use of chromaticism and by the free interchange of its line between strings and wind. This subject is dispelled by the sliding effect, now on woodwind, and, via a steep *crescendo*, the music enters a long codetta, a salient component of which is a *staccato* descent (flute, bassoon, violins) to a recollection of the opening subject. One detached chord brings a return to the start of the exposition, and after this has been repeated the chord is joined by two more, leading the music violently into F sharp minor, from which key the main theme sinks in despair amid fluid bassoon chords until valiantly fighting back with the strength of the bass strings. Battle is joined in earnest but no solution is reached. Violins repeat their opening phrase as woodwind echo it sadly, eventually evolving a wash of suspensions that seems about to resolve on a consoling close as impatient violins interrupt with the recapitulation. The fleeting chance of respite is lost. Still not satisfied that his amazingly versatile main theme has generated enough discussion, Mozart develops it yet more in the considerably modified recapitulation, allowing it to depart at length on woodwind in the coda.

We have encountered the layered canonic scheme of the opening of the Andante before—for instance, in Symphony No. 5 (see p. 81)—and Beethoven was to borrow the idea for the Andante Cantabile con Moto of his First Symphony. The mood of gradual expansion is at first most poignantly expressed in unclouded E flat, but chromaticism soon appears. As a subject, it is vague, difficult to commit to memory, so by way of consolation the woodwind intone a short but wonderfully complete melody, only three bars long, in B flat, a melody that turns out to be one of Mozart's throw-away ideas

clothed in a variety of colours that cannot be done justice in a brief example. This gem of a theme does not occur again: at the corresponding point in the recapitulation the violins vaguely hint at it—that is all. For the rest, the movement's argument is built on a tiny fragment of two demisemiquavers derived from the main theme. The similarity between parts of this movement and the first Adagio (in A) of Haydn's Symphony No. 45 in F sharp minor, the "Farewell," is clearer in performance than on paper, but it is worth noting that the two keys involved (A major and E flat major), although seemingly so remote from each other, are identical to those involved in the similarity noted earlier between the Finale of Symphony No. 19 and the slow movement of No. 20.

The Minuet (*allegretto*) returns to the grim home key of G minor. Moving doggedly through its first half, it deals bitter blows in the second as disruptive cross-rhythms and tight imitative entries compound the anger of the melodic lines until the solo flute single-handedly brings about an unexpected conclusion at *piano* level. In common with the equivalent section in Symphony No. 25, the Trio is a lightened episode for woodwind, but strings bring about this mood with a supple G major passage of shaded beauty, and in the second half it is to a rising line on bass strings that the wind responds.

Marked *allegro assai*, the Finale offers a tragic face different from that seen in the first movement. Whereas that had accepted its fate, this violent last movement fights against it with powerful and sinewy material that at first spans two octaves but is ever and again convulsed by a passage of quavers. Once it has presented all this material it enters combat with a will, quavers driving the violin passage-work into a frenzy of energy in which simple scales, both upward and downward, add yet more strength. Even their appearance in score resembles turrets and flying buttresses:

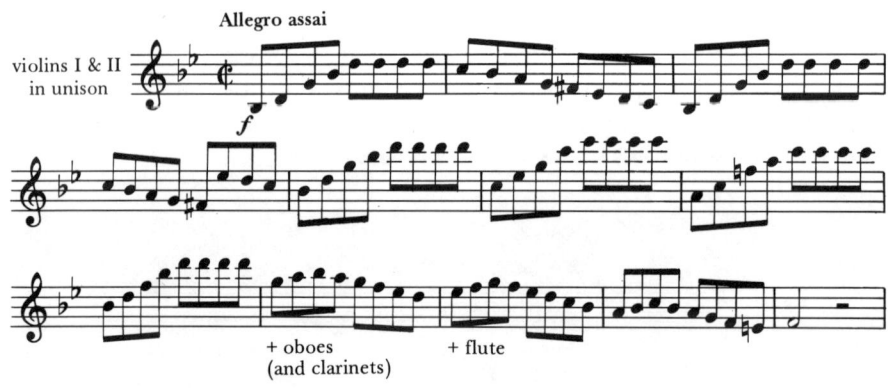

This immensely strong passage continues until a new theme appears: a pleading, feminine, counterpart, not quite as harrowingly lovely as the equivalent melody in the first movement but still of breathtaking radiance as it flows outward from violins to the whole orchestra. A codetta of angry quavers closes the exposition, which should be repeated. The start of the development brings the most notoriously disruptive passage in all the symphonies—perhaps in the whole of Mozart's music. For eight bars the movement writhes savagely, gripping the first theme. A series of isolated chords signals the total disintegration of tonality, halted only just in time by pleading oboes and bassoons. The first theme, disorientated in its fury, approaches various minor keys, finding each one unsatisfactory, and turmoil adds flames to its distress as the warring keys are shot through with *forte* horn notes vainly trying to support each fleeting tonality.* All at once four chords bring about a respite, but this is pitifully short-lived: the anguish returns with a dense passage of canonic argument that is at last terminated by a curious juddering phrase on violins and violas. For a moment at least the conflict is stilled in a bar-and-a-half of silence before the first theme announces the arrival of the recapitulation. For all its endeavour the development has solved nothing. The passion and tragedy remain throughout the recapitulation, and the end brings no answer.

SYMPHONY NO. 41 IN C was completed on August 10, 1788, and re-established Mozart's supreme confidence after the emotional dilemma he had faced so courageously in No. 40. The tonal ambiguities of that work are replaced with the least problematical of all keys, and the scoring has no room for the mellowness of the clarinets that were added to No. 40: its flute, oboes, bassoons, horns, and strings are here joined by trumpets and timpani. No. 41 has been compared to a Greek temple and a Roman god (the nickname "Jupiter" arose in 1819), and its character does indeed encourage thoughts of vast, echoing marble edifices enduring for unimaginable periods of time or of fabulous gods of superhuman power. Its instrumental colouration returns to the highly serious hues of the "Prague" Symphony, but this has little to do with the use of a "military" key since contemporary works by other composers in C and D rarely display a similarly dignified, almost arrogant, sonority. In Haydn's music, for instance, it is not until the "London" Symphony of 1795 that a similar seriousness is heard.

There is no slow introduction to the first movement, but the opening triplet gestures suggest that such opening *adagio* statements as that found in the "Prague" Symphony are already being assimilated into the structure of the opening Allegro Vivace theme. In answer to these triplets comes a structurally important phrase (marked a) that strives upwards:

---

* Neville Marriner brings out this aspect of the score with outstanding lucidity in his recording.

158 / mozart: the symphonies

The earnestness of the music is immediately established: the doubts amid which the previous two symphonies have emerged from silence are summarily dispelled by this commanding assertion of C major, and in bar 9 there commences a series of fanfares against a plunging *motif* on inner strings that drives the music into a *fermata* on the dominant. It is too soon for a second subject to appear, so C major returns for a quieter restatement of the first theme against rising and falling horn, then bassoon, octaves and a counter-theme on flute and oboe. A further restatement of the first subject in which the striving theme plays a part of increased importance eventually brings a secondary melody in which the striving *motif* is again suggested in the opening phrase. This leads to a developed continuation that alternates with the striving theme on lower strings, but an abrupt halt brings a forceful *tutti* attack reinforced by pounding drums that returns once again to the striving theme in diminution, and then to a sudden descent to yet another pause. Incongruously, a G major *buffo* theme trips in, yet towards its end the striving *motif* (marked *b*) is suggested yet again,

now perhaps a little prosaic and inconsequential. A headlong codetta terminates the exposition, which is to be repeated. Pausing only for a breath of woodwind, the development enters in E flat with the *buffo* melody, its tail-end (marked *c*) being grasped and strenuously developed in combination with *b*. This gradually dies away as the music prepares to recapitulate, cutting into the first subject at a point later than expected—at the quiet restatement, the counter-theme now on bassoons, then flute and oboes. But this is a false recapitulation in F major: the imperious opening triplets now demand prior attention, and get it, only to be ousted after all by the *buffo* fragment which has the honour of introducing the real reprise. Many twists and turns modify the original material, the first of the two subsidiary subjects being completely altered in outline, before, with violent emphasis, a coda closes the movement.

In F major, *minus* trumpets and drums, the Andante Cantabile utilises the withdrawn tone of muted violins and violas. Mozart breaks up the opening idea with off-beat *forte* chords, a feature which becomes inseparably associated with the melodic line. In spite of this the music unfolds with a flowing rhythm urged on by frequent sextuplets and by a great extension of a demisemiquaver pulse in the recapitulation. In mood the movement has a gentleness and grace that is a perfect relief from the harshness of the first movement. This relief is continued in the Minuet (*allegretto*), the smoothness of the opening of which recalls the Minuet of the Symphony in F, K75, of 1771, even to the extent that both *motifs* descend at the start in two-fold elegance. But a whole world has passed in the meantime: the artlessness of the earlier example is replaced in the later one by a feeling of inevitability in the rhythm and by the bitter-sweetness of freely-used chromaticism. Manifestly not meant for the dance hall, this Minuet is surely for twilight listening in a summer garden, the tranquillity of which the mock solemnity of trumpet and drum fanfares will only fleetingly disturb. The central Trio wears another face, however. Its seemingly immutable flute, bassoon and horn sighs alternate with a bantering violin-and-oboe phrase that itself sighs at the end, but the second strain brings a stern hint of the "Jupiter" theme against an insistent rhythm on brass and lower strings. Unperturbed, the Minuet returns, and we hear for the third time a passage of quiet beauty for woodwind alone.

Sometimes conveniently referred to as the "final fugue," Mozart's last symphonic movement is not by any means a strict fugue but a sonata-form piece, the components of which have evolved organically from his established symphonic procedures, some of which we have noticed in earlier pages. Appreciation of the movement starts after bypassing all formal analyses and listening to the music itself. It may be deepened by referring to an analysis, but full understanding will only come through examination of the score. All a writer can do is to list the themes that are involved and point out a landmark or two by which a listener new to the music may orientate himself. It comes as no surprise to discover that the composer expended so many different themes on this movement: multi-subject movements occur frequently in his work, the Finales of the G minor String Quintet and Symphony No. 33 being prime examples, and it was a logical progression to ensure that these subjects would combine with each other in fugal treatment. The skill with which this is carried out is one of Mozart's great miracles.

There are six distinct ideas. The opening subject presents two of them in succession, the first (I) is the famous "Jupiter" theme that we have encountered before, while the second (II) is an extended version of the short/short/short/long rhythm of, for instance, Symphonies Nos. 30 and 33:

Next comes a fanfare phrase (III):

and then a rising *motif* with a trill on the downbeat (IV):

The second subject comprises two ideas presented almost simultaneously (V and VI):

VI will often act as a kind of upbeat to draw attention to the entry of IV, and I, III and VI will later be turned upside-down.

At the start, as I is repeated *forte*, bass strings seize the little semi-quaver figure in bar two of II and thus forge a link to the plunging *motif* that accompanied the fanfare (bar 9ff.) in the first movement. When III has been stated, a pause brings the return of I, now continued with *staccato* crotchets that lead to IV. This terminates with a figure that is to be inverted shortly to become VI. The second group, V and VI, then arrives after another pause and is immediately combined with IV on bassoons and III high on flute, and while the *piano* dynamic is maintained flute and bassoon discuss IV in canon. V returns, *forte*, running on to II, and this is continued, gradually heightening in intensity until III takes over to complete the codetta. At this point the exposition is repeated. Even greater concentration of material is heard in the development, there being at one point, for instance, four canonic entries of III in two bars, and, at bars 189–91, a curiously condensed version of I on first oboe. Everything has a bearing on everything else. Eventually III brings about the recapitulation in which events take such a different course that the section assumes the stature of a second development. The entire development/recapitulation complex is now repeated. Yet the composer has still not done with his material: as the flute closes the recapitulation with III, the music inverts both this *motif* and I in preparation for a grand summation, a fugal apotheosis that combines all six subjects in a transcendental display of polyphony to form a magnificent peroration.

5: Conclusion

When considering Mozart's total symphonic achievement, comparisons will inevitably be drawn with the music of his contemporaries; and ultimately his status in the history of symphonic music will be defined by what he did within that form and how he affected its progress and development.

We described Mozart's second symphonic period, i.e. from 1772 to 1780, as a time in which he consolidated his early achievements and moved into a period of compositional perfection. Those early achievements were made on a purely personal level: Mozart as a very young lad heard the music around him with an absorbent but not over-critical mind and then imitated it as an exercise in technique rather than with any thought of his possible contribution to the sum of musical experience. His contemporaries at that time, many of them Italian or Italian-influenced, produced symphonies primarily as operatic overtures which fell into worn formulae: a standard mould that began with a fast section full of noise-generating instrumental tricks (unisons, triadic themes in octaves, semiquaver violin "walls" of attention-catching bustle, the whole set almost invariably in a key that allowed the utilisation of strident brass and drums), continued with a graceful slow section designed to encourage the audience to calm themselves, and then reintroduced brass and drums to conclude the work with a very fast piece, usually in 3/8 or 2/4 time, to produce a feeling of expectancy as the curtain rose.

The more local Salzburg and Viennese composers, while by no means ignoring these Italian conventions, in addition wrote concert and chamber symphonies that at first bore a more relaxed air and tended to replace the fast finale with a minuet, or extend the design to four movements by the inclusion of a minuet *and* a quick finale.

Learning all the devices in his early youth, Mozart copied them faithfully so that, as he moved into his second period, he had a highly developed technique as a foundation upon which to build his unique brand of harmonic and melodic perfection. Having achieved this perfection, his imagination sought ways of deepening it, but it did not occur to him to develop and extend the mould once it had been cast to his complete satisfaction. His later symphonies take a role as consolidators of established principles rather than as explorers of new worlds; and, miraculous creations though they are, they rarely stretch the mould.

By contrast, other composers attacked these formal conventions with a battery of imaginative tricks, the most prominent figure at the time being Joseph Haydn. He was a compulsive experimenter, rarely content to accept someone else's formula unless he could bring his own aggressive originality to bear upon it: in the first movements of Symphonies Nos. 31 and 45, for instance, Haydn modified sonata-form so radically that it is relegated to the position of a mere reference-point. Mozart's departures from formal convention, on the other hand, came very early in his symphonies and may be attributed to lack of experience (see the Finale of Symphony No. 1 and the slow movement of No. 5, for example). Mozart quickly appreciated the symmetry and dramatic possibilities of sonata-form and saw no reason to try to supplant it. He resisted most of Haydn's devices, too, such as the false recapitulation in the midst of the development (especially prominent in Haydn's symphonies of the 1770s), the dramatic use of silence, and experimentation with the order and layout of movements in symphonies such as Nos. 5, 15, 25, 46, 49 and 67. The fascination with rhythmic disorientation in the Andante of No. 35 and the Minuet of No. 65, the surprise endings of Nos. 23 and 35, extra-special effects like the tuning-up joke and the *accelerando* in No. 60, the palindromic Minuet of No. 47, and the selection of rare and exotic keys both for extended sections in more conventionally tonal works and for tonic keys of whole works, all show Haydn to have had a showman's nature. When Mozart indulged himself in such compositional games he did so circumspectly, as if anxious not to ripple the surface of his perfection. These rare instances are, therefore, not obvious to the casual listener, whereas Haydn's robust humour and special effects are designed to be recognised immediately.

Haydn also explored ways of extending the range of sounds from his instruments. The solo violin in Symphony No. 6, for instance, is given a solo so difficult that it leads one to suspect that Haydn may have been acquainted with Bach's Brandenburg Concerto No. 4, in which similar fiercely testing passage-work occurs, while his exploitation of the solo string bass (then a bass viol but today usually played on a double bass or even, unadventurously, on a cello one octave higher) in Symphonies Nos. 6, 7, 8, 31 and 72, the cello itself in No. 13, flute in Nos. 24, 30 and 41, oboe in No. 38, bassoon in Nos. 6 and 56, and horns in Nos. 5, 31, 51 and 72 (these lists are by no means exhaustive) show a deep interest in the characters of individual orchestral voices that Mozart did not share. Mozart's instrumentation was better integrated, each sonority sublimated for the benefit of the overall effect, but Haydn's scoring is more varied and interesting in its own right.

Yet Haydn went further still in the case of the horns, stretching his players' skill to, and perhaps even beyond, breaking-point in Symphony No. 51 and elsewhere; and he was interested in making even accompanying horn parts "tell": in bars 42 and 44 in the first movement of No. 31, first and third horns repeat the note a' (sounding) in a purely accompanimental role, *piano*, and at the start of the development of the first movement of Symphony No. 35 the first horn holds f" (sounding), *piano*, for eight bars. Other composers, Mozart amongst them, would choose lower, "safer" notes for mere harmonic support. Horns pitched in C alto were used by Michael Haydn, Masek and others, but most frequently by Joseph Haydn, notably in his "festive" symphonies. Mozart selected their hectic sonority only once, in Symphony No. 18, and then tentatively and probably as an afterthought.

In the matter of scoring, then, Mozart for the most part wrote well within the capabilities of his instrumentalists. The reason was probably that Mozart perforce wrote for many different musical centres in his short, travelling life; unlike Haydn, Pokorný and other experimenters, he did not have the opportunity of working for many years with one group of instrumentalists, probing their technique and encouraging them to extend their skills. There are, however, features in Mozart's symphonies that do strike one as daring: the unexpectedly extended and well-developed Finales of KE45B and No. 18; the use of a liturgical chant-like melody in the Trio of No. 18; fugal elements in the Finales of No. 27 and, especially, No. 41; dissonance as a dramatic effect in the Introduction of No. 39, and the incredibly disturbing rhythmic disruption in the Finale of No. 40—but not one of these effects is wholly original, and most appeared only after Mozart came to know Haydn's music.

Enough has been said to show that Mozart had little interest in extending the range of symphonic form, and if his symphonies are placed in historical perspective it will seem that, for all their emotional and technical achievements, the evolution of that form would have been unaffected if they had not existed. The musical historian will search in vain for a composer who picked up the symphonic story at the point at which Mozart laid it down. Perhaps none had the technical ability, or it was felt that the immense technical exertions involved had reached a point of diminishing returns in audience acceptance. Mozart's symphonies stand like a rock amidst rapids: washed and jostled by the stream of symphonic development racing all around but neither slowing nor hastening that tumultuous river on its journey from its source in Italy in the last years of the Seventeenth century to its broad delta a century later that emptied into the ocean of romanticism. It was Mozart's role to contribute to that romanticism in a quite different way: his keyboard style in the sonatas and concerti initiated a line that stretched, via Clementi, Dussek and Hummel, to Chopin and Liszt. It is a line in which symphonic thought can be seen quite clearly to be dying.

Appendix

Selected Writings

In the Introduction, acknowledgement is made to the invaluable contributions to Mozart research made by the cataloguer Ludwig Köchel, whose initial is used to precede the identifying number of every Mozart composition, and Alfred Einstein who organised the subsequent additions and amendments to Köchel's catalogue; by Emily Anderson who translated the letters of the Mozart family; and by Otto Erich Deutsch who gathered a daunting amount of Mozartiana for his "Mozart—A Documentary Biography." Also mentioned with gratitude are the studies of the symphonies carried out by Saint-Foix, Jens Peter Larsen and Hans Keller.

For a more general view of Mozart and his music the reader has a wide selection from which to choose. A start should be made with "Mozart—The Man—The Musician" by Arthur Hutchins, published in conjunction with Philips's issue of all the symphonies in performances by Neville Marriner and Josef Krips. This is two books in one with a bewildering profusion of paginations, dealing in turn with the biography and the music. It is extremely detailed, and its almost countless illustrations seem to include every known portrait of the composer. O. E. Deutsch, in a supplementary volume to the "Collected Edition" of Mozart's works, gives authenticating details of twelve surviving Mozart portraits, but in October 1979 the Swedish sculptor Torolf Engström purchased an anonymous portrait of an unknown man that he is certain depicts Mozart at the age of about thirty—but it shows a strabismic countenance that yet fails to reveal the slightly closed right eye to be seen in some of the authentic likenesses of the composer.

W. J. Turner's 1938 book, "Mozart—The Man and His Works," revised and edited by Christopher Raeburn (1965), offers a detailed and uncluttered study of the composer's life in parallel with a discussion of his music. Another study, full of insight and wisdom, is Alfred Einstein's "Mozart—His Character—His Work" (1944), well translated by Arthur Mendel and Nathan Broder and notable particularly for its level-headed discussion of the music.

A fascinating glimpse of the London that young Mozart would have known at the time he wrote his earliest symphonies is given in Charles Sandford Terry's "John Christian Bach" (1929); a second edition with Foreword and thirty-two-page corrigenda by H. C. Robbins Landon appeared in 1967. For a wider view of Mozart's environment, background and contemporaries, Erich Schenk's "Mozart and his Times" (translated and edited by Richard and Clara Winstone, 1960) is strongly recommended. Wider still is the uniquely valuable illumination thrown on the Eighteenth-century musical scene by the indispensable writings of Charles Burney, who was intimately involved with the composers about whom he wrote so perceptively. His "A General History of Music" (1776–1789), vital to the attainment of an Eighteenth-century musical pespective, is supplemented by his two "Present State of Music" volumes: in France and Italy (1771); and in Germany, the Netherlands and United Provinces (1773), since published in a modern edition with the addition of further original material.

The Music in Print

Printed editions of Mozart's symphonies were slow to gather momentum. The first to be published was the "Haffner" Symphony, issued by André of Offenbach in 1785; the "Paris" Symphony followed four years later, appropriately enough from the Paris firm of Seiber; and Imbault in the same city issued the *Overture in the Italian Style* at about the time of Mozart's death. At this time the familiar numeration did not exist: identification was by nickname only. The next symphony did not have a name, so when André published a Symphony in B flat in 1792 it was identified as *Op. 22* (this was later to be known as No. 33), and it was the firm of André that was responsible for publishing several more symphonies, each with an opus number that has now dropped from use, before the turn of the century: Op. 34 ("Linz") and Op. 38 ("Jupiter") in 1793; Op. 45 (No. 40) in 1794; Opp. 57 and 58 (Nos. 34 and 39) in 1797; and Op. 84 ("Prague") in 1800. A year or so earlier than this last Eighteenth-century publication, Günther and Böhme of Hamburg had brought out a group of four earlier symphonies under the description "Op. 64": these were Nos. 22, 25, 27 and 30. A mere fourteen symphonies, then, appeared during the Eighteenth century; a concerted publication programme had to wait for more than three-quarters of a century.

Breitkopf & Härtel's "Kritisch durchgesehene Gesamtausgabe" included all the numbered symphonies as "Serie VIII," published between 1879 and 1882, presenting them separately and in three volumes: I, containing Symphonies Nos. 1–21; II, Nos. 22–34; and III, Nos. 35–41. It will be noted that this series included all the symphonies now known to be spurious, but omitted the "Paris" Overture, KE311A (=K.Anh 8), which had been issued under the auspices of the Paris Conservatoire about 1805. The B&H "Serie XXIV—Supplement" incorporated seven of the unnumbered symphonies (KE42A/K76; KE73M/K97; KE73L/K81; KE73N/K95; KE74A/K87; K75 in 1881; and the very doubtful KE Anh 223B/K78 in 1888). A separate volume, "Serie V" (1883), offered all the overtures, including the "Symphony-Overtures" embraced in our discussion; likewise, the three serenades which were abbreviated to become symphonies were included with the rest of the occasional orchstral works in "Serie IX," which was completed by 1880. All these were in full-score format; miniature versions of them are published by Kalmus.

A rival edition of miniature scores by Ricordi was begun in 1951 with Symphony No. 41, continued the following year with No. 36, and in 1953 with Nos. 35, 38, 39 and 40. The series was completed in 1955 and was claimed later by the publishers to be the only complete series of Mozart symphonies in miniature score, yet it lacks K45B in B flat, the *Neuer Lambacher* Symphony in G, KE Anh 223B/K98 in F, KE74G in B flat, the three serenade-symphonies and several of the symphony-overtures, while including KE141A: *Il sogno di Scipione* (together with the Overture *La finta semplice* in its original form as Symphony No. 7, K45). The Ricordi Edition also embraced the two *Sinfonie concertante* which do not figure in our discussion. In offering this edition in two volumes (Volume I contained works up to and including Symphony No. 25), Ricordi, by using incredibly thin but adequately opaque paper, managed to cram the entire 1893 pages of music into less than two inches of shelf-space, complete with semi-stiff covers and cardboard dust-jackets. The convenience of this arrangement is mitigated somewhat by difficulties of handling and the ease with which the pages are damaged, and the decision to omit symphony numbers in the index, referring to the works only by their established "K" numbers and keys.

Rather more practicable is the small-format Kalmus Edition from the original "Gesamtausgabe," and the many other printings of the more popular symphonies.

At about the time Ricordi completed its series—coinciding roughly with Mozart's bi-centenary celebrations in 1956—the Salzburg Mozarteum began a collaboration with Bärenreiter Verlag of Kassel on a New Mozart Edition which, at the time of writing, is still incomplete. In addition to the Overtures *Mitridate* and *Ascanio in Alba*, which figure in the publications of the complete operas, the New Mozart Edition includes all the symphonies from No. 16 onwards, with the exception of the undoubtedly spurious No. 37 and the "Paris" Overture. The Overtures *Lucio Silla* and *Die Entführung aus dem Serail* and the earlier symphonies will doubtless appear in due course. Only Nos. 16–29, 31, 36 and 39–41, and the two overtures, have been issued as miniature scores in this edition. Meanwhile, 1965 saw the first-ever publication of a possibly authentic Symphony in G, the *Neuer Lambacher*, which is discussed together with its sister work, also in G, KE45A, on pp.64–68. This full score was issued by Nagels Musik-Archiv, No. 217.

Musical Instruments of Mozart's Time

A late Twentieth-century performance of a Mozart symphony displays many striking differences from the kind of sound Mozart would have known. With his facility of absolute pitch he would notice instantly that today's instruments play a semitone or so sharper; the violins are equipped with metal rather than gut strings and the method of playing them is quite different; woodwind tone is stronger but less well differentiated so that the voices of flute, oboe and clarinet, when playing in a register common to all, are not so readily distinguished; brass instruments are much more complicated to look at, smoother in sound and more reliable; and timpani heads are constructed of a material of which he could have had no experience (plastic), their tonal quality vastly more resonant and powerful. So different would the whole orchestra appear to him that he might be profoundly puzzled that the double bass still retains the sloping shoulders of the basic viol shape.

The players of these modern instruments show in varying degrees a deeply-rooted habit of applying *vibrato* to every note, no matter how short, thus prostituting a valuable effect that Mozart himself would have reserved for the heightening of expressive moments in his melodies. Furthermore, the whole band is "conducted" by a non-playing leader in a manner that Mozart might find somewhat ridiculous.

It is these modern conventions that enlightened musicians such as Christopher Hogwood (see Recommended Recordings) are overcoming in their search for authenticity in the performance of Mozart's music. Their endeavours are based on the researches of scholars such as the late David Munrow and Thurston Dart, and before them Adam Carse, whose books "The Orchestra in the 18th Century" (published in 1950) and "The History of Orchestration" (1925, reprinted 1964) are of continuing value.

An admirable pictorial and descriptive guide (in parallel English and French) is "Eighteenth Century Musical Instruments: France and Britain," published by the Victoria and Albert Museum, London, in 1973, in conjunction with an exhibition of period instruments. In the all-important matter of brass instruments, "Trumpets, Horns and Music" by J. Murray Barbour (1963), and "The Horn and Horn Playing and the Austro-Bohemian Tradition, 1680–1830" by Horace Fitzpatrick, 1970, will be found invaluable, while Paul R. Bryan's article, "The Horn in the Works of Mozart and Haydn: Some Observations and Comparisons" (in "Haydn Yearbook IX," 1975), offers stimulating but not wholly convincing arguments in favour of a less-strict approach to the "alto unless otherwise specified" guide-line set out in the present book.

Recommended Recordings

This discography of recommended recordings is designed to be a guide to the record enthusiast in his search for the best in Mozart symphony discs. Current availability of records has not been taken into account: discs come and go as the market fluctuates, and some that seem to have "gone" may well come back. Similarly, an exhaustive listing of local record numbers is not feasible: only U.K. and U.S. numbers are given, but these should be sufficient for a disc to be identified without ambiguity. All numbers are for U.K. issues unless prefixed by "US."

Inclusion in this list is dependant upon certain criteria:
a) a good standard of orchestral playing;
b) an orchestra of appropriate size, or a recorded balance that allows all Mozart's lines to be heard clearly;
c) attention by the conductor to matters of appropriate tempi, *da capi*, instrumentation, phrasing, authentic dynamics, etc.;
d) recorded sound of at least adequate quality.

Where a recorded performance is deficient in any of these factors but is still considered of sufficient merit to be recommended, a brief comment noting the deficiency is appended.

Several important series of Mozart symphonies have been recorded: these are discussed in the Introduction, where broad outlines are drawn as to their merits. These comments may be summarised as follows: Neville Marriner's Philips recording of the first thirty-one symphonies (Nos. 1–20 plus several unnumbered symphonies) may be given a blanket recommendation, along with the warning that his earlier disc for Argo (Nos. 13–16) should be avoided as being below par. Denis Vaughan's three-disc set (Nos. 16–24, plus two unnumbered symphonies) is excitingly played and recorded and, in common with Marriner's, uses a harpsichord continuo and pays attention to the vital matter of high horns, but the conductor's aproach to grace-notes is often unstylish. Karl Böhm's complete recording offers high musical rewards, but his "big orchestra" approach results in too comfortable and civilised a sound in most of the earlier works, and musicological matters are by-passed. Günther Kehr's Vox series contains some good things but is now outclassed and has been omitted from this listing. Christopher Hogwood's complete recording gives matters of authenticity prime importance yet never descends to dull historical correctness. His first issues are discussed in their places below. When complete, his series will contain six additional symphonies from serenades or operatic overtures, but will omit the Overture *Die Entführung aus dem Serail* and the *Alte Lambacher* and KE Anh 223B/K 98 Symphonies (presumably considered spurious) while including the certainly spurious No. 37.

In the following listing abbreviations are kept to a minimum. Couplings of other Mozart works are shown in brackets immediately before the name of the issuing company. Where only a number is given, this refers to another Mozart symphony. All records are 12" stereo LPs unless otherwise stated. (M) = monophonic. Sets in which the discs are not available separately are indicated by "nas" after the set numbers, and the number of discs therein.

The author would like to acknowledge the valuable assistance given by Antony Hodgson in the preparation of this section. Grateful thanks are also due to Andrew Dalton and Peter Wadland of The Decca Record Company for the considerable trouble they went to in order that the author might hear some of the first of Christopher Hogwood's Mozart series before release.

Symphony No. 1 in E flat, K16

Marriner—Academy of St. Martin-in-the-Fields
   (complete symphonies) Philips 6747374 (16, nas)
   (31 early symphonies) US: Philips 6747099 (8, nas)
   (4, 5, 10, KE73L) US: Philips 6500532

Symphony No.4 in D, K19

Marriner—Academy of St. Martin-in-the-Fields
   (complete symphonies) Philips 6747374 (16, nas)
   (31 early symphonies) US: Philips 6747099 (8, nas)
   (1, 5, 10, KE73L) US: Philips 6500532

Symphony No. 5 in B flat, K22

Marriner—Academy of St. Martin-in-the-Fields
   (complete symphonies) Philips 6747374 (16, nas)
   (31 early symphonies) US: Philips 6747099 (8, nas)
   (1, 4, 10, KE73L) US: Philips 6500532
Barshay—Moscow Chamber Orchestra
   (KE45B; *Alte Lambacher*) Melodiya CM 04091-2

Marriner's recording has the distinction of being the only version to play the music with the horn parts at the correct octave. All other recordings have these instruments in B flat basso, for which there is no musical justification. Nevertheless, Barshay's version deserves a recommendation on account of his otherwise outstanding reading. In the Andante the only repeat mark comes at the end of the movement: Barshay is the only conductor on disc to observe this simple instruction and play the movement through from beginning to end twice.

Symphony in F, KE42A (=K76)

Marriner—Academy of St. Martin-in-the-Fields
   (complete symphonies) Philips 6747374 (16, nas)
   (31 early symphonies) US: Philips 6747099 (8, nas)

Symphony No. 6 in F, K43

Marriner—Academy of St. Martin-in-the-Fields
   (complete symphonies) Philips 6747374 (16, nas)
   (31 early symphonies) US: Philips 6747099 (8, nas)

Paumgartner—Salzburg Mozarteum Camerata Academica
  (8, *Neue-* and *Alte Lambacher*) Archiv 198409

Symphony in G, KE45A (=KA221), "Alte-Lambacher"

Marriner—Academy of St. Martin-in-the-Fields
  (complete symphonies) Philips 6747374 (16, nas)
  (31 early symphonies) US: Philips 6747099 (8, nas)
Paumgartner—Salzburg Mozarteum Camerata Academica
  (6, 8, *Neue Lambacher*) Archiv 198409
Barshay—Moscow Chamber Orchestra
  (5, KE45B) Melodiya CM 04091-2

By a curious piece of logic Paumgartner decides to play the Alte Lambacher without harpsichord continuo but the Neue Lambacher with. Presumably the reason lies in the tradition, apparently still in force as recently as March 1967 when his performances were recorded, that orchestral music of c. 1768 should be played with a harpsichord continuo, perhaps to point up its antiquity, while W. Mozart's music of whatever date should not. Obviously, this makes musicological as well as musical nonsense since performing practices at Lambach Monastery are hardly likely to have undergone a revolution in style between performances of the two works during the Mozarts' one-day visit there. Further, Anna Amalie Abert on the sleeve of Paumgartner's disc argues that the attributions of the two works may in any case have been reversed by the Lambach copyist! This in turn negates any slight logic there may have been in Paumgartner's decision.

Marriner is fleet-footed and parsimonious with repeats, Barshay deliberate in tempi and, as is his usual practice, extremely generous with da capi. The latter more closely approaches the composer's allegro maestoso marking. Both balance the horns prominently. Paumgartner's tempi lie between these extremes but his horns are less powerful, although the exciting rusticity of his Finale is particularly convincing. Barshay joins Paumgartner in omitting continuo while Marriner's harpsichordist is not only finely balanced but musically imaginative.

Symphony in B flat, KE45B (=KA214)

Marriner-Academy of St. Martin-in-the-Fields
  (complete symphonies) Philips 6747374 (16, nas)
  (31 early symphonies) US: Philips 6747099 (8, nas)
Barshay—Moscow Chamber Orchestra
  (5, *Alte Lambacher*) Melodiya CM 04091-2

Marriner is excellent throughout but even he is surpassed by the splendid vitality and stylishness of Barshay, whose reading has to be recommended despite his most unfortunate decision to use B flat basso horns.

Symphony No. 7 in D, K45 (Overture: *La finta semplice*)

Böhm—Berlin Philharmonic Orchestra
 (early symphonies to KE173DA) US and UK: DG 2740109 (8, nas)
Marriner-Academy of St. Martin-in-the-Fields
 (complete symphonies) Philips 6747374 (16, nas)
 (31 early symphonies) US: Philips 6747099 (8, nas)

Böhm's recording is better balanced, the timpani in Marriner's being exceptionally backward in the first movement. The staid elegance of Marriner's Minuet is, however, an attractive element. Neither performance includes cembalo.

Symphony No. 8 in D, K48

Böhm—Berlin Philharmonic Orchestra
 (early symphonies to KE173DA) US and UK: DG 2740109 (8, nas)
Marriner—Academy of St. Martin-in-the-Fields
 (complete symphonies) Philips 6747374 (16, nas)
 (31 early symphonies) US: Philips 6747099 (8, nas)
Paumgartner—Salzburg Mozarteum Camerata Academica
 (6, *Neue*- and *Alte Lambacher*) Archiv 198409

Of these three performances, especially noteworthy is Paumgartner's stately, almost imperial, handling of the Minuet.

Symphony in G, "Neue Lambacher"

Marriner—Academy of St. Martin-in-the-Fields
 (complete symphonies) Philips 6747374 (16, nas)
 (31 early symphonies) US: Philips 6747099 (8, nas)
Paumgartner—Salzburg Mozarteum Camerata Academica
 (*Alte Lambacher*; 6, 8) Archiv 198409

Both performances are excellent. The proximity of the Alte Lambacher for comparison is in both cases useful. In Böhm's only slightly less recommendable version (absence of continuo is the main disadvantage) a single side is again shared by these two symphonies.

Symphony No. 11 in D, KE73Q (=K84)

Marriner—Academy of St. Martin-in-the-Fields
 (complete symphonies) Philips 6747374 (16, nas)
 (31 early symphonies) US: Philips 6747099 (8, nas)

Symphony in D, KE73M (=K97)

Marriner—Academy of St. Martin-in-the-Fields
   (complete symphonies) Philips 6747374 (16, nas)
   (31 early symphonies) US: Philips 6747099 (8, nas)

Symphony in D, KE73L (=K81)

Marriner—Academy of St. Martin-in-the-Fields
   (complete symphonies) Philips 6747374 (16, nas)
   (31 early symphonies) US: Philips 6747099 (8, nas)
   (1, 4, 5, 10) US: Philips 6500532

Symphony in D, KE73N (=K95)

Marriner—Academy of St. Martin-in-the-Fields
   (complete symphonies) Philips 6747374 (16, nas)
   (31 early symphonies) US: Philips 6747099 (8, nas)

Symphony in D, KE74A (=K87) (Overture: *Mitridate, rè di Ponto*)

Faerber—Württemburg Chamber Orchestra
   (overtures) US and UK: Turnabout TV 34628
Better than nothing, but an unremarkable performance. Hager is much more stylish but his recording is available only as part of the four-disc set of the complete opera.

Symphony No. 10 in G, K74

Marriner—Academy of St. Martin-in-the-Fields
   (complete symphonies) Philips 6747374 (16, nas)
   (31 early symphonies) US: Philips 6747099 (8, nas)
   (1, 4, 5, KE73L) US: Philips 6500532

Symphony No. 9 in C, KE75A (=K73)

(complete symphonies) Philips 6747374 (16, nas)
(31 early symphonies) US: Philips 6747099 (8, nas)

Symphony in F, K75

Marriner—Academy of St. Martin-in-the-Fields
  (complete symphonies) Philips 6747374 (16, nas)
  (31 early symphonies) US: Philips 6747099 (8, nas)

Symphony No. 12 in G, KE75B (=K110)

Marriner—Academy of St. Martin-in-the-Fields
  (complete symphonies) Philips 6747374 (16, nas)
  (31 early symphonies) US: Philips 6747099 (8, nas)

Symphony in D, K111 (Overture: *Ascanio in Alba*, plus Finale KE111A [=K120])

Marriner—Academy of St. Martin-in-the-Fields
  (complete symphonies) Philips 6747374 (16, nas)
  (31 early symphonies) US: Philips 6747099 (8, nas)

Symphony in C, KE111B (=K96)

Böhm—Berlin Philharmonic Orchestra
  (early symphonies to KE173DA) US and UK: DG 2740109 (8, nas)
Marriner—Academy of St. Martin-in-the-Fields
  (complete symphonies) Philips 6747374 (16, nas)
  (31 early symphonies) US: Philips 6747099 (8, nas)
Böhm makes this an exceptionally noble piece. Despite the excellence of the playing, Marriner's touch is a little lighter than is ideal for this work, although the performance remains recommendable.

Symphony No. 13 in F, K112

Marriner—Academy of St. Martin-in-the-Fields
   (complete symphonies) Philips 6747374 (16, nas)
   (31 early symphonies) US: Philips 6747099 (8, nas)

Symphony No. 14 in A, K114

Böhm—Berlin Philharmonic Orchestra
   (early symphonies to KE173DA) US and UK: DG 2740109 (8, nas)
Marriner—Academy of St. Martin-in-the-Fields
   (complete symphonies) Philips 6747374 (16, nas)
   (31 early symphonies) US: Philips 6747099 (8, nas)
Wöldike—Danish State Radio Chamber Orchestra
   (J. C. Bach; Dittersdorf; Haydn) Decca LXT 5135 (M)
All three versions are excellent, with Wöldike's, despite its age, having a sparkle and exuberance which improves even on the outstanding alternative recommendations and overcomes the disadvantage of Wöldike's uncharacteristic parsimoniousness with repeats.

Symphony No. 15 in G, K124

Marriner—Academy of St. Martin-in-the-Fields
   (complete symphonies) Philips 6747374 (16, nas)
   (31 early symphonies) US: Philips 6747099 (8, nas)

Symphony in D, KE141A (=K161) (Overture *Il sogno di Scipione*, plus Finale, K163)

Hogwood/Schröder—Academy of Ancient Music
   (K135; 18–24; 26; 27) L'Oiseau-Lyre Florilegium D 169 D3 (3, nas)
Marriner—Academy of St. Martin-in-the-Fields
   (complete symphonies) Philips 6747374 (16, nas)
   (31 early symphonies) US: Philips 6747099 (8, nas)
Vaughan—Orchestra of Naples
   (16–24; K196/121) RCA VICS 6201 (3, nas)
Vaughan's light tone and dry recording contribute to a neat performance,

with crisp timpani sound and extremely alert string playing. Of the three, Vaughan is the only one to take the first movement at a true allegro moderato, as marked, but he clips the grace-notes in the slow movement, as does Hogwood. Marriner's graceful approach to this central movement is ideal and his Finale goes with an infectious lilt, but the drums are poorly balanced, as they are, too, in Hogwood's recording. Hogwood, by adopting very fast tempi, skimps the phrasing, but he is the only one satisfactorily to realise the off-beat violin triple-stops in the final bars.

Symphony No. 16 in C, K128

Marriner—Academy of St. Martin-in-the-Fields
   (complete symphonies) Philips 6747374 (16, nas)
   (31 early symphonies) US: Philips 6747099 (8, nas)
Vaughan—Orchestra of Naples
   (17–24; KE141A; K196/121) RCA VICS 6201 (3, nas)

Marriner's is the brighter performance and is not to be confused with his dull version for Argo which omits continuo. Nothing in either of these admirable readings is able to mitigate Mozart's uncharacteristically academic writing with its unadventurous use of low horns.

Symphony No. 17 in G, K129

Marriner—Academy of St. Martin-in-the-Fields
   (complete symphonies) Philips 6747374 (16, nas)
   (31 early symphonies) US: Philips 6747099 (8, nas)

The alternative Vaughan version is less than immaculate in string intonation but does not invalidate the excellent set of which it is a part. Marriner does however give a more polished impression—a particularly fine example from his series.

Symphony No. 18 in F, K130

Hogwood/Schröder—Academy of Ancient Music
   (KE141A; K135; 19–24; 26; 27) L'Oiseau-Lyre Florilegium D 169 D3 (3, nas)
Marriner—Academy of St. Martin-in-the-Fields
   (complete symphonies) Philips 6747374 (16, nas)
   (31 early symphonies) US: Philips 6747099 (8, nas)
Vaughan—Orchestra of Naples
   (16–17; 19–24; KE141A; K196/121) RCA VICS 6201 (3, nas)

Vaughan is the least recommendable largely because of his abrupt handling of grace-notes, a fault shared to a lesser extent by Hogwood. Both Vaughan and Hogwood employ stylish harpsichord continuo, the former offering imaginatively varied embellishment on repeats and the latter adding a firm bassoon-enriched bass-line. Marriner eschews any continuo support but his recording balances the horns better than in rival versions: even Hogwood's natural horns are less telling. No conductor has yet had the courage to record B flat alto horns in the slow movement. Hogwood makes it a rule to repeat both halves of the Minuet after the Trio as well as before, considerably enhancing the balance of this movement, his treatment of repeats is everywhere most generous, and his exaggeration of the contrast between p and f is nowhere more telling than in the coda of the Andante grazioso, where, however, he allows an uncharacteristic dying fall on the last two notes.

Symphony No. 19 in E flat, K132

Hogwood/Schröder—Academy of Ancient Music
 (KE141A; K135; 18; 20–24; 26; 27) L'Oiseau-Lyre Florilegium D 169 D3
 (3, nas)
Marriner—Academy of St. Martin-in-the-Fields
 (complete symphonies) Philips 6747374 (16, nas)
 (31 early symphonies) US: Philips 6747099 (8, nas)

The "traditional" and the "authentic" views are here each represented with equal force, both conductors shaping the music well and accentuating the important horn parts, Marriner's modern instruments sounding the more brassy. Both conductors play the replacement Andante within the symphony and add the original Andantino Grazioso as an appendix. Since both movements are in B flat and basso horns are used by both conductors, none of the four performances is wholly successful. The sighing phrases for oboes in Hogwood's version of the Andantino Grazioso sound excruciating when juxtaposed with basso horns. On the other hand, Hogwood's use of a solo violin (Jaap Schröder) to lead the chant-like Trio is a daring experiment that comes off splendidly.

Symphony No. 20 in D, K133

Hogwood/Schröder—Academy of Ancient Music
 (KE141A; K135; 18; 19; 21–24; 26; 27) L'Oiseau-Lyre Florilegium D 169 D3
 (3, nas)
Marriner—Academy of St. Martin-in-the-Fields
 (complete symphonies) Philips 6747374 (16, nas)

(31 early symphonies) US: Philips 6747099 (8, nas)
Vaughan—Orchestra of Naples
   (16-19; 21-24; KE141A; K196/121) RCA VICS 6201 (3, nas)
Of these three successful performances the best is undoubtedly Hogwood's which, unlike its rivals, includes every indicated repeat (plus both in the Minuet after the Trio as well as before), and a timpani part, very well balanced. Its harpsichord continuo is also better focussed and the bass-line more firmly delineated. The overall effect under Hogwood is of a substantial festive symphony, something not quite achieved by either Marriner or Vaughan. The latter conductor allows several patches of untidy playing in the Finale. (A textual point: in bars 160-161 of the first movement a rising phrase on second oboe is delayed by half a bar. Hogwood "corrects" this Haydnesque little joke.)

Symphony No. 21 in A, K134

Goldberg—Netherlands Chamber Orchestra
   (5, 29) Philips SFL 14073; Europe: Philips 700201
Hogwood/Schröder—Academy of Ancient Music
   (KE141A; K135; 18-20; 22-24; 26; 27) L'Oiseau-Lyre Florilegium D 169 D3 (3, nas)
Mura—Miskolk Symphony Orchestra
   (*Idomeneo* Ballett Music) Hungaroton SLPX 11693
Stadlmair—Munich Chamber Orchestra
   (27) Oryx 3C 317; US: Nonesuch H 71244

Vaughan, though clear and lively, ruins the Finale through misconceiving the nature of the grace-notes. The recommended versions are all splendid: Szymon Goldberg, swift, forceful and with brilliantly clear sound, makes great impact. Hans Stadlmair is a little broader and attends very carefully to the wind parts. Péter Mura uses much legato phrasing; his is an exceptionally beautiful, extremely well recorded version. He, Stadlmair and Hogwood observe both repeats in the Finale. Hogwood also makes the Finale's gracenotes too short but his performance otherwise has such authority that a firm recommendation is possible, particularly for his extremely generous repeat schemes and the use of bassoon and harpsichord continuo.

Symphony in D, K135 (Overture *Lucio Silla*)

Hogwood/Schröder—Academy of Ancient Music
   (KE141A; 18-24; 26; 27) L'Oiseau-Lyre Florilegium D 169 D3 (3, nas)
Maag—London Symphony Orchestra
   (32; Serenades Nos. 6 and 8; *Thamos* Interludes) Decca Eclipse ECS 740

Another work in which "traditional" and "authentic" views are equally well represented, both conductors ideally realising the breathless nature of the work, although Hogwood's, being the more recent issue, is much better recorded.

Symphony No. 22 in C, K162

Böhm—Berlin Philharmonic Orchestra
 (early symphonies to KE173DA) US and UK: DG 2740109 (8, nas)
 (21; 23; 24) US and UK: DG 139405
Hogwood/Schröder—Academy of Ancient Music
 (KE141A; K135; 18–21; 23; 24; 26; 27) L'Oiseau-Lyre Florilegium D 169 D3 (3, nas)
Vaughan—Orchestra of Naples
 (16–21; 23; 24; KE141A; K196/121) RCA VICS 6201 (3, nas)
Böhm is weightier and therefore preferable to Vaughan but this does not make up for the lack of the essential timpani part—of all works where a conjectural drum part should be reconstructed its absence is most serious here. Hogwood rectifies this fault with a less-than-imaginative timpani part, but its mere presence makes his the most recommendable performance.

Symphony No. 26 in E flat, KE166A (=K184)

Böhm—Berlin Philharmonic Orchestra
 (25; 27–36; 38–41) US and UK: DG 2740110 (7, nas)
 (25; 27) DG 2530120
 (Serenade No. 6; Violin Concerto No. 2; March No. 5; Petits reins) DG 135126
 (31; 34) US: DG 139159
Hogwood/Schröder—Academy of Ancient Music
 (KE141A; K135; 18–24; 27) L'Oiseau-Lyre Florilegium D 169 D3 (3, nas)
No timpani reconstruction is applied in either recording but this omission is of no concern since the aurally superfluous nature of the trumpet parts seems even more illogical than their lack of underpinning. Hogwood's "authentic" approach, complete with a strong continuo force, is the more lively interpretation but Böhm elicits more emotion from the C minor Andante.

Symphony No. 27 in G, KE161B (=K199)

Böhm—Berlin Philharmonic Orchestra
 (25; 26; 28–36; 38–41) US and UK: DG 2740110 (7, nas)
 (25; 26) DG 2530120
Stadlmair—Munich Chamber Orchestra
 (21) Oryx 3C 317; US: Nonesuch H 71244
Böhm is reliable but Stadlmair is superb. With him this work takes on greater stature aided by his extreme generosity with repeats. Stadlmair should

be persuaded to make more Mozart recordings, perhaps with this orchestra, the wind section of which is exceptionally fine. Hogwood's performance, alone of his first issue of eleven symphonies and despite his generosity with repeats and careful attention to other details of authenticity, cannot be wholeheartedly recommended in the face of such competition because of his unduly hurried approach which reduces the poise of the first movement and the charm of the last.

Symphony No. 23 in D, KE162B (=K181)

Böhm—Berlin Philharmonic Orchestra
(early symphonies to KE173DA) US and UK: DG 2740109 (8, nas)
(21; 22; 24) US and UK: DG 139405
Hogwood/Schröder—Academy of Ancient Music
(KE141A; K135; 18–22; 24; 26; 27) L'Oiseau-Lyre Florilegium D 169 D3 (3, nas)

Another symphony requiring conjectural timpani reconstruction. Böhm, ignoring this need, despatches the music in a polished, professional way, as does Hogwood, but in the latter's hands, with the help of a well-balanced if slightly unadventurous drum part, the work has greater stature.

Symphony No. 24 in B flat, KE173DA (=K182)

Hogwood/Schröder—Academy of Ancient Music
(KE141A; K135; 18–23; 26; 27) L'Oiseau-Lyre Florilegium D 169 D3 (3, nas)
Vaughan—Orchestra of Naples
(16–23; KE141A; K196/121) RCA VICS 6201 (3, nas)

One of the best performances in Vaughan's set and a fine representation of this little-performed symphony. His stylish double-dotting of bars 11, 15, 86, and 90, etc., in the first movement and his neater playing put him above Hogwood's reading, but the latter's enthusiasm and better-balanced harpsichord have an appeal of their own. Technically, the grace-note in the main melody of the Andantino Grazioso perhaps should be shorter than the semiquavers which follow: Hogwood plays it thus while Vaughan equalises the values, and it is the latter that sounds the more stylish. Hogwood, unlike Vaughan, repeats the second half of the Finale.

Symphony No. 28 in C, KE189K (=K200)

Böhm—Berlin Philharmonic Orchestra
(25–27; 29–36; 38–41) US and UK: DG 2740110 (7, nas)

Hogwood/Schröder—Academy of Ancient Music
 (25; 29; 30; K196; KE213A; Serenade KE189B)
 L'Oiseau-Lyre Florilegium D 170 D 3 (3, nas)
Szell—Cleveland Orchestra
 (33; Overture: *Nozze di Figaro*) CBS 61197; US: Columbia MS 6858

Szell may include timpani (if distantly recorded) and, although rather steely, his performance sounds exciting. Böhm has no timpani but is more warmly recorded; neither conductor adds bassoon(s) to the bass-line. In some early pressings of the DG recording two bars near the end of the slow movement have been taped in twice. Later issues correct this. In Hogwood's authentic version drums and harpsichord stand out clearly—bassoons less so—and with its lively playing, clear recording and full repeats it is a reading of both character and stature.

Symphony No. 25 in G minor, KE173DB (=K183)

Davis—London Symphony Orchestra
 (29; 32) Philips SAL 3502; International: Philips 835262 AY; US: Philips 900133
Hogwood/Schröder—Academy of Ancient Music
 (28–30; K196; KE213A; Serenade KE189B)
 L'Oiseau-Lyre Florilegium D 170 D 3 (3, nas)
Klemperer—Philharmonia Orchestra
 (29; 31–37; 38–41) HMV SLS 5048 (6, nas)
 (Serenade No. 13) Columbia SAX 5252

Davis and Klemperer, while avoiding the pitfalls into which many performances fall (over-deliberate finale; misread appoggiature in the first movement) and accentuating the weightier aspects of the music, nevertheless overlook the bassoons other than where specified in the score (in the Andante and Trio). Hogwood, lighter and leaner, allows bassoons into the continuo line along with harpsichord, and the result is better balanced than any other version. Both passion and pathos are stressed, and the authentic timbres of oboes and horns in particular make this a moving, if bitter, utterance. All repeats are observed.

Symphony No. 29 in A, KE186A (=K201)

Barbirolli—Hallé Orchestra
 (41) Pye GSGC 15028; US: Vanguard S 180
Barshay—Moscow Chamber Orchestra
 (Boccherini) US and UK Artia ALPS 185
Beinum—Concertgebouw Orchestra
 (K320) Philips ABL 3174 (M); US: Epic LC 3354 (M)
Goldberg—Netherlands Chamber Orchestra

(5; 21) Philips SFL 14073; Europe: Philips 700201
Hogwood/Schröder—Academy of Ancient Music
  (25; 28; 30; K196; KE213A; Serenade KE189B)
  L'Oiseau-Lyre Florilegium D 170 D 3 (3, nas)
Klemperer—Philharmonia Orchestra
  (33) Columbia SAX 5256; US: Angel S 36329
  (25: 31–36; 38–41) HMV SLS 5048 (6, nas)
Barshay observes all the repeats, and his tempi are fairly broad, while Barbirolli provides only the first da capo of the Finale and those in the Minuet, but both performances are powerfully persuasive. Klemperer's breadth in the opening Allegro Moderato is ideal. Goldberg is light of touch and elegant in rhythm throughout, Beinum is swifter and very vivid. His warm acoustic is colourful, enabling one to overlook the age of the recording. Both Philips versions suffer from a clumsy tape-join in the third movement. Only Hogwood adds a bassoon to the bass-line, and, like Barshay, he takes all repeats. Minuet gracenotes are stressed, and only Klemper's cornists show greater abandon in the finale.

Symphony No. 30 in D, KE186B (=K202)

Hogwood/Schröder—Academy of Ancient Music
  (25; 28; 29; K196; KE213A; Serenade KE189B)
  L'Oiseau-Lyre Florilegium D 170 D 3 (3, nas)
Hogwood employs timpani, and bassoons and harpsichord continuo (except in the Andantino), and he observes every repeat, thereby bringing full weight to this work for the first time on disc.

Symphony in D, K196 (Overture: *La finta giardiniera*, plus Finale, KE207A [=K121])

Hogwood/Schröder—Academy of Ancient Music
  (25; 28–30; KE213A; Serenade KE189B)
  L'Oiseau-Lyre Florilegium D 170 D 3 (3, nas)
Marriner—Academy of St. Martin-in-the-Fields
  (complete symphonies) Philips 6747374 (16, nas)
  (31 early symphonies) US: Philips 6747099 (8, nas)

Symphony in C, K208 (Overture: *Il rè pastore*, plus Finale KE213C [=K102])

Hogwood/Schröder—Academy of Ancient Music
  (32–36; KE248B; K320)
  L'Oiseau-Lyre Florilegium D 171 D 4 (4, nas)
Marriner—Academy of St. Martin-in-the-Fields
  (complete symphonies) Philips 6747374 (16, nas)
  (31 early symphonies) US: Philips 6747099 (8, nas)

Symphony in D, KE213A (=K204) (movements I, V, VI and VII of Serenade in D)

Complete Serenade:
Waart—Dresden Staatskapelle
  (March KE213B) Philips 6500967
This large-scale, but musical, performance is simply a representation of a current published score. No timpani are included and the three movements for concertante violin (which do not form part of the "symphony") are slightly more stylish than the remainder.
Symphony Version:
Hogwood/Schröder—Academy of Ancient Music
  (25; 28–30; K196; Serenade KE189B)
  L'Oiseau-Lyre Florilegium D 170 D 3 (3, nas)

Symphony in D, KE248B (=K250) (movements I, V, VI, VII and VIII of "Haffner" Serenade in D)

Complete Serenade:
Boskovsky—Vienna Mozart Ensemble
  Decca JB 31
Wöldike—Danish State Radio Chamber Orchestra
  (March K249) Philips WL 1194 (M); US: Vanguard VRS 483 (M)
Both performances are stylish, Wöldike's additional forcefulness making the work very symphonic. The brief trumpet cadenza at the fermata near the end of the first movement typifies Wöldike's imaginative approach to music of this period.
Symphony Version:
Hogwood/Schröder—Academy of Ancient Music
  (32–36; K208; K320)
  L'Oiseau-Lyre Florilegium D 171 D 4 (4, nas)

Symphony No. 31 in D, KE300A (=K297) "Paris"

Böhm—Berlin Philharmonic Orchestra
  (25–30; 32–36; 38–41) US and UK: DG 2740110 (7, nas)
  (26; 34) US: DG 139159
Krips—Concertgebouw Orchestra
  (complete symphonies) Philips 6747374 (16, nas)
  (38) US: Philips 6500466
Schmidt-Isserstedt—Bamberg Symphony Orchestra
  (35) Harmonia Mundi 0666471
Krips obtains magnificent sonority, Schmidt-Isserstedt greater definition and

inner detail. Böhm's powerful recording is notable for an exceptionally slow but very convincing Finale. A good, but not outstanding, recording by Guschlbauer adds the original slow movement for reference but like its coupling (No. 36) falls just outside the recommended list.

Symphony No. 32 in G, K318 (Overture in the Italian Style)

Hogwood/Schröder—Academy of Ancient Music
 (33–36; K208; KE248B; K320)
 L'Oiseau-Lyre Florilegium D 171 D 4 (4, nas)
Krips—Concertgebouw Orchestra
 (complete symphonies) Philips 6747374 (16, nas)
 (33, 34) US: Philips 6500526
Maag—London Symphony Orchestra
 (*Lucio Silla*; Serenades Nos. 6, 8; *Thamos* interludes) Decca Eclipse ECS 740; US: London STS 15087

Hogwood's opening flourish is strongly dotted in rhythm, a most stylish procedure. Timpani are used in all three recommended versions despite signs of unauthenticity in the part (the crescendo rolls at bars 53–56 and 240–243 seem particularly out of style).

Symphony No. 33 in B flat, K319

Barshay—Moscow Chamber Orchestra
 (30) Melodiya 022569–70 (M)
Beinum—Concertgebouw Orchestra
 (Haydn Symphony No. 103) Decca ACL 107 (M)
Dixon—Prague Chamber Orchestra
 (34) Supraphon 1 10 1125
Hogwood/Schröder—Academy of Ancient Music
 (32; 34–36; K208; KE248B; K320)
 L'Oiseau-Lyre Florilegium D 171 D 4 (4, nas)
Jochum—Bavarian Radio Symphony Orchestra
 (36) Heliodor 478435 (M) US: Decca 9920 (M)
Krips—Concertgebouw Orchestra of Amsterdam
 (complete symphonies) Philips 6747374 (16, nas)
 (32, 34) US: Philips 6500526

Six excellent readings. Barshay and Dixon make both finale repeats, Jochum clarifies inner parts superbly, Beinum offers lively rhythmic precision, Krips elicits glowing orchestral fullness, and Hogwood, with period instruments, unfailingly captures Mozart's style and observes more repeats than anyone else.

Symphony in D, K320 (movements I, V, VII from "Posthorn" Serenade in D)

Complete serenade:
Beinum—Concertgebouw Orchestra
   (29) Philips ABL 3174 (M) US: Epic LC 3354 (M)
Schönzeler—London Philharmonic Orchestra
   (Marches KE 320A) Classics for Pleasure CFP 40258
Symphony Version:
Hogwood/Schröder—Academy of Ancient Music
   (32–36; K208; KE248B)
   L'Oiseau-Lyre Florilegium D 171 D 4 (4, nas)

Symphony No. 34 in C, K338

Böhm—Berlin Philharmonic Orchestra
   (25–33, 35–36, 38–41) DG 2740110 (7, nas)
Dixon—Prague Chamber Orchestra
   (33) Supraphon 1 10 1125
Hogwood/Schröder—Academy of Ancient Music
   (32; 33; 35; 36; K208; KE248B; K320)
   L'Oiseau-Lyre Florilegium D 171 D 4 (4, nas)
Krips—Concertgebouw Orchestra
   (complete symphonies) Philips 6747374 (16, nas)
   (32, 33) US: Philips 6500526

Böhm's grandeur exceeds even Krips's broad reading but is less beautifully recorded. Dixon and Hogwood observe both finale repeats at exciting, rapid tempi but Hogwood has the edge in clarity and drama; his harpsichord continuo is an unexpected asset.

59.   Symphony in C, K384 (Overture: *Die Entführung aus dem Serail*)

Lehmann—Berlin Philharmonic Orchestra
   (Overtures) Heliodor 478074 (M) US: Decca 9849 (M)
Newstone—Hamburg Pro Musica Orchestra
   (overtures) Saga 5373 US: Forum S 70010

The overture is designed to flow directly into the opera, but both performances use a brief concert ending. Newstone's version is notable for its force, Lehmann's for its elegant liveliness.

Symphony No. 35 in D, K385, "Haffner"

Hogwood/Schröder—Academy of Ancient Music
   (32–34; 36; K208; KE248B; K320)
   L'Oiseau-Lyre Florilegium D 171 D 4 (4, nas)
Marriner—Academy of St. Martin-in-the-Fields
   (40; March KE385A) US and UK Philips 6500162

Schmidt-Isserstedt—Bamberg Symphony Orchestra
   (31) Harmonia Mundi 0666471
There are no da capo markings in the first movement in most published scores and on records an exposition repeat is observed only by Szell and Fricsay in their otherwise unremarkable readings. There are many enjoyable recordings: Marriner's is of especial interest in that he uses the original Serenade scoring which excludes flutes and clarinets. Though employing a larger orchestra, Schmidt-Isserstedt (using Mozart's final scoring) achieves more lucid detail and this makes his recording preferable to the satisfactory but slightly restrained versions by Krips and Boult. Hogwood, in attempting to return to the original serenade version, does so only partially by restoring the March (KE385A = K408, No. 2)—but only at the beginning—and omitting flutes and clarinets, but not restoring the first movement's repeats. Timpani tone is not crisp enough, but a strong bass-line, divided violins, a harpsichord continuo and very alert playing of period instruments offer many rewards.

Symphony No. 36 in C, K425 "Linz"

Hogwood/Schröder—Academy of Ancient Music
   (32–35; K208; KE248B; K320)
   L'Oiseau-Lyre Florilegium D 171 D 4 (4, nas)
Jochum—Bavarian Radio Symphony Orchestra
   (33) Heliodor 478435 (M) US: Decca 9920 (M)
Krips—Concertgebouw Orchestra
   (complete symphonies) Philips 6747374 (16, nas)
   (21) US: Philips 6500525
Mackerras—London Philharmonic Orchestra
   (38) Classics for Pleasure CFP 40079

Jochum's "Linz" must surely be one of the finest interpretations of a Mozart symphony ever recorded. It proves that a small body of modern instruments can effectively represent Mozart's textures, and the recording, made at the Würzburg Festival in 1956, has yet to be surpassed for naturalness and explicit balance. Mackerras and Krips are both excellent but lack Jochum's magical lightness of touch. Mackerras uses harpsichord and repeats both halves of the Finale. Krips convinces in his unusually fast Andante and handles the large orchestra with a fine sense of balance which justifies and exploits the full textures—a valid modern interpretation. By observing every repeat, Hogwood realises the work's stature (it lasts 38 minutes), and his authentic timbres bring out admirably he fiercely ceremonial nature of the work without coarseness.

Symphony No. 38 in D, K504, "Prague"

Krips—Concertgebouw Orchestra
   (complete symphonies) Philips 6747374 (16, nas)

(31) US: Philips 6500466
Maag—London Symphony Orchestra
   (Clarinet Concerto) Decca SDD 331
   (32) US: London STS 15087
Mackerras—London Philharmonic Orchestra
   (36) Classics for Pleasure CFP 40079

Mackerras is very true to style, includes the first movement repeat, and makes both in the Finale. He uses harpsichord continuo and adopts fairly swift tempi. Maag's older recording (a more recent one, on Vox, is not recommendable) is clearer in the bass and the performance gives a Beethoven-like impression. Krips is warm and noble in the modern style without losing clarity. His flowing Andante is preferable to Maag's more static approach.

Symphony No. 39 in E flat, K543

Guschlbauer—Bamberg Symphony Orchestra
   (38) Erato STU 70653
Jochum—Bavarian Radio Symphony Orchestra
   (Violin Concerto No. 4) Heliodor 89620

Jochum's version has immaculate clarity and a superb sense of proportion. The 1952 recording re-mastered from mono with amazingly effective stereo representation is still impressive. All pressings other than 89620 have had repeats removed by the editors. Guschlbauer's is a good though more stolid modern alternative, but his omission of the short second repeat in the Andante con Moto is illogical. Collegium Aureum (coupled with No. 38) play every repeat and use authentic instruments but there are several anachronistic mannerisms in the performance and the balance is poor.

Symphony No. 40 in G minor, K550 (original version)

Barenboim—English Chamber Orchestra
   (39) HMV ASD 2424
   (Piano Concerto K467) US: Angel S 36814
Furtwängler—Vienna Philharmonic Orchestra
   (Serenade, K525) HMV XLP 30104 (M)
Marriner—Academy of St. Martin-in-the-Fields
   (35; March KE385A) US and UK Philips 6500162

Furtwängler's is the only performance to take the initial molto allegro indication seriously and the result is breathtaking (though Barenboim is fairly close to Furtwängler's high speed). In the Minuet Furtwängler's absolutely firm tempo throughout is revelatory. Marriner is lighter in touch and more literal—a faithful representation with slightly more character than the good Barenboim alternative.

Symphony No. 40 in G minor, K550 (revised edition, with clarinets)

Guschlbauer—Bamberg Symphony Orchestra
   (41) Erato STU 70738
Keilberth—Bamberg Symphony Orchestra
   (38; 39; 41) Telefunken DT 6 48109 (2, nas)
Mackerras—London Philharmonic Orchestra
   (41) Classics for Pleasure CFP 40253
Strauss—Berlin State Opera Orchestra
   (41) DG 642010 (M)

Britten (not recommended) is the only recorded conductor to include every repeat. Mackerras balances the instrumental sections well, observes both Finale repeats, and phrases stylishly. Guschlbauer adopts similar tempi and is warmer but less clear. Richard Strauss (recorded in 1927) shapes the phrases like an operatic singer. Mozart might hardly have recognised his own music but the performance is tremendously revealing. Keilberth is heir to this performance: solid and noble but without the mannerisms of tempo which make Strauss controversial.

Symphony No. 41 in C, K551, "Jupiter"

Barbirolli—Hallé Orchestra
   (29) Pye GSGC 15028; US: Vanguard S 180
Barshay—Moscow Chamber Orchestra
   (2 sides) Melodiya C 01515–6
Boult—London Philharmonic Orchestra
   (35) HMV ASD 3158
Guschlbauer—Bamberg Symphony Orchestra
   (40) Erato STU 70738
Jochum—Concertgebouw Orchestra
   (35) Philips 839522
Krips—Concertgebouw Orchestra
   (complete symphonies) Philips 6747374 (16, nas)
   (35) US: Philips 3500429

Barshay and Boult both observe every repeat, the former's reading occupying both sides of the disc while HMV finds room for a coupling of Symphony No. 35. Where Boult is thorough and lucid, albeit within the context of a large-scale performance, Barshay offers greater conviction largely through firmer rhythm and bold use of open strings in the Finale. Jochum and Krips omit slow movement and second Finale repeats but both see the structure whole. Krips is broad and rich in texture—a successful if arguable exploitation of the modern orchestra. Guschlbauer observes first movement and Minuet repeats only but shows a clear sense of line. Barbirolli (Minuet repeats only) provides superior forcefulness and his old recording is very well balanced. An imposing account.

Spurious Symphonies

Symphony "No. 2" in B flat, KE Anh 223A (=K17)

Leinsdorf—London Philharmonic Orchestra
  (1, "3," 4, 5) HMV SXLP 20093; US: Westminster XWN 18861 (M)
A rustic, rather ham-fisted work of unknown pedigree that should doubtless include alto horns in its scoring. Leinsdorf drops these instruments an octave, but is otherwise recommendable if only to illustrate the type of music the young Mozart heard and how far he rose above it.

Symphony "No. 3" in E flat, KE Anh109I (=K18)

Lehan—Consortuim Musicum
  Electrola C 053 28396
Leinsdorf—London Philharmonic Orchestra
  (1, "2," 4, 5) HMV SXLP 20093; US: Westminster XWN 18861 (M)
Written by Karl Friedrich Abel (op. 7/6, c. 1764), this symphony is scored for oboes, horns and strings. The eight-year-old Mozart copied it out, transferring the woodwind parts to clarinets presumably as a transposition exercise. Both these recordings use Mozart's scoring.

Symphony in B flat, KE311A (=KA8), "Paris Overture"

Swarowsky—Vienna State Academy Orchestra
  (54; 70) Lyrichord LL 32 (M)
This brilliant overture with its shades of Pleyel and Méhul has slightly French overtones and there are some turns of phrase similar to Mozart with whom it is quite clear that the piece is not connected. Köchel rightly placed the work in his Appendix of doubtful compositions; Einstein's instatement of it in the main catalogue is a musicologically eccentric act which can surely only result in confusion. Nevertheless, Swarowsky's performance has a rough grandeur due to forthright use of alto horns and timpani, and should be sought as a rewarding curiosity.

Symphony "No. 37" in G, KE425A (=K444)

Jones—Little Orchestra of London
  (M. Haydn Symphony No. 33; Violin Concerto) Pye GSGC 14131
Mackerras—English Chamber Orchestra
  (M. Haydn Symphonies Nos. 13 and 20) US and UK: Archiv 2533109
Only the introduction of this Michael Haydn symphony is by Mozart and the placing of a scroll on the disc prior to the succeeding Allegro con Spirito of this charming symphony is an intelligent point in the excellent Pye production. Mackerras also gives a stylish performance with harpsichord continuo, but we await a reading that allows the Allegro con Spirito first movement its proper weight without the unduly hurried tempi to be heard on both these discs.

Reconstructed Timpani Parts

These timpani parts are offered merely as suggested reconstructions for those Mozart symphonies whose scoring includes trumpets but excludes a surviving timpani part. The need for these reconstructions has already been described in the main text and the author would like to support it by drawing attention to a practical demonstration which proved instructive.

In November 1978 Antony Hodgson directed a week-end course entitled "Haydn I," held at the Maltings, Snape, in Suffolk. The course examined the textures of Haydn's early orchestral music, with reference also to authenticity of performance, and for Symphony No. 30 a radical experiment was carried out. Scored for two oboes, two horns in C basso, and strings, No. 30, the "Alleluia" Symphony, nevertheless displays strong links in style and even in thematic fragments with the "Maria Theresia" Symphony, No. 48, which is scored for two oboes, two horns in C alto, timpani and strings. The conductor Christopher Fry persuaded the young cornists of the Snape Maltings Training Orchestra to play the parts of Symphony No. 30 "up," i.e. in C alto, and János Keszei, one of Britain's leading percussionists, played a timpani part reconstructed by the author and designed to support the horns playing in the trumpet register.

In a unique experiment, students were encouraged during rehearsals to comment upon the effects produced, and it was agreed that Symphony No. 30 made a splendid and much more striking effect when the scoring was brought into line with that of Symphony No. 48. Details in the reconstructed timpani part, which Mr. Keszei described as being stylistically appropriate, were amended for this particular performance, although in other conditions (acoustics, size of orchestra, type of timpani, etc.) these alterations may not be relevant.

It is in precisely this spirit that the following parts for Mozart's symphonies are put forward for consideration: details may well need altering in certain circumstances, but it is submitted that, in each of these symphonies, a timpani part is vital. It may be argued that the above experiment, since it concerned a Haydn work, bears no relevance to the music of Mozart, but we must not overlook the fact that both composers occupied the same *milieu*: in their environment orchestral trumpets in D major and C major works (and, for that matter, C alto horns holding the trumpets' position in C major symphonies) were essentially supported by timpani just as the lower strings were invariably supported by bassoons. In both instances, a literally unwritten law was in operation.

SYMPHONY in D, KE 73N (= K 95).

Timpani Part reconstructed by
ROBERT DEARLING, 1978

I: Allegro

II: Andante
Tacet

III: Minuetto

IV: Allegro

SYMPHONY No. 20 in D, K 133.
Timpani Part reconstructed by
ROBERT DEARLING, 1978

I: Allegro

II: Andante
Tacet

III: Minuetto

IV: (Allegro)

SYMPHONY No. 22 in C, K 162. Timpani Part reconstructed by ROBERT DEARLING, 1978

I: Allegro assai

II: Andante grazioso
Tacet

III: Presto assai

SYMPHONY No. 23 in D, KE 162b (= K 181). Timpani Part reconstructed by
ROBERT DEARLING, 1978

I: Allegro spiritoso

II: Andantino grazioso
Tacet

III: Presto assai

SYMPHONY No. 28 in C, KE 173e (= K 200).   Timpani Part reconstructed by ROBERT DEARLING, 1978

I: Allegro spiritoso

II: Andante
Tacet

III: Minuetto

Trio Tacet   D.C. Minuetto

IV: Presto

SYMPHONY No. 30 in D, KE 186b (= K 202). Timpani Part reconstructed by
ROBERT DEARLING, 1978

I: Molto Allegro

II: Andantino con moto
Tacet

III: Minuetto

IV: Presto

SYMPHONY in D, from Serenade KE 213A (= K 204). Timpani Part reconstructed by ROBERT DEARLING, 1978

I: Allegro assai

II (V): Andante
Tacet

III (VI): Menuetto

IV (VII): Finale

OVERTURE in C, "Il rè pastore", K 208, with Finale KE 213c (= K 102).
(Concert version of the end of the first movement)

Timpani Part reconstructed by
ROBERT DEARLING, 1978

I. Molto Allegro

II: Andantino
Tacet

III: Presto assai

Köchel Numbers

Few can escape alarm and confusion when contemplating the proliferation of Köchel numbers associated with Mozart's symphonies. The easy reference table below is an attempt to clarify the situation by listing them all in numerical order regardless of the various subsystems. These systems may, however, still be identified by reference to the prefix and suffix letters, as follows:

K = Köchel (the original Köchel numbering system, given in German-speaking countries as KV [=Köchel-Verzeichnis]).

KA = Köchel-Anhang (the Appendix to Köchel's original catalogue).

KE = Köchel-Einstein (Einstein's revision of Köchel's listing).

KE Anh = Köchel-Einstein Anhang (the Appendix to Einstein's revision). (Suffix letters denote works slotted into the basic numeration.)

KE AC = Köchel-Einstein Anhang, as revised by Giegling, Wienmann and Sievers in the Sixth Edition, 1964. This latest edition's revisions account also for the occasional appearance of double suffices.

Identification numbers in the right-hand column show the position of each work in the Table of Mozart's Symphonies which follows.

KA	8 = KE 311A	70
KE AC	11.03: Symphony in B flat (KE 74G; KA 216)	25
K	16: Symphony No. 1	1
KE	16A: Symphony in A minor (KA 220)	4
KE	16B: Symphony in C	5
K	17 = KE Anh 223A	67
K	18 = KE Anh 109 I	68
K	19: Symphony No. 4	2
KE	19A: Symphony in F (KA 223)	69
KE	19B: Symphony in C (KA 222)	3
K	22: Symphony No. 5	6
KE	42A: Symphony in F (K 76)	7

K	43: Symphony No. 6	8
K	45: Symphony No. 7 (KE 46A = K 51)	11
KE	45A: Symphony in G (KA 221)	9
KE	45B: Symphony in B flat (KA 214)	10
KE	46A see K 45	11
K	48: Symphony No. 8	12
K	51 see K 45	11
KE	66C: Symphony in D (KA 215)	14
KE	66D: Symphony in B flat (KA 217)	15
KE	66E: Symphony in B flat (KA 218)	16
K	73 = KE 75A	24
KE	73L: Symphony in D (K 81)	19
KE	73M: Symphony in D (K 97)	18
KE	73N: Symphony in D (K 95)	20
KE	73Q: Symphony No. 11 (K 84)	17
K	74: Symphony No. 10	22
KE	74A: Overture in D (K 87)	21
KE	74G: Symphony in B flat (KA 216; KE AC 11.03)	25
K	75: Symphony in F	26
KE	75A: Symphony No. 9 (K 73)	24
KE	75B: Symphony No. 12 (K 110)	27
K	76 = KE 42A	7
K	81 = KE 73L	19
K	84 = KE 73Q	17
K	87 = KE 74A	21
K	95 = KE 73N	20
K	96 = KE 111B	29
K	97 = KE 73M	18
K	98 = KE Anh 223B	23
KA	100 = KE 383G	60
K	102 see K 208	51
KE Anh	109 I: Symphony "No. 3" (K 18)	68
K	110 = KE 75B	27
K	111: Overture in D (KE 111A = K 120)	28
KE	111A see 111	28
KE	111B: Symphony in C (K 96)	29
K	112: Symphony No. 13	30
K	114: Symphony No. 14	31
K	120 see K 111	28
K	121 see K 196	50
K	124: Symphony No. 15	32

K	128: Symphony No. 16	34
K	129: Symphony No. 17	35
K	130: Symphony No. 18	36
K	132: Symphony No. 19	37
K	133: Symphony No. 20	38
K	134: Symphony No. 21	39
K	135: Overture in D	40
KE	141A: Overture in D (K 161; K 163)	33
K	161 = KE 141A	33
KE	161A: Symphony No. 26 (K 184)	41
KE	161B: Symphony No. 27 (K 199)	42
K	162: Symphony No. 22	43
KE	162B: Symphony No. 23 (K 181)	44
K	163 see KE 141A	33
KE	173DA: Symphony No. 24 (K 182)	45
KE	173DB: Symphony No. 25 (K 183)	46
K	181 = KE 162B	44
K	182 = KE 173DA	45
K	183 = KE 173DB	46
K	184 = KE 161A	41
KE	186A: Symphony No. 29 (K 201)	47
KE	186B: Symphony No. 30 (K 202)	48
KE	189K: Symphony No. 28 (K 200)	49
K	196: Overture in D (KE 207A = K 121)	50
K	199 = KE 161B	42
K	200 = KE 189K	49
K	201 = KE 186A	47
K	202 = KE 186B	48
K	204 = KE 213A	52
KE	207A see K 196	50
K	208: Overtures in C (KE 213C = K 102)	51
KE	213A: Serenade (K 204)	52
KE	213C see K 208	51
KA	214 = KE 45B	10
KA	215 = KE 66C	14
KA	216 = KE 74G; KE AC 11.03	25
KA	217 = KE 66D	15
KA	218 = KE 66E	16
KA	220 = KE 16A	4
KA	221 = KE 45A	9
KA	222 = KE 19B	3

KA	223 = KE 19A	69
KE Anh	223A: Symphony "No. 2" (K 17)	67
KE Anh	223B: Symphony in F (K 98)	23
KE	248B: Serenade (K 250)	53
K	250 = KE 248B	53
K	297 = KE 300A	54
KE	300A: Symphony No. 31 (K 297)	54
KE	311A: Overture in B flat (KA 9)	70
K	318: Symphony No. 32	55
K	319: Symphony No. 33	56
K	320: Serenade in D	57
K	338: Symphony No. 34 (KE 383F = K 409)	58
KE	383F see K 338	58
KE	383G: Symphony in E flat (KA 100)	60
K	384: Overture in C	59
K	385: Symphony No. 35	61
K	409: see K 338	58
K	425: Symphony No. 36	62
KE	425A: Symphony "No. 37" (K 444)	71
K	444 = KE 425A	71
K	504: Symphony No. 38	63
K	543: Symphony No. 39	64
K	550: Symphony No. 40	65
K	551: Symphony No. 41	66

Table of Mozart's Symphonies

The following list of Mozart's symphonies includes all those discussed in the text: numbered and unnumbered symphonies, symphonies derived from operatic overtures, and those extracted from serenades. In addition to the keys (G=G major; g=G minor) and the Köchel numberings (with the chronologically more accurate "KE" system first), dates and places of composition are given together with scoring details. The standard code is used in the matter of scoring: woodwind first (flutes, oboes, clarinets, bassoons), then brass (horns, trumpets), percussion, and strings in four or five parts (à 4 or à 5).

In order to obtain a historical musical perspective for Mozart's symphonies, approximately contemporary works in other *genres* are listed and contemporary Haydn symphonies are shown so that comparisons may be drawn both before and after the cross-influences between the two composers took place. In the final column are listed works in the wider musical scene—not an exhaustive list but enough to assist in the establishment of a perspective.

No.	Key	KE	K	Scoring	Composition	Major Page Refs.	Mozart Works	Contemporary Haydn Syms.	Other Works
1	E flat	—	16	0200–20 str à 4	London, end of 1764 or start of 1765	20, 33, 60f, 78f, 87f, 105, 106, 163	Klavier/Violin Sonatas, K10–15; London Notebook	21, 22, 23, 24	J. C. Bach: Syms., op. 3 (published). Schobert: Syms., opp. 9, 10
2	D	—	19	0200–20 str à 4	London, start of 1765	20, 33, 61f, 65, 78, 82, 89		36?	
3 lost	C	19B	Anh 222	0200–20 str à 4	London, start of 1765	33, 62		72?	Clementi's earliest keyboard works
4 lost	a	16A	Anh 220	0200–20 str à 4	London, 1765	62		28, 29	R. Hoffstetter's first quartets
5 sketch	C	16B	—	0200–20 str à 4	London, 1765	62		30, 31	
6	B flat	—	22	0200–20 str à 4	The Hague, Dec. 1765	20, 33, 62f, 78, 81f, 87, 90, 155, 163	Aria: Conservati fedele, K23; Keyboard Variations on a Dutch Song, K24	34	J. C. Bach: Syms., opp. 6 and 8 (published)
7	F	42A	76	0202–20 str à 4	Salzburg (or Vienna?), autumn 1767	35, 63, 82, 84, 91	Church Sonata in D, KE41K (=K69)	35, 38?	Haydn: La canterina. Boccherini's first sym. (Gér. 500) (published). F. X. Dušek's first sym.

8	6	F	—	43	(2)200–20 str à 5	Olmütz and Vienna, autumn or Dec. 1767	20, 63f, 65, 78, 82, 84, 90n	Soprano duet: *Ach, was müssen wir erfahren?*, KE43A (=K Anh.24A)	58?, 59?	Gluck: *Alceste* (Vienna). Mysliveček: *Bellerofonte* (Naples)
9	—	G	45A	Anh 221	0200–20 str à 4	Vienna, start of 1768, "Alte Lambacher"	35, 64f, 67, 78, 82, 172		26, 39?	Gassmann: Sym. in A flat (Hill 65)
10	—	B flat	45B	Anh 214	0200–20 str à 4	Vienna, start of 1768	66f, 78, 85, 87, 91, 164			Mysliveček's first sym.
11	7	D	—	45	0200–22 timp str à 4	Vienna, 16/1/68[1]	20, 65, 67, 78, 82, 85, 87, 91n, 129			M. Haydn: Symphony *Hochzeit auf der Alm*
12	8	D	—	48	0200–22 timp str à 4	Vienna, 13/12/68	20, 35, 67f, 76, 78, 85, 87, 90, 99, 106	Mass in C, K47A; Offertorium, K47B; Trumpet Concerto (lost); *Missae breves* KE47D (=K49); KE61A (=K65)	49?	Haydn: *Lo speziale*
13	—	G	—	—	0200–20 str à 4	Vienna, late 1768?, spurious? "Neuer Lambacher"	35, 68, 73, 78, 85, 87, 111, 172	7 Minuets, KE61B (=K65A)	41	

[1] Used later for the Overture to *La finta semplice*, KE46A (=K51).

14	lost	D	66C	Anh 215	0202–20 str à 4	Salzburg, end of 1769	68	Te deum, KE66B (=K141)	Haydn: Quartets, op. 9
15	lost	B flat	66D	Anh 217	2000–20 str à 4	Salzburg, end of 1769	68, 76	Aria: Ah, più tremar non voglio, K71	Vaňhal: Syms. in A minor, C minor, E minor
16	lost	B flat	66E	Anh 218	2202–20 str à 4	Salzburg, end of 1769	68	Keyboard Allegro in G, K72A	R. Hoffstetter: Quartets, op. 1
17	11	D	73Q	84	0200–20 str à 5	Italy, first half of 1770	20, 71f, 78, 83, 87, 91n, 129	Arias KE73A–E (=K143, 78, 88, 79); KE73 O–P (=K82, 83); Kyrie, KE73K (=K89)	Haydn: Le pescatrice 48?
18	—	D	73M	97	0200–22 timp str à 4	Rome, April 1770	69, 78, 85, 87, 90, 91	Quartet in G, KE73F (=K80); Contretanz, KE73G (=K123)	
19	—	D	73L	81	0200–20 str à 4	Rome, 25/4/70	71f, 82, 87, 90		K. Stamitz: Orch. Quartets, op. 4
20	—	D	73N	95	2 or 200–02 str à 4 (timp)	Rome, 25/4/70	69ff, 78, 83, 85, 87, 91		U. Hoffstetter: Syms., op. 1
21	—	D	74A	87	2200–20 str à 4	Milan, mid-Dec. 1770[2]	72f, 78, 87, 90, 95		J. C. Bach: Syms., op. 9 (published)
22	10	G	—	74	0200–20 str à 5	Milan, Dec. 1770	20, 73, 78, 83, 87, 90		Richter: Quartets, op 5

[2] Overture: Mitridate, rè di Ponto.

23	—	F	Anh 223B	98	0200–20 str à 4	Milan?, 1771. Doubtful	22, 73, 78, 85			Boccherini: Quartets, opp. 8, 10
24	9	C	75A	73	0200–22 timp str à 4	Salzburg, early summer 1771?	20, 73f, 78 86, 87, 90, 129	*La Betulia Liberata*, KE74C (=K118) *Regina coeli*, KE74D (=K108)		Haydn: Keyboard Sonata, L33
25	—	B flat	74G AC 11.03	Anh 216	0200–20 str à 5	Salzburg, early summer 1771	20, 23, 73f. 86, 90	*Litaniae Laurentanae*, KE74E (=K109)	42	Haydn: Quartets, opp. 17, 20
26	—	F	—	75	0200–20 str à 4	Salzburg, early summer 1771	73f, 78, 86, 87, 90, 159	*Offertorium*, KE74F (=K72); *Missa brevis*, KE90A (=K116)	43	M. Haydn: Requiem in C minor
27	12	G	75B	110	(2)20(2) –20 str à 4	Salzburg, July 1771	73f, 75n, 78, 86, 88, 90	*Kyries*, K90; KE93B (=K221)	44	Boccherini: Syms., op. 12 (published)
28	—	D	—	111	2200–22 timp str à 4	Milan, end of Aug. to 23/9/71[3]	75, 78, 83, 87, 95			Cambini's first quartets
29	—	C	111B	96	0200–22 timp str à 4	Milan, late Oct. or early Nov. 1771	75, 78, 83, 86, 90	Divertimento in E flat K113		
30	13	F	—	112	0200–20 str à 4	Milan, 2/11/71	19, 23n, 76, 78, 87, 88. 91			

[3] Overture: *Ascanio in Alba*, + Finale KE111A (=K120).

31	14	A	—	114	2(2)00–20 str à 4	Salzburg, 30/12/71	19, 20, 23n, 76f, 78, 83, 87, 91, 106, 119	Missa solemnis KE114A (=K139)		
32	15	G	—	124	0200–20 str à 4	Salzburg, 21/2/72	23n, 104, 112, 114	Church Sonatas KE124A–B (=K144; 145); K124C	C. Stamitz: Syms., op. 6	
33	—	D	141A	161	2200–22 timp. str à 4	I, II: Salzburg, March 1772 III: Milan, end 1772[4]	21, 93, 95	Litaniae, K125; Divertimenti ("Salzburg Symphonies"), KE125A–C (=K136–8)	Vaňhal: Quartets, op. 9	
34	16	C	—	128	0200–20 str à 4	Salzburg, May 1772	21, 23n, 104f, 106, 114	Regina coeli, K127		45
35	17	G	—	129	0200–20 str à 4	Salzburg, May 1772	20f, 104, 105f, 106		Vaňhal: Syms., op 10	46
36	18	F	—	130	2000–40 str à 4	Salzburg, end of May 1772	18, 20, 21, 113f, 116, 119, 133, 134, 143, 164	6 Minuets, KE130A (=K164) Divertimento in D, K131		47
37	19	E flat	—	132	0200–40 str à 5	Salzburg, July 1772	20f, 115f, 118, 119, 133f, 156			65?

[4] Overture: *Il sogno di Scipione*, + Finale K163.

38	20	D	—	133	(1)200–22 (timp) str à 4	Salzburg, July 1772	19f, 22, 117f, 135 156		51?	
39	21	A	—	134	2000–20 str à 4	Salzburg, Aug. 1772	20f, 23, 77, 106, 110n, 116, 119f		52?	
40	—	D	—	135	0200–22 timp str à 4	Milan, start of Nov. 1772[5]	94, 96, 102	Quartets in D, KE134A (=K155) in G, KE134B (=K156); in C, K157		
41	26	E flat	161A	184	2202–22 str à 5	Salzburg, early 1773	19f, 23, 96f, 99, 100, 131, 150	Wind Divertimenti in B flat, KE159B (=K186); E flat KE159D (=K166)		Vaňhal: Syms., op. 16
42	27	G	161B	199	2000–40 str à 4	Salzburg, April 1773	19f, 23, 104, 106, 110, 120, 164, 170			Haydn: L'infedeltà delusa
43	22	C	—	162	0200–22 timp str à 5	Salzburg, early 1773	20f, 23, 95, 99, 100	String Quartets in F, K158; in B flat, K159; in E flat KE159A (=K160); Exsultate, jubilate, KE158A (=K165)	50	Vaňhal: Syms. in A flat
44	23	D	162B	181	0200–22 timp str à 5	Salzburg, 19/5/73	20f, 23, 57, 99, 100	Concertone in C, KE166B (=K190)		C. P. E. Bach: 6 Syms. W182 (published)

[5] Overture: *Lucio Silla*.

45	24	B flat	173DA	182	(2)200–20 str à 5	Salzburg, 3/10/73	19f, 23, 57, 99, 100	Missa brevis, KE166D (=K115); Missa Trinitatis, K167		Haydn: *Philemon und Baucis*
46	25	g	173DB	183	0202–40 str à 5	Salzburg, 5/10/73	19f, 23, 97, 121f, 131f, 133, 156, 170	Quintet, K174; Concerto in D, K175		
47	29	A	186A	201	0200–20 str à 4	Salzburg, 6/4/74	19f, 23, 104, 121, 123f		54, 55	Grétry's only Sym. published Paisiello: *Il mondo della luna*
48	30	D	186B	202	0200–22 timp str à 4	Salzburg, 5/5/74	19, 23, 125, 149, 159, 170	Sonata for four hands, KE186C (=K358); *Litaniae Laurentanae* KE186D (=K195); Bassoon Concerto, KE186E (=K191)	56, 57	Gluck: *Iphigénie en Aulide*
49	28	C	189K	200	0200–22 timp str à 4	Salzburg, 17/11/74	19, 23, 104, 110n, 114, 120f	Divertimento, KE173A (=K205); 6 Variations for keyboard, KE173C (=K180)		
50	—	D	—	196	0200–20 str à 4	Salzburg/Munich, Sept. 1774–Jan. 1775[6]	21, 100	Sonatas KE189E–H (=K280–3); Missa brevis, KE196B (=K220)	60	Gluck: *Orphée et Eurydice* (Paris)

[6] Overture: *La finta giardiniera*, + Finale KE207A (=K121).

51	—	C	—	208	0200–22 timp str à 4	Salzburg, 23/4/75[7]	100	Bassoon and Cello Sonata, KE196C (=K292); Wind Divertimenti KE196E–F (=KAnh 226–7); Violin Concerto, K207	64?	R. Hoffstetter: Quartets, op. 3 (attrib. Haydn)
52	—	D	213A	204	(2)201 –22 (timp) str à 4	Salzburg, 5/8/75[8]	135	Wind Divertimento, K213; Marches, KE213B (=K215), K214; Violin Concerto, K216		Haydn: *L'incontro improviso* C. P. E. Bach: 4 Syms., W183 (published)
53	—	D	248B	250	(2)202 –22 timp str à 4	Salzburg, July 1776[9]	39, 135f	Offertorium *Venite populi*, KE248A (=K260); Divertimento in D, K251; Wind Divertimento, K253	61, 62?	Haydn: *La vera costanza* Gluck: *Alceste* (Paris) Soler: Organ Quintets
54	31	D	300A	297	2222–22 timp str à 4	Paris, before 12/6/78 "Paris"	15, 19f, 23f, 43, 104, 108f, 120, 170	Sinfonia Concertante, KE297B (=K Anh 9); Flute and Harp Concerto, KE297C (=K299)	63?, 66?, 67?, 68?, 69?	

[7] Overture: *Il rè pastore*, + Finale KE213C (=K102).
[8] First, fifth, sixth and seventh movements of Serenade in D.
[9] First, fifth, sixth, seventh and eighth movements of "Haffner" Serenade in D.

55	32	G	—	318	2202–42 timp str à 4	Salzburg, 26/4/79, "Overture in the Italian Style"	19, 23, 57, 94, 101f, 108, 133, 170	Two-Piano Concerto, KE316A (=K365); Coronation Mass, K317; Violin Sonata, KE317D (=K378)		Gluck: Iphigénie in Tauride
56	33	B flat	—	319	0202–20 str à 5	I, II, IV: Salzburg, 9/7/79 II: Vienna 1782	19f, 23, 79, 106, 126f, 149, 159, 170	Divertimento, KE320B (K334)		Haydn: L'isola disabitata
57	—	D	—	320	0202–22 timp str à 4	Salzburg, 3/8/79[10]	135, 137	Sinfonia Concertante, KE320D (=K364); Thamos, König in Ägypten. KE336A (=K345)	71?, 75 70	C. P. E. Bach: Sonatas, W55 (published) R. Hoffstetter: Quartets op. 2
58	34	C	—	338	0202–22 timp str à 5	Salzburg, 29/8/80[11]	19f, 23, 104, 110f, 126, 170	Violin Concerto, KE365B (=K268); Idomeneo, K366	74	Haydn: La fedeltà premiata
59	—	C	—	384	piccolo, 0222–72 timp triangle str à 4	Vienna 29/7/81–29/5/82[12]	90, 139	Serenade KE370A (=K361); Violin Sonatas, KE374D–F (=K376,377, 380); Concert Rondo, K382	73	J. C. Bach: Syms., op. 18 (published) Haydn: Quartets, op. 33 Salieri: Der Rauchfangkehrer (Vienna)

[10] First, fifth and seventh movements of "Posthorn" Serenade in D.
[11] + Minuet in C, KE383F (=K409).
[12] Overture: Die Entführung aus dem Serail.

60	lost	E flat	383G	Anh 100	1201–20 str à 5	Vienna, May 1782	140, 143	Serenade, KE384A (=K388)	76	Haydn: *Orlando Paladino* Cherubini: *Armida*; *Adriano in Siria*; *Il Messenzio*
61	35	D	—	385	(2)2(2)2 22–timp str à 4	Vienna, July or Aug, 1782, "Haff-ner"	19f, 23, 140f, 170	Marches, K384B; KE385A (=K408/11); Violin Sonata, KE385C (=K403)	77, 78	Haydn: Keyboard Concerto in D Paisiello: *Il barbiere di Sevilla*
62	36	C	—	425	0202–22 timp str à 4	Linz, 3/11/83, "Linz"	15, 19f, 23, 45, 83, 110, 143f, 146n, 170	Duos, K423–4; *Lo Sposo deluso* KE424A (=K430)	79, 80, 81	Haydn: *Armida* Pleyel's first sym. published Kraus: Sym. in C minor M. Haydn: Sym. No. 20 (1784)
63	38	D	—	504	2202–22 timp str à 5	Vienna, 6/12/86, "Prague"	19f, 23, 83, 146f, 157, 170	Keyboard Trio, K502; Piano Concerto K503	82, 84, 85, 86	Haydn: Quartets, op. 50 Martín y Soler: *Una cosa rara* Dittersdorf: 12 "Ovid" Syms.; *Doktor und Apotheker*
64	39	E flat	—	543	1022–22 timp str à 4	Vienna, 26/6/88	19f, 23, 49, 145, 146n, 150f, 164, 170	Coronation Concerto, K537; Keyboard Trio, K542 Sonata, K545	90, 91	Cherubini: *Ifigenia in Aulide* C. P. E. Bach: Double Concerto, W47
65	40	g	—	550	12(2)2 –20 str à 4	Vienna, 25/7/88	19f, 23, 49, 97, 123, 133, 154f, 164, 170	Violin Sonatina, K547; Keyboard Trio, K548		Cherubini: *Démophon*

66	41	C	—	551	1202-22 timp str à 4	Vienna, 10/8/88 "Jupiter"	19f, 23, 49, 79, 106, 107, 110, 127, 157f, 164, 170	15 Canons; Divertimento K563	L. Koželuh: Syms., op. 24

SPURIOUS SYMPHONIES

No.		Key	K	K	Instr.	Place, Date	Pages	Notes
67	2	B flat	Anh 223A	17	0220-20 str à 4	?, 1764/5	20f, 58n, 60	
68	3	E flat	Anh 109I	18	0021-20 str à 4	London, copied 1764	20f, 33, 57f	By Abel: 0201-20 str à 4 (op. 7/6)
69	—	F	19A	Anh 223	0200-20 str à 4	London, start of 1765	62, 66	Discovered 1981 in the Bavarian State Library
70	—	B flat	311A	Anh 8	2222-22 timp str à 4	Paris, end of Aug. or Sept. 1778 "Paris Overture"	171f	
71	37	G	425A	444	(1)200 -20 str à 4	Linz, start of Nov. 1783	20f, 45, 58n, 83, 143, 145f	By M. Haydn. Perger 16, 23/5/83. Slow introduction only by Mozart

Index of Mozart's Works

Orchestral and Concertos

(for Symphonies, see pp. 209–219)

Clarinet Concerto	153
Concertone in C	43n
Deutsche Tanz, K603, No. 3	27n
Divertimenti ("Salzburg Symphonies")	105, 106, 119, 135
Eine Kleine Nachtmusik	14, 117
Haffner March, KE383A	140
Horn Concertos: No. 3	46n
No. 4	14
Keyboard Concertos: KE21B	33
K37, 39, 40, 41	35n
K238, 246, 271	39
K467	14
K537	48
Kontretanz, La Bataille	27n
Minuet and Trio, KE383F	111
Musikalischer Spass, Ein	54
Serenade, KE62A (=K100)	82, 135n
Sinfonia Concertante for strings	171
Sinfonia Concertante for wind	43n, 171
Triple Concerto	39f
Violin Concertos	39, 136

Chamber Music

Clarinet Quintet	153
Divertimento for string trio	49
Duets for violin and viola	45
Horn Quintet	45n
String Quintet in G minor	97, 159
Violin Sonatas	31
Wind Divertimenti	48n

Stage Works

Apollo et Hyacinthus	35b, 82n
Ascanio in Alba	37, 75
Bastien und Bastienne	35
Clemenza di Tito	51
Così fan tutte	49
Don Giovanni	47
Finta giardiniera, La	38
Finta semplice, La	67
Idomeneo	44
Lucio Silla	37
Mitridate, Rè di Ponto	36f, 72
Nozze di Figaro, Le	47, 49
Rè Pastore, Il	39
Schauspieldirektor, Der	47
Schuldigkeit des ersten Gebotes, Die	35n
Sogno di Scipione, Il	37
Zaide	102
Zauberflöte, Die	50f

Church Music

Missae breves	35, 39, 40
Requiem	51

Keyboard Works

Sonatas	14
London works	33
Variations, Les Mariages Samnites	44n

General Index

The reference "Table: 4", for example, refers to an entry in the Table of Mozart's Symphonies starting on page 209, the numeral being that of the identifying number on the left-hand side of that Table. Discography references have *not* been indexed.

Abel, C. F.	32f, 58f, 66
Abert, A. A.	68
Ackermann, O.	20
Alexandre, C.-G.	81, 131
Allegri, G.	36
Amalia, Princess of Prussia	31
Anderson, E.	16, 169
Anfossi, P.	67
Ansermet, E.	20n
Archiv Produktion (Record Co)	27n, 68
Arco, Count	44
Argo (Record Co)	23n
Arne, T.	91
Asplmeyer, F.	132
Azaïs, P.-H.	131
Bach/Abel Concerts	32, 58, 80
Bach, C. P. E.	35n, 111, 131, 132 Table: 44, 52, 57, 64
Bach, J. C.	32f, 43, 58f, 62, 66, 70, 80, 82f, 88, 94, 98, 100, 103, 112, 131, Table: 1, 6, 21, 51
Bach, J. S.	106, 148
Bagpipes	113n
Bailleux, A.	131
Bambini, F.	131
Barthélémon, F.-H.	132
Beck, F.	80, 131
Beecham, Sir T.	18, 19f
Beecke, I. N. F. von	39, 132
Beethoven, L. von	13f, 24, 47f, 76, 106, 125, 131, 143n, 155
Bernasconi, A.	28, 67, 70
Bianchi, F.	101
Biber, H. I. F.	27
Boccherini, L.	43n, 77, 132, Table: 7, 23, 27

Böhm, K.	22
Bonno, G.	35, 110
Boskovsky, W.	136n
Brahms, J.	106
Breitkopf Catalogues	71, 80
Broder, N.	170
Bruckner, A.	18
Brunetti, G.	132
Bryan, P.	133n, 173
Burney, Sir C.	42, 170
Byrd, W.	24
Cambini, G. G.	43, Table: 28
Cannabich, J. I. C.	30, 41, 77, 108
Caroline of Nassau-Weilburg, Princess	33, 42
Carse, A.	23, 70n, 173
Cherubini, L.	Table: 60, 64, 65
Chopin, F. F.	165
Clementi, M.	45, 165, Table: 3
Cocchi, G.	32
Collins, A.	14
Colloredo, Archbishop (Bishop of Gurk)	36f, 39, 44, 113
Colombo, P.	20
Concert Hall (Record Co)	20
Concert Spirituel	42f
Conti, Prince de	31
Cornelys, Mrs.	32
Crispi, P. M.	, 67
Danzi, I.	41
Dart, R. T.	173
Davesne, P.-J.	131
Decca (Record Co)	24
Denkmäler der Tonkunst in Bayern	96n
Deutsch, O. E.	16, 169

Dittersdorf, K. D. von   37, 47, 69, 71,
        131, 132, Table: 63
Drasil, F.   46n
Dušek, F. X.   47, 58n, Table: 7
Dussek, J. L.   165
Dvořák, A.   143n

Eckard, J. G.   35n
Eichner, E.   77, 131, 132
Einstein, A.   16, 169
Electrola (Record Co)   103n
Elvira Madigan (film)   14
Engström, T.   169
Esipov, V.   81n
Esterházy, Prince   38, 45

Fendler, E.   19
Ferdinand, King of Naples   35, 50
Ferrari, G. J. G.   102
Fils, A.   41, 77, 103, 117, 131
Firmian, Count L. A. von   27, 37
Fitzpatrick, H.   173
Flanders and Swann   14
Fränzl, I.   41
Frederike, Queen   49
Friedrich II, King of Prussia   31
Friedrich Wilhelm II   49
Froment, L. de   20
Fry, C.   195
Furtwängler, W.   20

Gassmann, F. L.   37, 48, 131, Table: 9
Gazzaniga, G.   67
George III, King of England   32
Gérard, Y.   77, 132
Gibbons, O.   24
Glass harmonica   38
Gluck, C. W. von   37, 48, 129, 132,
        Table: 8, 48, 50, 53, 55
Goethe, J. W. von   130
Gorvin, C.   72n
Gosec, F.-J.   96n, 131
Gra(a)f(f), C. E.   34
Grétry, A. E. M.   Table: 47
Gros, J. le   42f
Guglielmi, P. A.   101
Guillemain, L. G.   131

Haffner, E.   39, 136
Haffner, S.   136, 140
Hamann, J. G.   130
Handel, G. F.   32f, 148
Hasse, J. A.   35, 37

Haydn, F. J.   17, 21n, 27n, 34n, 38,
        45, 46f 50, 66, 73n, 75, 76,
        80, 83, 84, 86, 105n, 106,
        110, 111, 113, 117, 118–128
        passim, 132f, 137, 143, 145,
        146n, 148, 153f, 155, 157,
        163f, 195, Table: passim
Haydn, J. M.   20n, 36, 38, 45, 51,
        83, 90, 113, 132, 145f, 164,
        Table: 11, 26, 62
Hennig, C. F.   132
Herder, J. G.   130
Hodgson, A.   195
Hoeckh, K.   131
Hoffmeister, F. A.   132
Hofstetter, R.   Table: 4, 16, 51, 57
Hofstetter, U.   96n, Table: 20
Hogwood, C.   24f, 118, 172
Holzbauer, I. J.   41, 97
Honauer, L.   35n
Horns   18, 132f
Huber, T.   132
Hummel, J. N.   165
Hurdy-gurdy   113n
Hutchins, A.   169

Ingle, "Red"   14
Jommelli, N.   30, 70
Jones, L.   21n
Joseph II, Emperor   39, 48

Kaffka, J. C.   132
Karajan, H. von   19
Karl Theodor, Duke
    (Elector of Mannheim)   30, 41f
Kehr, G.   22
Keller, H.   16, 153, 169
Keszei, J.   195
Kisch, R.   19n
Kleiber, E.   20n
Klemperer, O.   20
Klinger, F. M. von   131
Knappertsbusch, H.   19
Köchel, L. R. von   15f, 30, 58, 92,
        99, 169
Koussevitzky, S.   19f
Koželuh, L. A.   77n, 132, Table; 66
Kraus, J. M.   132; Table; 62
Kreusser, G. A.   132
Krips, J.   19, 23, 169
Kuntz, A. K.   96n

Lachnith, L. V.   132

general index / 223

Lang, J. J. 132
Langenmantel, J. W. 40
Larson, J. P. 16, 34n, 169
La Rue, J. 34n, 71
Leemans, H. 81
Leinsdorf, E. 21
Leitgeb, A. 51n
Lemiérre, A. M. 96
Lenz, J. M. R. 131
Leopold II, Emperor 50f
Leutgeb, J. 45n, 46, 53
Lichnovsky, Prince 49
Liszt, F. 165
Lorenziti, J. A. 132
Louis XV, King of France 31
Lully, G. B. 70n, 143
Lund, G. 20

Maag, P. 22
Mahaut, A. 131
Maldere, P. van 31, 131
Maria Theresia, Empress 29, 35
Marie Antoinette 29
Marriner, N. 22f, 76n, 86, 90n, 91n, 101, 116n, 117n, 142n, 143n, 157, 169
Martin, F. 80, 102
Martini, Padré 39
Martini il Tedesco 131
Martín-y-Soler 47; Table: 63
Mašek, V. 164
Maximilian, Archduke
 (Elector of Cologne) 39, 47
Maximilian Joseph III 28, 42
Melkus, E. 27n
Melodiya (Record Co) 81n
Mendel, A. 170
Mesmer, F. A. 38
Miča, F. A. 132
Michael, H. 20
Milandre, L. T. 132
Miroglio, J. B. 81
Mitchell, D. 16
Montillot, M. de 97
Mozart, Anna Maria 27f, 40, 43
Mozart, Constanze 45, 47f, 52
Mozart, Franz Xaver
 (later W. A.) 51
Mozart Jahrbuch 71
Mozart, Leopold 26f, 48, 55, 60f, 66, 71, 80, 84, 88, 113, 140
Mozart, Maria Anna Thekla 41
Mozart, Maria Anna (Nannerl) 28f, 33, 44, 46, 55

Mozart, Theresa 49
Mozart, Wolfgang Amadeus
 Character 53f; Composing methods 55; Falsification of age 32n, 34n; Fecundity 15; First compositions 28, 30; First recital 29; Illnesses 30, 33, 35, 46, 48, 51f; Influenced by Mannheim School 30f, 74; Last years 50f; Name variants 26n; Neglect 15; Physical appearance 55f; Popular appeal 13f; Symphonies: authentic performance 17f, 21f, 195; gramophone availability 19f; Use of: "Alberti bass" 65, 67, 69, 113; crescendo 62, 85, 90, 94, 99, 100f, 103, 105, 109, 119, 121, 138, 155; horns 18, 64f, 113f, 132f; Scotch snap 63, 94, 99, 101, 105, 110, 113, 118, 120, 121, 122, 125, 142; timpani 18, 70, 95, 96f, 195; "Turkish music" 84, 90, 139
Mozart, W. A., and freemasonry 46; and Joseph Haydn 46f; and money 47f
Münchinger, K. 136n
Munrow, D. 173
Murray Barbour, J. 173
Mysliveček, J. 36, 40, 132, Table: 8, 10

Nardini, P. 30n
Neefe, C. G. 132
Neel, B. 19n.
New Mozart Edition
 (Bärenreiter) 140n
Nissen, G. N. 52
Nixa (Record Co) 20n
Nonesuch (Record Co) 21n, 43n

Oiseau-Lyre (Record Co) 20, 24
Olmütz 35
Orrey, L. 16
Otvós, G. 103n

Paisiello, G. 102, Table: 47; 61
Perger, H. L. 113n
Period (Record Co) 20n
Philips (Record Co) 23, 169
Pifferi 113n
Pleyel, I. J. 132, Table: 62
Pokorný, F. X. 164
Pompadour, Madame 31
Puchberg, J. M. 49, 53f
Punto, G. 43
Pushkin, A. 52

Querfurth, F. 96n

Raeburn, C. 169
Rague, L.-C. 132
Ramm, F. 42f
Rasmussen, M. 46n
Raupach, H. F. 35n
Reichardt, J. F. 132
Rettensteiner Catalogue 46n
Richter, F. X. 41, 131, Table: 22
Rigel, H.-J. 132
Righini, V. 47
Rimsky-Korsakov, N. 52
Ristenpart, K. 43n, 103n
Ritter, G. W. 41f
Robbins Landon, H. C. 16, 170
Roeser, V. 96n
Rosetti, F. A. 132
Rousseau, J. J. 130
Royale (Record Co) 20

Saint-Foix, G. de 16, 169
Salieri, A. 45, 47, 50, 52f, Table: 59
Salomon, J. P. 50f
Salzburg Mozarteum 172
Sammartini, G. B. 33, 36, 83, 103
Sargent, Sir M. 20n
Sarti, G. 101
Schenk, E. 170
Schenker, ?. 131
Scherchen, H. 19f
Schikaneder, E. 50
Schmitt, J. 131, 132
Schobert, J. 31, 35n, Table: 1
Schrattenbach, Archbishop 35, 37
Schroeder, J. 116n
Schubart, C. D. F. 38
Schubert, F. 16, 126, 131, 138, 143n
Schumann, R. A. 106
Seidl, F. 36
Shakespeare, W. 130
Shostakovich, D. D. 106
Simpson, R. 17
Sohier, C.-J. B. 131
Soler, A. Table: 53
Sophia Charlotte, Queen of England 32
Stadlmair, H. 120n
Stamic, J. V. A. 24, 30, 41, 77, 90, 96n, 115, 117, 134
Stamitz, C. 131, Table: 19, 32
Stein, A. 40
Stein, F. 19
Stock, F. 20n
Strauss, R. 20
Sturm und Drang 38n, 43, 119, 129f, 154
Supraphon (Record Co) 103n
Sussmayer, F. X. 53
Swoboda, H. 19f
Szell, G. 19, 120n

Talon, P. 80, 131
Tchaikovsky, P. I. 13f
Terry, C. S. 80, 170
Thun, Count 45
Thurn-Valsannia, Count Johann 27
Toeschi, C. G. 58n, 77, 96n
Toscanini, A. 20
Trombe lunghe 125n
Turner, W. J. 169

Umlauf, I. 50
Unger, M. 38

Vachon, P. 81
Vaňhal, J. K. 47, 67, 69, 131, 132, 133, Table: 15, 33, 34, 41, 43
Vaughan, D. 21f, 94n, 99n, 100n, 105n, 116n, 117n, 120n
Vivaldi, A. L. 129, 131
Vogler, G. J. 41f
Vox (Record Co) 22

Wagenseil, G. C. 27, 29, 64, 97, 131
Walsegg-Stuppach, Count F. 51n
Walter, B. 19, 20n
Weber, Aloysia 42, 44
Weber, Carl Maria 24
Weber, Constanze 44f
Weber, Fridolin 42, 44
Weber, Marie Cäcilia 44f
Weingartner, F. 19
Wendling, J. B. 42f
Westminster (Record Co) 20, 21, 103n
Winstone, C. 170

Young, E. 130
Yppold, F. d' 48

Zazlaw, N. 24f
Zelenka, J. D. 134
Zimmermann, A. 96n, 132
Zingoni, G. B. 34
Zöschinger, Father 40